Stealing Through Time

Stealing Through Time

On the Writings of Jack Finney

JACK SEABROOK

McFarland & Company, Inc., Publishers
Jefferson, North Carolina, and London

All material quoted in Chapter Sixteen has been provided courtesy
of Special Collections and Archives, Knox College Library, Galesburg,
Illinois, and is reproduced with permission.

LIBRARY OF CONGRESS CATALOGUING-IN-PUBLICATION DATA

Seabrook, Jack.
    Stealing through time : on the writings of Jack Finney /
Jack Seabrook.
        p.   cm.
    Includes bibliographical references and index.

    ISBN 0-7864-2437-0 (softcover : 50# alkaline paper)

    1. Finney, Jack — Criticism and interpretation.   2. Science
fiction, American — History and criticism.   I. Title.
PS3556.I52Z87 2006
813'.54 — dc22   2006007837

British Library cataloguing data are available

Cover image ©2006 PhotoDisc

Manufactured in the United States of America

*McFarland & Company, Inc., Publishers
    Box 611, Jefferson, North Carolina 28640
    www.mcfarlandpub.com*

To Lorrie, as always

Acknowledgments

Writing this book was a labor of love. I first discovered Jack Finney's work when I bought a paperback copy of *The Night People* in the late 1970s and thoroughly enjoyed it. I read *Forgotten News: The Crime of the Century and Other Lost Stories* when it was published in 1983, devoured *Three By Finney* and *About Time* a few years later, and fell in love with *Time and Again* somewhere in between. *From Time to Time* was my Valentine's Day present to my wife in 1995.

I wanted to learn more about Jack Finney, but my search for a biography or a critical work came up empty, so I decided that I would write one myself.

Tracking down the novels was not difficult now that the Internet has made book collecting much easier. Tracking down the short stories was a bit tougher, but fortunately I had help from the reference staffs of several libraries. The Trenton Public Library in Trenton, New Jersey, still has bound copies of the slick magazines of the 1950s, and it is there that I found most of what I needed. The New York Public Library Express was able to provide the elusive "The House of Numbers." The Lawrence, New Jersey, branch of the Mercer County Library System was very helpful, as was Rutgers University's Alexander Library and the Moore Library at Rider University. Matt Norman at the Knox College Archives provided the letters and other documents that are found in Chapter Sixteen.

Jack Finney fan extraordinaire Leah Sparks provided support, as did my children. My wife, Lorrie, proofread the manuscript and put up with all of the research and writing with grace and enthusiasm. Without her encouragement, this book would not exist.

Contents

Preface

Stealing Through Time: On the Writings of Jack Finney covers the career of the author who lived from 1911 to 1995 and wrote ten novels, more than fifty short stories, two plays, and a nonfiction book. Jack Finney kept details of his personal affairs closely guarded, but careful research has revealed aspects of his life that are reflected in his writing. Each of the novels is examined in detail, and all of his short stories have been located and studied to present a complete picture of the author's work.

Research has also led to the discovery of details of his long-forgotten play, *This Winter's Hobby*, as well as to some reasons why it did not succeed. From his alma mater, Knox College, comes a series of letters exchanged between Finney and various persons associated with the college. These letters show a side of the author that has rarely been seen, and they also demonstrate his personal interest in some of the themes that recur in his fiction.

Stealing Through Time begins with an overview of Finney's life and career. A discussion of his early short stories is then followed by in-depth analyses of his first two novels. More short stories are analyzed, culminating in his first short story collection.

His third and fourth novels are discussed, and the rest of his short stories are covered in a chapter that also begins to discuss his last play. Finney's next five novels are featured in subsequent chapters, after which his lone nonfiction book is examined. Following a discussion of his last novel, the letters from Knox College are reproduced in full and analyzed. Finally, separate chapters discuss the ways that Finney's work has been adapted for the stage, television, and film.

The book concludes with the first comprehensive list of Jack Finney's writing ever published, credits for adaptations of his work, a list of works cited, and an index.

ONE

A Life Kept Hidden

Throughout much of his career as a writer, Jack Finney guarded his privacy carefully. Biographers were able to find little beyond the most rudimentary details of his life, and he made few public appearances (Ickes 36).

Yet a close analysis of his published work over the course of fifty years reveals some details of his private life, details that may shed some light on themes that recur in his writing.

Finney was born in Milwaukee, Wisconsin, on October 2, 1911 ("Finney, Walter Braden." *Contemporary Authors* 150: 138), as John Finney, and he was given the nickname Jack as a baby. His father died when Jack was just two years old (Ickes 37), and Jack was renamed Walter Braden Finney, in honor of his late parent. However, the nickname Jack remained with him for the rest of his life (Sparks).

His mother then took him to the Chicago suburb of Forest Park, Illinois, to live with her parents. She married again, to a man named Frank D. Berry, who worked for the railroads and the Illinois telephone company. Finney's mother (now Mrs. Berry) was described as an accomplished seamstress and woodworker who never worked outside the home (Sparks). As an adult, Jack Finney fondly recalled visiting Galesburg, Illinois, every summer when he was a child in the 1920s (Finney, Jack. Letter to Douglas L. Wilson).

Finney appears to have had a half-sister, Elaine Mitchell, who was said to be living in Alaska as of 2002. He grew up in Forest Park (Sparks), and attended Proviso Township High School in Maywood, Illinois ("Finney, Jack"); this high school served several Chicago suburbs including Forest Park ("Proviso").

He presumably was graduated from high school around 1929, the beginning of the Great Depression. He then attended Knox College in Galesburg, Illinois, where he took writing courses, enrolled in a fraternity, and participated in the ROTC. He was also on the swim team and the staff of the *Student,* presumably a journal or newspaper (*The 1935 Gale*). He completed his studies in 1934 (Breen 27). He spent the next twelve years working as a copywriter for one or more advertising agencies in Chicago and New York ("Walter B. Finney, '34"), and by 1946 he was living in New York City and working for the Dancer-Fitzgerald-Sample agency. At some point he is said to have tried writing for the radio, but no details of this have survived (Breen 24–25).

Details also have not survived about his first marriage, which most likely ended sometime in the late 1940s.

Jack Finney's career as a fiction writer is much easier to document than his private life, simply because publications exist as a record. In 1946, when he was 35 years old and had been working as an ad copywriter for twelve years, he sold his first story to the relatively new digest, *Ellery Queen's Mystery Magazine.* Entitled "The Widow's Walk," the story won a special prize in the magazine's second annual contest and was published in July 1947 (Breen 25).

Finney's first story to reach publication was "Manhattan Idyl," which appeared in the popular weekly magazine *Collier's* on April 5, 1947. His lack of interest in self-promotion was evident from the first. The editor's page in *Collier's* included a photograph of Finney on a fake postage stamp, and noted that:

> ... he's from Forest Park, Illinois, 35, Knox College-bred, and wedded to a gal he'd like us to meet: She likes everything he writes, including the singing commercials he once ground out for the radio.
>
> Right now this exhibitionistic philatelist writes advertising copy directly across the street from the Collier's office. "I can look into your windows," he confides. "Frequently I do — and sometimes I wave" [Shane].

Finney immediately set his sights on selling stories to the popular magazines of the day, and by the end of the 1940s he had published eight more stories in *Collier's*, *Ladies' Home Journal*, and *Good House-keeping*. His wife was mentioned again in the August 28, 1948 issue of *Collier's*, when he won "the first of our new Star Story $1,000 Awards with his hilarious whodunit rib, 'It Wouldn't Be Fair'..." (Shane).

He won a second Star Story $1,000 Award for "Long-Distance Call," a story published in the November 6, 1948 issue of *Collier's* (Shane). He is said to have divorced his wife in Reno, Nevada, and met his second wife there (Ickes 34). She was also divorcing, and her name was G. Marguerite Guest. She was Canadian ("Walter B. Finney, '34"), possibly from Toronto (Finney, Jack. Letter to M.M. Goodsill. 27 Apr. 1960). At some point, probably in the late 1940s, Finney moved with Marguerite to Mill Valley, California, where he would settle and remain for the rest of his life. In 1966, he wrote that he had lived in New York, Reno, San Francisco, and Mill Valley (*Playbill*. This Winter's Hobby 34).

Mill Valley is mentioned in "My Cigarette Loves Your Cigarette," which appeared in the September 30, 1950 issue of *Collier's*, and again in "Husband at Home," in the April 1951 *Ladies Home Journal*. The main characters in "Stopover at Reno" travel by bus from New York to San Francisco and have an adventure in the title town; this story appeared in the January 5, 1952 *Collier's*. Mill Valley is located in Marin County, north of San Francisco.

Finney's daughter Margie was born around 1951 (Ickes 34), and in the early 1950s the writer was a prolific contributor of short stories to popular magazines — nineteen stories were published between 1950 and 1952. In the summer of 1953, his first extended work, "5 Against the House," was serialized in three issues of *Good Housekeeping*. This became his first novel when it was published the following year.

"The Body Snatchers" was his second novel-length work, and it was serialized in three issues of *Collier's* at the end of 1954. Finney's son Kenneth was born around this time (Ickes 34–35), and the novel version of this serial was published in 1955. In this time period Finney appears to have begun using agent Don Congdon, who would represent him for the rest of his life (Ickes 37).

With the 1955 release of the film *5 Against the House*, Jack Finney's work began to reach a new audience, which grew with the 1956 release of the popular science fiction film, *Invasion of the Body Snatchers*. According to J. Sydney Jones, this film "changed everything for the forty-three-year-old writer and ... allowed him to support his family solely on his writing" (74).

The rest of the 1950s found Finney dividing his time between short stories and novels. He published seven more stories in 1955–1956 and even had a play entitled *Telephone Roulette* published in 1956 (Fidell 103). The story "Such Interesting Neighbors" was adapted for television as "Time Is Just a Place," first airing on April 16, 1955, as part of the series, *Science Fiction Theatre*. The long story "The House of Numbers" appeared in the July 1956 issue of *Cosmopolitan*, then was published in novel form in 1957 to coincide with the release of *House of Numbers*, the third film to be based on Jack Finney's work.

Nine more short stories appeared in magazines between 1957 and 1959, and *The Third Level* was published in 1957. This short story collection focused on Finney's science fiction and fantasy, and it won an award for best short story collection in 1958 from the magazine, *Infinity Science Fiction* (Jones 73).

In August and September of 1959, the *Saturday Evening Post* serialized "The U-19's Last Kill" in six consecutive issues. This was revised and published as the novel *Assault on a Queen* that same year.

Jack Finney turned 49 in 1960 and was by then established as a popular author of short stories with four novels under his belt and three motion pictures based on his work. The market for short stories was changing, as old standbys like *Collier's* fell by the wayside and were replaced by new magazines like *Playboy*. Finney published ten short stories between 1960 and 1962, and another collection, *I Love Galesburg in the Springtime*, appeared in 1962. Like *The Third Level*, this group of short stories focused on those with themes of science fiction and fantasy. As a result, Finney's other short stories have, with few exceptions, not been reprinted since their initial appearances in magazine form. Also in 1962, the story, "All My Clients Are Innocent," was adapted for television and broadcast as part of the *Alcoa Premiere* series on April 17, 1962.

Finney's fifth novel, *Good Neighbor Sam*, was published in 1963, and marked the first time that one of his novels did not also appear as a serial. The author admitted having written this book with popular actor Jack Lemmon in mind, and the film starring Mr. Lemmon was released in 1964 (Wilson).

Jack Finney's last published short story, "Double Take," appeared in *Playboy* magazine's April 1965 issue. He then wrote a play entitled

This Winter's Hobby, which closed in Philadelphia during a pre-Broadway tryout in 1966 (Zolotow). At this point, Finney was 54 years old, and his writing output dwindled. He would not publish any more short stories or have any more plays performed. He continued writing for another thirty years, but only five novels and one non-fiction book appeared during that time.

The first of these novels was *The Woodrow Wilson Dime*, published in 1968. It was a reworking of his short story, "The Other Wife." *Time and Again* followed in 1970 and, along with *The Body Snatchers*, it would become the author's most famous work.

Finney turned 62 in 1973, the year that *Marion's Wall* was published; he followed this with *The Night People* in 1977. In 1983, he published a non-fiction book, *Forgotten News: The Crime of the Century and Other Lost Stories*, and a short story collection entitled *About Time* was released in 1986, but it only included selections from his two earlier short story collections.

The film *Maxie* was released in 1985; this was an adaptation of his novel *Marion's Wall*. The short story "Such Interesting Neighbors" was adapted for television in 1987, the same year that Finney was presented with the World Fantasy life achievement award (Jones 74).

Jack Finney turned 83 in 1994, the year that the French translation of *Time and Again* was awarded the Grand Prix de l'Imaginaire ("The Locus Index to SF Awards"), and he made a splash in the publishing world in 1995 when *From Time to Time* was published. This sequel to *Time and Again* was his last novel. He had lived in the same home with his wife Marguerite for about 40 years (Ickes 36), and died of pneumonia on November 14, 1995 ("Finney, Walter Braden." *Contemporary Authors* 150: 138).

Jack Finney's writing has continued to intrigue television and movie producers even after his death. *The Love Letter* premiered as a made-for-TV movie in 1998, and a musical adaptation of *Time and Again* opened Off Broadway in New York City in January 2001 (Brantley). Walking tours of New York City locations in that novel were popular in the city for years,* and several of the author's books remain in print as of this writing.

---

*For example, see ads in the *New York Times* on 28 May 1999: E37; 4 Aug. 2000: E40; and 3 Aug. 2001: E35.

Jack Finney wanted his private life kept private, and he was successful at shielding many details of his background from the press and the public. He wanted his work to speak for itself, and this book will concentrate on his writing, starting with his earliest short stories in the 1940s.

TWO

Early Short Stories
(1947–1952)

"The Widow's Walk" is credited with being Jack Finney's first short story, sold to *Ellery Queen's Mystery Magazine* and winner of that publication's second annual short story contest. It was published in the July 1947 issue, and thus missed being his first story to see publication by about three months.

In this story, Finney appears to have been writing for his intended market, and the themes are not those to which he would later return. Narrated in the first person by Annie, an unhappy 32-year-old wife, it tells of the calculating mother-in-law whom she dreams of killing. Life was good with husband Al until Mother moved in; now, she won't leave the young couple alone.

Annie reads about widow's walks in a magazine, and convinces her husband to build one at the top of their house. Mother eventually develops a habit of sitting up on the high perch and listening to the radio. Annie's plans to push Mother to her death are foiled when Mother obliges by having a heart attack and falling off on her own, but in the twist ending Al also falls to his death while trying to save her. At the story's end, Annie paces the widow's walk alone.

Finney's first story shares the characteristic of a first-person narrator with much of his later work, yet its subject of murder sets it apart

from most of his writing. Still, there's no real murder in the story—
only a lot of planning for one, and the twist ending is a trick he would
use again.

The first story of Jack Finney's to see publication was actually
"Manhattan Idyl," which appeared in the April 5, 1947 issue of *Collier's*, a popular weekly magazine of the time. *Collier's* had been founded
in 1888 and, during World War Two, its circulation had reached
2,500,000 ("Collier's Weekly"). By appearing in *Collier's*, Finney's work
was assured of a huge audience.

"Manhattan Idyl" is also notable for being the first appearance in
print of the Ryans, a young married couple who would appear in eleven
short stories, making them Jack Finney's busiest recurring characters.
They live in an apartment in Manhattan and Timberlake (Tim) is often
portrayed as a prankster. In this first tale, they combat boredom by taking a taxi to the Ambassador Hotel and dancing, then by taking a trolley ride down Third Avenue, and finally by walking along the East
River and imagining they're the last people on Earth. This is a charming little story of a couple in love. Finney's prose is elegant and the dialogue is sharp.

It is interesting to note that some of the themes that would recur
throughout Finney's fiction actually get their start in this long-forgotten story. Eve Ryan recalls "the small Illinois town where she'd spent
her childhood summers" (35), demonstrating that Finney's characters
from the first were already nostalgic for earlier times. Eve also recalls a
Hoot Gibson movie serial she'd seen as a child, and Tim fills in the
details of the serial's final chapter, probably inventing them as he goes
along.

Tim also pretends to be a tourist pointing out the sights (and getting them all wrong)—St. Patrick's Cathedral, Wall Street, the Flatiron Building—these would reappear almost fifty years later in Finney's
last novel, *From Time to Time*.

Best is the following paragraph, where Tim Ryan waxes poetic
about the good and bad in the world:

> "So long, world," said Tim. "You were quite a place while you lasted.
> Noisy, dirty, and ugly most of the time. Mixed up and confused and
> afraid. Evil and vicious and callous. But pretty wonderful, too. There
> was a humanity in your people that could never quite be repressed no
> matter who tried it. There were mornings and evenings; there was snow

at night, and sun that felt good — and unexpected moments of peace and happiness. People were alive and doing things — and we —"

His wife Eve breaks the spell: "'You dope,'" said Eve, "'you'd just love to get a tear out of me, wouldn't you?'" (36). But the picture has been painted and, in this story published just two years after the end of the Second World War, Manhattan looks like a pretty nice place to be when you're young and in love.

Finney's next story, "I'm Mad at You," also features Tim and Eve Ryan. This time, Eve is angry with Tim until she realizes she just wants him to court her a little bit more than he's been doing recently. The themes of "Manhattan Idyl" are repeated: Eve loves Tim and enjoys thinking about him; Tim likes to tease Eve and exaggerate. There is a good bit of humor and a light and wistful tone. Tim reads a book called *Murderer's All* and pretends to talk like a private eye (Finney would soon return to the subject of private detectives in a satiric way), and at one point he imagines buying "'...an eight-room frame house in Galesburg, Illinois. Built in the eighties; lots of fancy scrollwork on the eaves and front porch'" and moving it to the middle of Manhattan (17). He'll "'mow the grass and then sit out on the curbstone smoking my pipe. I'd be the living representative of what New York subconsciously yearns for'" (54). Tim goes on with his daydream until his friend Mrs. Mellett agrees that "'those were better days, I guess. Things were quieter. More peaceful'" (54).

Tim concludes by remarking that "'For a moment, the steel and concrete would be blotted out and they'd remember the peaceful people everywhere for whom they should be working'" (54). In a way, this exchange involving the Ryans and their Manhattan friends the Melletts sets up one of the dominant themes of Jack Finney's fiction — we need to slow down, because progress has taken our focus away from the things in life that truly matter.

A note in the April 5, 1947, issue of *Collier's* reported that Finney was working in a Manhattan advertising agency at the time (Shane), and it is tempting to see the comments in "I'm Mad at You" as evidence of the frustration of a man feeling trapped in New York City and voicing nostalgia for his Midwestern youth.

We must be careful not to assume too much, however, since the Ryans are very happy in their Manhattan apartment and Tim's nostalgic daydream is presented as part of his clearly farcical behavior in front of their friends.

Finney's next story was the brief tale, "Cousin Len's Wonderful Adjective Cellar," published in the April 1948 issue of *Ladies' Home Journal*. Reprinted in his 1957 collection, *The Third Level*, this is a story about a columnist who buys what he thinks is a salt cellar in a Second Avenue pawnshop in New York City but later learns that it can be used to remove all of the adjectives and verbs from his prose, much like a literary vacuum cleaner.

His prose improves and his readers notice the difference. He empties the cellar out of his window over Second Avenue, where the words sometimes float into conversations, but he remarks that they could never be enough to supply ad agencies. This short, humorous piece with a folksy tone has, at its center, a fantastic object whose existence no one questions. This is Finney's first published piece of fantasy, and it demonstrates what Stephen King called "[o]ne of Finney's great abilities as a writer ... his talent for allowing his stories to slip unobtrusively, almost casually, across the line and into another world ..." (236).

So, by only his fourth published short story, Finney has introduced ideas of nostalgia, time travel, and fantasy, ideas that would inform much of the best of his writing for the next fifty years.

He returned to Tim and Eve Ryan for his next story, "Breakfast in Bed," which appeared in the May 15, 1948 issue of *Collier's*. This time, the Ryans spend Sunday morning in bed, reading the newspaper and imagining a party at which they each meet interesting strangers. As in the later story, "Something in a Cloud," Tim refers to a miniature cloud forming above his head (42). To Tim, "'It looks, as on every other day, like a very depressing world. A good one to stay out of, if only for a day'" (47). By the end of the story, the Ryans never do manage to get out of bed. In an editor's note, Finney tells *Collier's* that he has never had breakfast in bed himself (Shane).

The "hilarious whodunit rib" (Shane) entitled "It Wouldn't Be Fair" came next, in the August 28, 1948 issue of *Collier's*. For this story, Finney won the first weekly Star Award, a $1000 bonus over the magazine's usual rate of payment and a great incentive for the new fiction writer to continue in this vein. Finney tells the editor that he plans to use the money to take a mail-order private eye course, because his wife always solves mysteries and he's always left confused (Shane).

The story itself is a bit of fluff, satirizing detective stories as lovely Annie, who is good at solving murders she reads about in mystery books, shows the police that her mental skills apply to real life situations as well.

Finney's next story, "Long Distance Call," was published in the November 6, 1948 issue of *Collier's*, and again won a $1000 Star Award for what the editor called the "fourth of his domesticomedies" (Shane) to feature the Ryans. This forgettable tale finds Tim proving his fidelity to his wife while out of town by squiring a lovely young woman and then taking her with him to pick up Eve.

"Something in a Cloud" then appeared in the March 1949 *Good Housekeeping*. This story is one of the most familiar of Jack Finney's pre-1950 pieces, simply because of its inclusion in *The Third Level*. The cloud of the title refers to a narrative device used to show the picture each character forms in his or her mind about the other before actually meeting them. The gimmick takes the place of interior monologues and quickly wears thin.

Finney's next story to be published was the equally forgettable "You Haven't Changed a Bit," about a young, urban couple in love, not unlike Tim and Eve Ryan. Here, Charley and Ann Knowles attend the wedding of their old flames and conclude that the bride and groom have aged badly, unlike themselves. The twist at the end finds the bride and groom thinking the same thoughts about Charley and Ann.

"The Little Courtesies" ended Finney's string of ten short stories published in the 1940s with his fifth tale about Tim and Eve Ryan. In this installment, they sit in their apartment and trade witty banter about movie stars Fredric March and Katharine Hepburn. Their humorous byplay makes this an entertaining entry in the series.

Nineteen-fifty was an important year for Jack Finney, since it marked the appearance of his first story dealing with fantasy and time travel, "The Third Level." But first came four more light comedies, led by "Sneak Preview" in the April 29th issue of *Collier's*. Al and Debbie fill in for the Ryans here as another smart, young, urban couple facing the birth of their first child and getting a taste of things to come when they baby-sit a four-year-old girl.

The Ryans returned for their sixth go round in "Week-end Genius," in which Tim is tired of working and wishes he were rich. He imagines inventing a panoramic camera that can take three-dimensional pictures of people's front and back (a similar invention will appear in Finney's 1968 novel, *The Woodrow Wilson Dime),* then decides it might be better to uninvent things. He remarks that "'Each invention makes life more unbearable: telephones, printing presses, bombs'" (57) and concludes that, if he can turn back the tide of progress, he could say that "'The good old days — are almost here!'" (57). Here again Finney is toying with ideas and themes that would later become central to his work.

In "I Like It This Way," Charley and Ann Masik are the young, urban couple of the moment who talk a lot, just like the Ryans. The enticingly titled "My Cigarette Loves Your Cigarette" marks the seventh appearance of Tim and Eve Ryan. Eve refers to Tim's youth in Mill Valley, suggesting that Finney had moved to California from New York by the time this story was written.

This story finds Tim and Eve feeling nostalgic for their youth (Tim is over thirty), and includes the following passage, where Tim tells Eve about how things were when he was single:

> "Oh"—he shrugged—"I met people in New York after I'd been here a while; I made friends and a lot of them, but even then I was lonely a lot of the time. I'm not kidding myself; I had fun, too, and there *was* a special exciting kind of feeling about those days that you never quite have again. But right along with it, there was strain and doubt and worry, too; people forget that" [54].

Up to this point, Jack Finney's stories (with the exception of "The Widow's Walk") had been light comedies, aimed at the young, urban readers of slick, high-circulation magazines. With "The Third Level," published on a single page of the October 7, 1950 issue of *Collier's,* his writing began to change, as he veered into the realm of the fantastic.

In "The Third Level," narrator Charley (aged 31, and thus a contemporary of Tim Ryan) tells the reader that he has discovered a third level at New York's Grand Central Station. His psychiatrist told him that it was a sign of wish fulfillment, due to his unhappiness with the pressures of the modern world. "Everybody I know wants to escape," he says. One evening, by mistake, he walked through a corridor and into the nineteenth century: "everyone in the station was dressed like eighteen-ninety-something..."

He sees the front page of a newspaper (The *World,* which was no longer being published in 1950), and later confirms that its date was June 11, 1894. He goes to a ticket clerk to buy tickets for himself and his wife to travel to Galesburg, Illinois (where Finney went to college):

> Have you ever been there? It's a wonderful town still, with big old frame houses, huge lawns, and tremendous trees whose branches meet overhead and roof the streets. And in 1894, summer evenings were twice as long, and people sat out on their lawns... To be back there with the first World War still twenty years off, and World War II over forty years in the future ... I wanted two tickets for that.

Charley's 1950 money isn't honored in 1894 New York, though, and even though he returns to the present and buys vintage money, he's never able to find the strange corridor to the past again. A twist ending reports that Charley's psychiatrist Sam managed to find his way back to 1894 through the same portal and invites Charley and Louisa to follow him.

"The Third Level" is unlike anything Jack Finney had published before it. It is personal (both Charley the narrator and Finney the writer went to school in Galesburg, Illinois), and it goes one step beyond imagination by making nostalgia real. By dint of its being the title story in a 1957 collection, it has attracted some interest from critics; Stephen King, in *Danse Macabre,* discusses the story and calls the imaginary third level of Grand Central Station "a kind of way station in time, giving egress on a happier, simpler time ..." (236). He calls the story the precursor to the television series *The Twilight Zone* and adds that: "Finney's most important accomplishment ... is that Daliesque ability to create the fantasy ... *and then not apologize for it or explain it*" (236).

An article in volume 110 of *Contemporary Authors* refers to the "escape from the complex, harsh present to an idyllic past" ("Finney, Walter Braden" 182) and John Clute, writing in *The Encyclopedia of Fantasy,* uses the term "timeslip" to describe "an act of entry into something like Eden" (352).

"The Third Level" also forms a bridge from the musings of Tim Ryan in "Manhattan Idyl" and "I'm Mad at You" to the theme of *From Time to Time,* Finney's last novel, which opens with a quotation stating that the years before the First World War were the best time to be alive.

Finney's next story, "Such Interesting Neighbors," is also in the fantasy vein. This time, the narrator tells of his new neighbors, who seem to be rather unfamiliar with current events and customs, even though they claim to have been born and raised in the United States.

The Hellenbecks turn out to be fugitives from the future, where people live sick with fear of self-destruction. They were more than happy to return to 1951, where there are only bombs to worry about.

The story is told with great understatement, and nothing is ever said straight out — most of what we learn about the future comes from an article that appears to have come from the future and that explains the history of time travel. Finney makes an in-joke when neighbor Ted Hellenbeck receives a book called *The Far Reaches* by Walter Braden (Finney's legal name) and says that it could be worth $5000 to $8000 in 140 years.

At the end of the story, we learn that the future is so bad that everyone escapes to the past, "leaving an empty earth of birds and insects, wind, rain and rusting weapons" (47). "Such Interesting Neighbors" is filled with humorous touches that contrast with its serious message, and at the end, after the Hellenbecks move away, the narrator remarks that his new neighbors are "kind of dull" (47). This story was adapted twice for television, in 1955 and 1987. Both versions are discussed in chapter eighteen.

Finney followed these two fantasies with another comedy featuring a young, married couple sitting around the house and trading clever remarks; Ben Bennell and wife Reagh in "Husband at Home" are interchangeable with the Ryans and the other couples that peopled such stories in Finney's early years.

Similarly undistinguished is "One-Man Show," the eighth appearance of Tim and Eve Ryan. Playful humor makes this story breezy but forgettable. The rather odd "Swelled Head" followed; in it, office workers play a prank on a recently-promoted co-worker by changing his hats in order to convince him that he really has developed the title problem.

"Quit Zoomin' Those Hands Through the Air" combines Finney's comedic side with elements of fantasy and time travel. In this story, an old man tells his grandson to stop bragging about his World War Two flying exploits. The old man recounts his experience in the Civil War with a Harvard professor who used a time machine to transport them both ninety years into the future to the 1950s. The professor brings the Wright Brothers' plane from the Smithsonian Institute back with him to 1864. They get the plane airborne and meet General Ulysses Grant, who scoffs that air power will never replace the foot soldier.

They scout out rebel forces using the plane, then return it to the 1950s museum "'before daylight or the space-time continuum will be broken and no telling what might happen then'" (48). The battle the next day is a disaster due to faulty intelligence — the narrator later learns that the plane got drunk when he used whiskey instead of gasoline for fuel. As a result, Grant and General Robert E. Lee decided that air power was a bad idea and never spoke of it again. The narrator concludes the story by telling his grandson that he was the first pilot.

This story falls under the heading of "tall tales," serving as a precursor to *Time and Again* and *From Time to Time* in its use of time travel and the suggestion that it can be used to alter the course of history.

"I'm Scared," published six weeks after "Quit Zoomin' Those Hands Through the Air" in *Collier's*, takes a much more serious approach to the theme of time travel. The narrator of this story is 66 years old, making him much older than Finney's usual characters, and he is scared by events he's been observing in the world around him.

He heard a broadcast of Major Bowes' Amateur Hour on the radio, and then realized that Bowes had been dead for ten years. He then investigated a story about a house that had been painted gray but had begun to develop a white strip, where the house's prior color had gotten lost in time. He begins to catalogue and explore similar events, such as a man killed in a car accident who was dressed in 1870s style. The man had suddenly appeared in Times Square in 1950 and research showed that he had gone missing in 1876.

The narrator concludes that more and more people are longing for a simpler time, "'when you could bring children into the world and count on the future....'" He adds that "People didn't talk that way when I was young! The present was a glorious time! But they talk that way now" (81). He concludes the story by arguing that the overwhelming desire of people to escape their lives is putting pressure on the boundaries of time, and when the "clock of time" breaks, "I leave to your imagination the last few hours of madness that will be left to us..." (81).

In his article on Jack Finney in *Twentieth-Century American Science-Fiction Writers*, Michael Beard calls the conclusion to "I'm

Scared" "uncharacteristic of Finney, but the portrait of an entire society straining semiconsciously to escape the present is a compact argument for the sensibility behind most of his writing" (184). Beard is
correct; "I'm Scared" demonstrates Jack Finney moving into more serious areas with his fiction, areas that he would continue to explore for
the remainder of his career.

He returned to light comedy with the ninth story about Tim and
Eve Ryan, "Sounds in the Night." This time, they can't sleep and plan
to go out on the town at three a.m. Tim leans his head out of the window and hears a woman across the street call out of her own window
to a cop on the beat. Finney describes the cop as "irritable authority,"
with a "chilling, impersonal ruthlessness" (51). The woman dumps a
bucket of water on his head. His description and reaction prefigure the
portrayal of the police in Finney's later novel, *The Night People,* demonstrating that the questioning of authority in that book was not simply
a nod to 1970s attitudes by the author.

Though Finney's early stories appear to have attracted no critical
attention at the time they first appeared, two letters from the readers
of *Collier's* were published in the January 5, 1952 issue and discuss this
story. In the first letter, reader Ruth Crane writes that Finney "reminds
me most of Somerset Maugham, American style. He writes about prac-
tically nothing, yet he does it wonderfully well" (4). In the second letter, reader Francis T. Bettack remarks that the story was "terrific" and
recalls "another wonderful story ... My Cigarette Loves Your Cigarette"
(4). Finney's work was beginning to be noticed.

It's odd that "Stopover at Reno" has never been reprinted or discussed, because it is one of Jack Finney's most exciting short stories. Ben
Bennell (who shares the same name as the main characters in "Husband
at Home" and *The Woodrow Wilson Dime,* as well as having the same
last name as the main character in *The Body Snatchers*) and his wife Rose
rent a room in Reno, Nevada. They've left Newark and spent four days
on the bus, heading for San Francisco. They're nearly broke. While Rose
sleeps, Ben visits the casino in the hotel where they're staying.

He is gradually drawn into betting at the craps table, and Finney
brilliantly chronicles his agony and ecstasy as he compulsively gambles
with nearly the last scrap of money they have. He almost loses everything, then wins his way up to $1500 before losing it all over again. At
the end of the story he tells his wife that he lost a dollar.

In addition to the obvious parallels to Finney's life that were discussed in chapter one of this book, this is a tale of great psychological suspense that serves as a neat tune up for Finney's first novel, *5 Against the House*.

A *Collier's* short short is how the magazine described "Obituary," co-written by Finney and C.J. Durban, about whom I have been able to discover absolutely nothing. In this spooky little tale, average guy Charley dreams every night that he's really successful Edward V. Carmody. His wife worries that his dreams depict his desires, so she gives him sleeping pills and he sleeps well and dreamlessly for a month. She then sees the real Carmody's obituary in the newspaper — he resembled Charley but lived the life of the man in his dreams, and he'd spent a month in a coma before dying. The twist ending of this story puts it in the category of those found on the television series, *The Twilight Zone*, but it doesn't really fit well with Jack Finney's other writing.

More consistent is "Tiger Tamer," in which the narrator recalls an incident thirty years before in Galesburg, Illinois (there's that town again), when a boy named Charley hypnotized a tiger and attracted national media attention. "I remember that day, and all those long-ago, deep-summer days in Galesburg, Illinois, with a terrible nostalgia" (72) writes the narrator, and he proceeds to tell how Charley did the trick. He concludes that Charley (now an adult) would make a great president, adding: "I don't say his methods would always stand the full light of day, but ... His aims ... are right, and he usually achieves them..." (73). "Tiger Tamer" would later be reprinted in the collection, *I Love Galesburg in the Springtime* under the title, "A Possible Candidate for the Presidency."

"There Is a Tide" is a wistful tale set in New York City, where the narrator is a 28-year-old assistant at a "big candy and cough-sirup company" (50) who sees a ghost in his apartment on East 68th Street. Concerned about beating boss Ted Haymes out of his job, he is awake at three a.m. wrestling with his ethical dilemma when he sees a chunky, middle-aged ghost who also appears to be having an ethical problem. The experience makes the narrator decide to preserve his boss's job, but the same boss's behavior at work the next day makes the narrator change his mind again.

He decides that the ghost is that of Harris L. Gruener, the prior tenant in his apartment, and he tracks down Mr. Gruener in Brooklyn where he is an unhappy man in his seventies. Gruener explains that, when he lived in the narrator's apartment, he had pondered suicide for three nights in a row and now he regrets not having killed himself because he is a burden to his son and his son's family.

Gruener had looked for a sign on the third night but had received nothing. Gruener speculates that

> "a particularly intense human experience can sometimes leave behind some sort of emanation or impression on the environment it happened in. And that under the right conditions it can be evoked again, almost like a recording that is left behind in the very air and walls of the room" [52]

and wonders if the narrator's experience "brought back the actual time itself..." (52). That night, the narrator looks up the title quote in *Julius Caesar* ("There is a tide in the affairs of men..." [IV.iii.218]), sees the ghost, and thinks out loud the words, "Do it!" (53).

The next day, a look in the phone book finds no entry for Gruener and a trip to Brooklyn reveals that he died twelve years before. The narrator realizes that his comment drove the man to suicide, and he thinks, "*I* don't know if time shifts sometimes; if events that have already happened can be made to happen again, this time in another way" (53). He concludes that "There is a tide, all right, but whether a man should take it or not depends on where he wants to go" (53). *Time and Again* is foreshadowed in this effective story, as present and past are both altered by the actions of the narrator.

After a ten-month hiatus, Tim and Eve Ryan returned for the tenth time in "Man of the Cocktail Hour." This uneventful story features a flirtatious actress named Ann Darrow, after Fay Wray's character in the film *King Kong*.

Another mysterious co-author, this time named F.M. Barratt, was listed with Finney in the byline of his next story, "Diagnosis Completed," which appeared in the October 18, 1952 issue of *Collier's*. This mystery features an elderly doctor and a younger doctor solving the mystery of whether a woman died accidentally, committed suicide, or was murdered. This story has few Finney touches and it's tempting to think that he helped Mr. Barratt polish a story that the latter had written.

By the time "Behind the News" appeared in the November 1952

issue of *Good Housekeeping*, Jack Finney's name was well-known enough to sell magazines, since this is the first time it was listed on the cover. In this humorous tale, Johnny Deutsch edits the *Clarion,* a small-town newspaper, and is fond of composing phony stories that he never prints, such as "Police Chief Slain by Wolf Pack."

He recalls that his father, the former editor, once threw a chunk of lead into the Linotype machine and claimed that the rock was a meteor. Somehow, this type begins to make Johnny's fanciful story come true, and once he realizes that this is the case he begins to use it to his advantage. Stephen King's comment about Finney's technique of presenting an unusual situation and not explaining it is recalled when Johnny remarks that, in any science fiction story, "'the dullest part is always the explanation...'" (186).

This bit of fantasy or wish fulfillment features a small-town newspaper background reminiscent of science fiction/mystery author Fredric Brown, who was writing some of his finest novels at about the same time.

Jack Finney published twenty-nine stories from 1947 to 1952, then turned to novels and did not publish another short story until 1955. In these early stories one can see him finding his voice and experimenting with the themes that he would continue to explore for the rest of his career. He wrote many stories with a comedic flavor, something that he would return to in *Good Neighbor Sam.* The suspenseful "Stopover in Reno" clearly sets the stage for his first novel, *5 Against the House,* and his many fantasy stories dealing with aspects of time travel foreshadow *Time and Again.*

Finney would not publish anything between November 1952 and July 1953, when "5 Against the House" began to appear as a serialized novel in the pages of *Good Housekeeping.*

THREE

5 Against the House

In 1947, when "The Widow's Walk" was published, Jack Finney was a 35-year-old married man without children who had been working in advertising for over ten years. By 1953, he had divorced and remarried, and he had a baby daughter. He had published twenty-nine stories in magazines read by millions of people, and he was well-known enough to have his name on the cover. He had moved from the East Coast to the West Coast, and it was time for him to take the next step as a writer and begin writing longer works.

In July 1953, a big box on the cover of that month's *Good Housekeeping* announced, "The terrific suspense story of the year!" This was "5 Against the House," which would run as a serial in three consecutive issues of the magazine.

The story is told by 19-year-old college junior Al Mercer, who lives in a fraternity house at a college in Illinois (where Finney had attended Knox College). It is early June and he and his friend, Guy Cruikshank, are bored. True crime buff Jerry Weiner arrives and, after seeing a Brinks truck out the window, relates an armored car robbery that happened years before in Brooklyn. Al thinks, "There's a handful of moments scattered through your life that stick in your mind forever" (159).

A fourth fraternity brother then arrives — he is Brick Vogeler, older than the rest at twenty-two and an ex-football star. Jerry finishes his story and the four friends began to plan their own big crime as a way to pass the time.

This is how Jack Finney sets up "5 Against the House," which features the youngest group of protagonists to appear in any of his stories. They are about a decade younger than the urban married couples who peopled many of his early short stories, and their youth plays a role in the choices they make.

The foursome then drives to the Brinks office in town and observes the goings on while trading ideas for a robbery. They are interrupted and interrogated by the police, who provide a quick dose of reality that angers Brick but that the younger members of the gang take in stride, since they're still treating the idea of robbery as a lark.

The fifth member of the title group is introduced as Tina Greyleg, a beautiful waitress whom Al is dating. The story then shifts back to the four men, who recall working in Reno, Nevada, the summer before. Brick dealt cards at an ornate casino named Harold's Club, while the others merely had menial jobs. Brick suggests that they rob Harold's Club, arguing that they would have a better chance at success because they already know the place and its workings. Jerry (the true crime buff) explains that the real trick is getting away with the robbery, because one can always be traced back to one's origins. Al realizes that Jerry is serious about planning the heist, and the foursome split up to think about how to arrive in Reno seemingly out of thin air.

Al takes Tina out to dinner and proposes marriage, but she hesitates, telling him that she wants a man with money and prospects for the future, not just a college student. Al tells her he'll have money soon, and this may be the first time that Al is serious about the robbery himself. His motives are thus suspect: the idea is hatched out of boredom but becomes more appealing when it may lead to Tina's taking his marriage proposal more seriously.

Al's ethics are questionable as he explains the plan to Tina: "'I think gambling is wrong. I always have; this isn't a new idea with me. I think it's vicious. As evil socially as narcotics'" (180).

For a nineteen-year-old junior in college, Al has strong feelings. He continues with this bit of ethical gymnastics: "'So I say [casinos are] fair prey. Harold's Club has only a technical legal right to that money, no more real right to it than I do.'" He continues: "'But this isn't stealing to me; by any standard I respect, that money doesn't belong to Harold's Club; and I'll take it if I can, and it will never bother my conscience for a moment'" (180).

This curious rationalization by Al Mercer hurts the story, especially because he never wrestles with his conscience again. Jack Finney would use a similar excuse in *Assault on a Queen,* and it is problematic there as well. To enjoy "5 Against the House," the reader is required to accept Al's argument, and (fortunately) the story is good enough that one soon forgets about the ethical dilemma and gets wrapped up in the events.

Tina concocts a method of arriving in Reno unnoticed and tells Al, but Finney keeps the reader in suspense by not telling us at this point in the story. Tina thus becomes the fifth member of the title group.

Her plan is revealed a few pages later, and she explains that they can cross the country hidden in a trailer, emerging only at night for supplies. They plan to abandon the trailer in Reno and then rob Harold's Club disguised as cowboys during the Rodeo Week celebration on the Fourth of July. The group decides to go through with the planned robbery, and part one of the serialized novel ends with Al and Tina struggling with the idea of marriage.

Part two appeared in the next issue of *Good Housekeeping,* published in August 1953. This section begins as Al and his friends collect supplies and work out the details of the trip to Reno and the robbery. Jerry flies to Reno and takes photographs at Harold's Club; when he returns, he explains his plan to his friends but again the details are withheld from the reader. Eventually, the gang begins driving cross-country, with Jerry behind the wheel and everyone else hiding in the trailer.

During the trip, Al gets to know Tina better and falls deeply in love with her. They decide that the robbery is too risky and Al tries to back out, but Brick refuses to allow this and threatens to harm Tina if Al does not cooperate. Al stays with the group against his better judgment as the trailer crosses the state line into Nevada.

After reaching Reno and Harold's Club, the men don their cowboy suits and Tina heads for a boarding house. Jerry waits with the car as Al enters the club and surveys it, followed by Guy. Al watches a man pushing a cart and sees him go in and out of the cash room. The cart contains silver dollars that are used to replenish supplies at the gambling tables. Al approaches the man with the cart and tells him that Guy will kill him if he does not smile and cooperate. The man walks out of the casino with Al into an alley, where Brick threatens him.

At this point, the details of the plan start to become clear to the reader. There is a duplicate cart waiting in the alley, and Jerry is allegedly hiding inside the cart. However, the reader learns that it's actually a tape recorder inside the cart that plays a recording of Jerry's voice. "Jerry" threatens to kill the casino employee and himself if the man does not cooperate. They convince the man to go back into the casino with Al, who watches anxiously as he enters the cash room.

The man emerges and wheels the cart over to where Al is standing. Al takes the money sack from the cart, gives the man a warning about raising an alarm, and exits into the alley. As part two ends, Al finds himself alone, the getaway car having disappeared.

The last of the three-part serial appeared in the September 1953 issue of *Good Housekeeping*. From the alley, Al climbs a fire escape and looks down as people pour out of the casino. Al runs up onto the roof and hides the money in the netting that surrounds a big balloon advertising Harold's Club. Al removes his costume and climbs back down to the alley when the coast is clear. He then re-enters the club in street clothes and goes unnoticed; he plays a slot machine and hits the jackpot but walks away from the money to avoid calling attention to himself.

Reaching the boarding house where Tina is staying, he joins her and they spend the night together. They are wed at the courthouse the next day and honeymoon in Virginia City. A description of the city foreshadows themes that will be central to Finney's next novel, *The Body Snatchers:*

> Virginia City is a ghost town; eighty years ago forty thousand people lived there, and mined and fought for the millions in silver they dug out of these hills from the famous Comstock Lode. Now, surrounded by the still raw-looking old slag heaps, maybe five hundred people live in the dead town, running bars, restaurants, and curio shops for tourists. Off the main street we walked past empty old houses, gray and paintless, their windows gone, their porches sagging, their once expensive ornamental porch railings hanging twisted and loose. We stared at roofless walls that had once held a family, trying to imagine it. At one end of

town we walked up a broken flight of stone stairs leading to nothing but weeds, rubble, and humming insects, the house that had stood there long since gone [171].

In "5 Against the House," this scene depicts something that Al and Tina see on their honeymoon, but in *The Body Snatchers,* similar scenes would have more ominous connotations.

Back in Reno, Al walks to a pre-arranged meeting place, where he sees Brick. Brick explains that a patrol car had made Jerry leave the alley. Al refuses to tell Brick where the money is hidden (Brick, after all, had forced Al to remain involved), and the next day Al and Tina travel to Lake Tahoe to continue their honeymoon.

Back at the same meeting point, a little boy points out Brick to a policeman, and he is caught. Brick identifies Al, who manages to escape and tries to leave town with Tina in a taxicab. The alert cabbie signals a police car, however, and the newlyweds are arrested, taken to the police station, and interrogated. The plan failed because a nine-year-old boy had written his name in the dust on the trailer in Salt Lake City. He was then able to identify Brick as the driver for the police after the robbery.

Al and Tina are taken to an office, where they learn that Brick had given everyone's names to the police. Al agrees to tell them where the money is in exchange for Tina's freedom. After the money is recovered, Al gets a lecture and the club decides not to prosecute anyone in order to avoid bad publicity. Al flies home that evening and never sees Brick again. The story ends with Al holding Tina's hand and realizing that "now I knew what is important and what life is for..." (190) — he has matured in the course of the story and now realizes that love matters more than money.

The three-part serial in *Good Housekeeping* was successful enough for Jack Finney to turn it into his first novel, which was published by Doubleday the next year, in February 1954. The novel is not significantly different than the serialized story, and all of the major plot twists are unchanged. Minor revisions abound, though, often adding expletives or salacious details to scenes that were more innocent in the family magazine.

In chapter seven of the novel, background details about Guy's family are added, as are more details to strengthen Jerry's motivations for robbery. This chapter also deletes the details of the plan to go cross-country in a trailer; this is held back from the reader until chapter eleven, when the five friends actually make the trip. This method of creating suspense mirrors that used by Finney in holding back the details of the actual robbery from the reader.

Finney would use this same technique in his other three caper novels, *The House of Numbers, Assault on a Queen,* and *The Night People,* with varying degrees of success.

The main change in the middle part of the novel concerns a dream that Tina has while they are driving to Reno; she has a nightmare that Al will be killed in the robbery, and this leads him to try to back out of the scheme. The latter part of the novel has few differences from the serialized version.

Reviewers at the time were supportive of Jack Finney's first novel. Anthony Boucher, writing in the *New York Times,* called Finney "the admirable short-story writer," remarked that "the elaborately ingenious gimmicks with which the raid is carried out would stir the admiration of Raffles or even of Arsène Lupin," and concluded that "the high enterprise and dazzling execution of the crime itself will stay with you." James Sandoe of the *New York Herald Tribune* called *5 Against the House* a "pretty sad work" but admitted that "the essential gimmick is worth a look for its preposterous ingenuities and Mr. Finney gives the events some nice panic-striking swerves." Sergeant Cuff of the *Saturday Review* added that "implausabilities abound, but story is well paced."

Perhaps even more important to Jack Finney's life was the sale of *5 Against the House* to Columbia Pictures; it was made into a motion picture of the same name and released in May 1955. A paperback edition of the novel was issued by Pocket Books in July 1955 to coincide with the film. Stirling Silliphant, John Barnwell, and William Bowers wrote the screenplay and Phil Karlson directed it. Finney was said to have disliked the film (Bosky 173).

Viewed today, it is a disappointing adaptation of the novel that turns Brick into a psychotic Korean War veteran and Tina into a glamorous lounge singer. The climax is utterly different and clichéd — Brick steals the money and runs for it; he is cornered in a parking garage by Al and the police and talked out of using his gun. The film is most interesting when it follows the novel closely, in the trip to Reno and the robbery of Harold's Club. The film is discussed in more detail in chapter nineteen.

5 Against the House is a mediocre novel that has not been reprinted in America since 1955. Its chief value is that it set Jack Finney's career as a novelist in motion and set the scene for the series of caper novels that he would write over the next twenty-five years. His second novel would be much more memorable.

FOUR

The Body Snatchers

Jack Finney's next published work came in the November 26, 1954 issue of *Collier's,* the bi-weekly magazine that had published so many of his early short stories. He had not published anything since *5 Against the House,* which had been issued as a novel in February of that year, and his last story for *Collier's* had appeared on October 18, 1952 ("Diagnosis Completed").

"The Body Snatchers" was billed as "a new three-part serial," and would appear in three consecutive issues of *Collier's* (part two was published in the December 10, 1954 issue, followed by part three in the December 24, 1954 issue). Little did readers know that this would eventually become Finney's best-known tale, a story that would work its way into the cultural mind-set of the latter half of twentieth-century America.

The story is told in first-person narration by Miles Bennell, a 28-year-old doctor in the small town of Santa Mira, California. His former girlfriend, Becky Driscoll, arrives at his office just before closing time on a Thursday to report that she is worried about her cousin Wilma, who has come to believe that her Uncle Ira is an impostor.

After going to see Ira and finding him unchanged, Miles refers Wilma to a psychiatrist named Mannie Kaufman in nearby Valley Springs. On Friday, another patient tells Miles that her husband is not himself. By Tuesday, he has referred five more patients to Dr. Kaufman for the same problem.

On Wednesday night, Miles and Becky go on a date to the movies but are summoned by Jack Belicec, who takes them to his home and shows them a strangely unformed body that has appeared on the billiard table in his basement. Miles examines the body and decides that it is somehow not yet alive. He, Becky, Jack, and Jack's wife Theodora agree that they do not want to call the local police. Miles notices that the body appears to be a model of none other than Jack Belicec.

At three a.m. on Thursday morning, Jack and Theodora arrive at Miles's house and Miles has to sedate Theodora. She is frantic because she had trouble waking Jack after he fell asleep. On a hunch, Miles runs to Becky's house, breaks into her basement, and finds a double of Becky there. He takes Becky home and meets Jack, Theodora, and Mannie Kaufman. They return to Jack's house, only to find the body gone from the basement.

In part one of "The Body Snatchers," Finney sets the stage for a tale of horror and moves the story along quickly. All of the main characters are introduced and the small town setting is depicted quite well. The ending is a cliffhanger that is sure to make readers anxious for the arrival of part two.

The second part of the serial begins with Mannie Kaufman providing a logical explanation that the people of Santa Mira are suffering from mass hysteria. Jack produces a file he has amassed of clippings reporting unusual events (much like those found in the books of phenomenologist Charles Fort), including a local story about seed pods from outer space.

After Miles and Jack finally report the body in Jack's basement to the police, the tide in Santa Mira starts to turn. First a patient tells Miles that all is well, then he hears the same story from Wilma. That night, however, Jack finds four giant seed pods in Miles's basement. Miles and Jack recall the news clipping about seed pods from outer space as they watch the pods begin to take human form before their eyes. Miles destroys the pods and attempts to telephone the FBI in San Francisco, but the lines are tampered with and the call is unsuccessful.

Miles, Becky, Jack, and Theodora pile into Jack's car and drive out of Santa Mira, traveling eleven miles on Highway 101. They stop and check the trunk of the car, where they find two more pods that Miles destroys. They decide to return to Santa Mira to get help.

Jack drops off Miles and Becky back in town, and they walk the streets, noticing that everything around them seems dead. There is nothing happening, homes are in disrepair, and lawns have not been maintained. They are shocked to realize that they had not noticed the gradual change in Santa Mira. Returning to Becky's house, they stand outside a window and hear Becky's relatives make fun of Becky's concerns. Miles and Becky realize that the voices they hear do not belong to human beings. They run, calling Jack Belicec along the way to tell him what's happening.

Miles and Becky visit the home of Professor Budlong (an appropriate name for someone who has been replaced by a seed pod), who discusses how long it might have taken spores to drift through space toward Earth and then admits that he's one of them. Having been replaced by a space seed, he no longer feels emotion and explains that the pods' only goal is the survival of their species.

Budlong remarks that life "'takes any form necessary'" (124), including copying a pattern from human bodies. The pods plan to take over the world but can only survive on Earth for five years, after which they will move on into space, having used up this planet. As part two ends, Miles and Becky leave Professor Budlong's house and see Jack, chased by police and driving frantically through Santa Mira. Miles and Becky climb into the hills on the edge of town, tiring, realizing that nowhere is safe.

In part two of the serial, Finney methodically disposes of any reasonable explanation for what is happening and ratchets up the terror that Miles, Becky, and the reader feel as the characters come to realize that they are up against a seemingly unbeatable foe.

The conclusion of the three-part serial begins on Saturday, just over a week after the story began. Miles and Becky return to Miles's office, where they are soon trapped by Mannie Kaufman, Professor Budlong, and two other pod people. Miles and Becky use their wits to defeat the first attempt to replace them with pods and escape by attacking their captors as they try to transfer them to a jail cell.

Miles and Becky head for the hills and hide in a field until darkness falls. They walk toward Highway 101 and see pods growing in a field. They fill the field's irrigation ditches with gasoline and set the pods on fire, burning them as they grow. A crowd catches Miles and Becky but lacks emotion, almost as if uncertain about what to do with the humans.

At the last minute, Jack Belicec arrives with FBI agents to rescue Miles and Becky. Everyone watches as the remaining pods drift off into space, leaving a clearly inhospitable planet behind. As the serial ends, Miles recalls the incident from a vantage point years later, recalling how the pod people eventually died off and Santa Mira came to life again. He and Becky are together and he can hardly believe it ever happened.

> But this much I know: once in a while, the orderly, immutable sequences of life *are* inexplicably shifted and altered. You may read occasional queer little stories about them, or you may hear vague distorted rumors of them, and you probably dismiss them. But — some of them — *some* of them — are quite true [73].

The editors of *Collier's* must have known that they had something special on their hands, because Jerome Beatty, Jr., wrote, in an editor's note in the December 24, 1954 issue, that

> Mr. Finney's realistic tale scared the devil out of *us*. For reassurance, we showed it to Dr. Harry A. Charipper, chairman of the department of biology of New York University, and asked him about the "transmutation" of "substance" from one form of life to another, which is how the body snatchers are taking us over. He says: "Readers need not be reminded that twenty-five years ago that which is real now was but fantasy. The scientific analysis on which this story is based is most intriguing and certainly within the realm of possibility." Gulp.

Movie producer Walter Wanger also seems to have purchased the rights to the story by the time it appeared in *Collier's*; William Relling, Jr., notes that Wanger traveled to Jack Finney's home town of Mill Valley, California, "just after New Year's Day in 1955" with screenwriter Daniel Mainwaring and director Don Siegel to talk about the story and to scout filming locations (63). Kevin McCarthy, who would star in the film, recalled that he was living in New York in 1955 when Siegel telephoned him from California "'about a story that had been recently serialized in *Collier's*, the popular weekly magazine.'" McCarthy told an interviewer that "'I guess Siegel *sent* me the pertinent issues of the mag or I dug 'em up myself!'" (McCarty 233).

Invasion of the Body Snatchers, the film that was made from the original story, has become a cult classic among cinema enthusiasts. What was it about the three-part serial in November and December 1954 that excited a movie producer and led to countless articles in scholarly journals and books?

When asked about the many theories that have been advanced by critics, Jack Finney replied that he intended "The Body Snatchers" to be a good story and nothing more. "'I have read explanations of the 'meaning' of this story, which amuse me, because there is no meaning at all; it was just a story meant to entertain, and with no more meaning than that'" (King 290).

At the same time that Daniel Mainwaring and Don Siegel were getting ready to film the story, Finney was working on an expanded version, which would be published as Dell paperback first edition number 42 in 1955. This is the version of the story that has received a great deal of critical attention, and it is interesting to note the changes made in the transformation from magazine serial to paperback novel.

Unlike the novel *5 Against the House,* which has few significant changes from the prior serialized version, the novel *The Body Snatchers* has major revisions that change the focus of the story and alter its conclusion.

Chapter one of the novel is expanded, with entire paragraphs and many details added. Among the details are male and female skeletons (the male named Fred) that Miles keeps in his closet (11–12). These skeletons play an important role later in the novel, but Finney's light-hearted introduction of them in the early part of the book gives no hint of their later purpose. Finney also may be suggesting that Miles has psychological skeletons in his closet that will later be revealed.

Wilma's character is filled out in chapter two with an anecdote from her childhood that she shares with Miles — she recalls going to a hardware store with her Uncle Ira and wanting a tiny door in a frame that she saw there (16). This hint that Wilma is about to enter an *Alice in Wonderland*-like situation is strengthened by her other recollection, when she tells Miles of another time that she saw a cloud "'shaped like a rabbit'" (16).

Miles's intelligence and trustworthiness are highlighted by a passage added to chapter three, where he recalls diagnosing Theodora Belicec with Rocky Mountain spotted fever the year before. It was an unusual diagnosis, but Miles was certain and Jack believed him (27). This story helps to create a bond of trust between Miles and the Belicecs that will serve to bolster their confidence in each other when strange things start to happen.

Among the passages in chapters four and five that are added, expanded, or reworked is one which has been cited by critics as a key moment in the novel. In the middle of the night, Miles is awakened by his telephone ringing. He answers, but there is no one on the other end of the line. In the novel, the following section is added:

> A year ago the night operator, whose name I'd have known, could have told me who'd called. It would probably have been the only light on her board at that time of night, and she'd have remembered which one it was, because they were calling the doctor. But now we have dial phones, marvelously efficient, saving you a full second or more every time you call, inhumanly perfect, and utterly brainless; and none of them will ever remember where the doctor is at night, when a child is sick and needs him. Sometimes I think we're refining all humanity out of our lives [43].

Miles thinks of the new telephone system as "inhumanly perfect," foreshadowing the alien pod people he will encounter later in the novel.

Chapter six expands the search of Becky's basement and adds two full pages of description of Becky's pod and its resemblance to the real person (52–54). Two more paragraphs added at the chapter's end remove the cliffhanger that had concluded part one of the serial, as Mannie prepares a rational explanation for Miles.

The next eight chapters expand the portion of the story that had appeared as part two of the serial. In chapter seven, Finney adds a story told by Mannie Kaufman of a bizarre character known as the Mattoon Maniac; in chapter eight, additional Fortean stories are added to flesh out Jack's collection of clippings reporting unusual occurrences (71). Two more paragraphs are added later in chapter eight that feature Miles talking to his reflection in the mirror as he shaves. Miles's comments have also been cited by Glen M. Johnson in his insightful comparison of the novel and film (8). Miles says to himself:

> "You can marry them, all right; you just can't stay married, that's your trouble. You are weak. Emotionally unstable. Basically insecure. A latent thumb-sucker. A cesspool of immaturity, unfit for adult responsibility" [76].

Once again, a passage that has been cited as central to understanding the themes of the novel is one that was absent from the original serial. Another important passage is added to chapter nine, where Miles walks along Main Street and observes that "it seemed littered and shabby" (77). He thinks that it's just due to his mood, however, and attaches no significance to the run-down appearance of downtown Santa Mira.

Chapter ten begins with another passage that is not present in the serial and that has a similar effect. Here, Miles goes up to his attic and looks out of the window at the town below. He recalls all of the places and friends he has known since he was a boy, thinking "I knew them all, at least by sight, or to nod or speak to on the street. I'd grown up here...." He contrasts what he has always known with the present Santa Mira and thinks "And now I didn't know it any more" (89). The formerly friendly faces and places have become menacing and now menace Miles.

Another big change in chapter ten occurs when Miles, rather than Jack, attempts to call the outside world for help. In the serial, Jack tries to call the FBI in San Francisco (119). In the novel, Miles calls old school friend Ben Eichler at the Pentagon (92–97) and only when this conversation fails does Jack try the FBI.

Chapter twelve of the novel is almost entirely new, focusing on the changes in Santa Mira brought on by the pod people. According to Miles,

> "In seven blocks we haven't passed a single house with as much as the trim being repainted; not a roof, porch, or even a cracked window being repaired; not a tree, shrub, or a blade of grass being planted, or even trimmed. Nothing's *happening*, Becky, nobody's *doing* anything. And they haven't for days, maybe weeks" [108].

A scene in a drugstore is added, where a salesman from out of town complains that nobody in Santa Mira is buying anything anymore (110–12), and a scene in the library is added, where Miles discovers that all news of the pods has been snipped out of the newspapers (112–15). Finney makes an in-joke here when he has Becky reading *Woman's Home Companion* and Miles "glancing through *Collier's*" (113); one would not be surprised if they found stories by Jack Finney in the magazines' pages.

Scenes like those in chapter twelve led Glen M. Johnson to write that "when the town turns shabby ... such neglect becomes a product of something sinister" (9). Stephen King was more lighthearted about it, writing that "From where Finney stands, the scariest thing about the pod people is that chaos doesn't bother them a bit and they have absolutely no sense of aesthetics..." (303).

One of the most often discussed scenes in the novel doesn't appear at all in the original serial. The comparison of the overheard conversation among the pod people with Miles's memory of an overheard conversation involving Billy, the shoeshine man, is memorable, and Finney's observations about race relations in 1950s America are worth noting. Briefly, Miles recalls a moment when he saw beyond the facade created by a black man for his white customers; Miles notably recalls that, after the incident, "I never again had my shoes shined at Billy's stand" (119). To quote Glen M. Johnson again,

> This astounding passage has only the most tenuous relationship to the plot of the novel; indeed, Finney has to go to awkward lengths to set it up. But the segment is all the more significant for its awkwardness and intensity. Here, in a work of popular literature from 1954 [sic], is a compulsive association of American blacks with fictional characters who are both victims and subversives [7–8].

Like virtually all of the passages in *The Body Snatchers* that have attracted critical attention, this section of the novel did not appear in the original serial. Chapter fourteen of the novel also includes one other major change from the serial. In the novel, Miles and Becky meet Professor Budlong and discuss his theories of seed pods' arrival from outer space. Budlong tells Miles that it's impossible for pods to change into duplicates of human beings, and Miles and Becky leave, with Miles feeling rather foolish. Almost immediately thereafter, he sees Jack being chased in his car by pod people and he knows the threat is real.

In the serial, the scene with Professor Budlong is quite different. Miles catches Budlong in a lie and confronts him; Budlong admits that he's a duplicate and has a long and rational discussion with Miles about the purpose of the invasion. He explains that the pods left a dying planet and moved across the universe with their only goal being survival of their race. However, he explains that the duplicates cannot live for very long due to instability in their makeup, and that they will all be dead within five years. The pods will use up life on Earth and then move on into space to look for new hosts. "'They are the parasites of the universe, and they'll be the final survivors in it'" (125).

Miles and Becky leave Professor Budlong's house (as in the novel), and the story then continues in the same fashion in both versions. Why did Finney delete this scene from the novel when he was working hard to expand his story? Perhaps the explanation of the pods' mission was too trite, too much the stuff of many science fiction stories that had come before. Or perhaps he thought that the calm discussion between Miles, Becky, and Professor Budlong hurt the suspenseful tone that he was developing. In any case, part two of the serial ends as does chapter fourteen of the novel, with Miles and Becky tiring as they head for the hills at the edge of town.

The third and final part of the serialized version of *The Body Snatchers* was expanded to comprise chapters fifteen through twenty-one of the novel. This section includes fewer changes and new passages than the sections before it, moving quickly to the conclusion. The climax of the novel is substantially different than that of the serial, however, and the changes deserve some attention.

In the novel, Miles and Becky have set fire to the field of pods and, when they are finally captured, they watch as the pods drift off into space, choosing to leave an inhospitable planet. In the serial, they are rescued at the last minute by the arrival (with a "squeal of tires" [73]) of three cars containing Jack Belicec and a number of FBI agents with riot guns and machine guns. They round up the pod people and move them back toward town. As they walk, everybody stops and it is only then that the pods begin to drift off into space.

The serial's climax is straight out of a pulp magazine and the novel is better off without it. The subsequent last chapter of the novel follows the conclusion of the serial rather closely, and they end in the same way.

As readers, we are thus faced with two versions of the same story — the three-part serial originally appearing in *Collier's* in November and December 1954, and the expanded novel appearing in 1955. Jack Finney clearly did a great deal of work to expand the serial to novel form, and a careful examination of the two side by side reveals significant changes.

First and foremost is the emphasis that Finney put on the decline of the town of Santa Mira when he expanded his story to novel form.

Several important passages demonstrate that this theme was important to the author, for he chose it as a method of fleshing out the details of his story. But who are the invaders who "threaten an established, cherished way of life"? (Johnson 5). Are they the Communists who were so feared in 1950s America? This is doubtful, since later novels such as *Time and Again* and *The Night People* suggest that Jack Finney's politics were more liberal than conservative. Are they the right-wing followers of Senator Joseph McCarthy, who hunted down Communists in America in the 1950s? This, too, is inaccurate, according to the author.

When asked about the hidden meaning in *The Body Snatchers*, Jack Finney replied that "'I wrote the story purely as a good read'" (Oliver). Judging from his loving portrayal of small towns in stories and novels throughout his career, it is unlikely that Finney would have agreed that the novel "could also easily be read as a clever assault on the dehumanizing conformity of small town life in America in the 1950s" (Sloan 186). Even the idea that a "theme of the novel is the way that small-town life nourishes the spirit of the individual and strengthens him to stand up to terrifying threats" (Otten 437) was addressed by Finney, who wrote that "'the idea of writing a whole book in order to say that it's not really a good thing for us all to be alike, and that individuality is a good thing, makes me laugh'" (King 290).

In the end, then, Glen Johnson is most likely correct when he writes that *The Body Snatchers* "encompasses and exposes for analysis the peculiar anxieties and accommodations of the early cold war period" (5). Despite Jack Finney's assertions that the story is pure entertainment, the themes that he keeps returning to in the novel version demonstrate an interest in the preservation of small town life and the way that it was beginning to disappear in the 1950s.

According to Robert Otten, *The Body Snatchers* was "favorably reviewed in the leading science fiction magazines" (436) of the time but, as a paperback original, it did not receive a large amount of attention in mainstream publications. The main reason that it became famous was the film adaptation, which was released in 1956, the year after the novel was published. Despite the fact that the producer visited Finney in Mill Valley to discuss the adaptation of novel into film, "Finney had nothing to do with" the screenplay (Ickes 36) and sold the film's rights in 1955 for $7500.

The film, titled *Invasion of the Body Snatchers*, was written by Daniel Mainwaring and starred Kevin McCarthy, who later said that the script was "'*less subtle* and *sophisticated* ... than Jack Finney's serialized novel, which had come out in a paperback edition by that time'" (McCarty 238). McCarthy's take on the story is interesting, especially in light of Finney's background writing advertising copy: "'I viewed it as an attack on or satire of Madison Avenue attitudes. *The whole idea of programming us to eat the same foods, drink the same beverages, conform to certain modes of behavior'*" (252–4).

Whatever it meant, the film version of *The Body Snatchers* eventually was recognized as a classic of science fiction cinema, and has been the subject of critical attention ever since its appearance in 1956. Probably due to the popularity of the film, Finney's novel has remained in print in various editions since it was first published.

In 1975 or 1976, movie producer Robert Solo decided to remake and update *Invasion of the Body Snatchers* (Timpone 126), and the result was a 1978 film of the same name, directed by Philip Kaufman. Again, Finney had nothing to do with the filmed version of his novel, which was updated to the 1970s and set in San Francisco. This film veers far from the source novel and suffers in comparison. According to Solo, Finney was angry at not being paid for the new version of his story and refused to come when he was invited to be in a scene in the film (Timpone 136).

Not to be outdone, Finney took his 1955 novel and revised it for reissue in 1978 to tie in with the new film. He retitled the novel *Invasion of the Body Snatchers* and changed the name of the town where the story occurs from Santa Mira to Mill Valley, where Finney had been living since about 1950. While most of the changes are minimal, mainly updating references that would seem dated to 1978 readers, Finney does have a bit of fun in chapter three when he makes the movie that Miles and Becky attend a filmed version of his own novel, *Time and Again*: "it was a good picture ... about a guy who finds a way to visit the past" (28). Ironically, Finney's 1970 novel *Time and Again* has never been filmed.

Under its new title, the novel continued to remain in print through the 1980s and 1990s, and a third film version was released in 1993, with the title shortened to *Body Snatchers*. According to Bernadette Lynn Bosky, Finney earned an additional $3750 for "each of the remakes due to a loophole in the copyright law" (173), making his grand total for three movie adaptations of the novel only $15,000. All three films are examined in detail in chapter nineteen.

Serial, novel, revised novel, and three film adaptations — as well as an aborted television series (Timpone 138) — *The Body Snatchers* has been Jack Finney's most famous work and certainly what he is most known for. According to J. Sydney Jones, *The Body Snatchers* "changed everything" for Finney and "allowed him to support his family solely on his writing" (74). Oddly enough, after achieving success with the serials "5 Against the House" and "The Body Snatchers," both of which were expanded into novels and adapted as motion pictures, Finney returned to writing short stories and would not publish another novel for two years.

FIVE

More Short Stories and *The Third Level*

In 1953 and 1954, Jack Finney published his first two serialized novels, "5 Against the House" and "The Body Snatchers," but he did not publish any other short stories. In February 1955, he resumed publishing short stories with "Legal and Tender" in *Good Housekeeping*. It features young married couple Benjamin and Ruth Callandar in the first of their four appearances. The Callandars are quite similar to the Ryans, who had already appeared in ten earlier stories by Finney; perhaps the author was trying to create a new series for *Good Housekeeping* as he had done with the Ryans for *Collier's*.

"Legal and Tender" is a light, romantic comedy in which Ben becomes interested in the phrase "lawful money" that appeared at that time on the American five-dollar bill. Printed on the bill was the phrase, "redeemable in lawful money," and Ben embarrasses Ruth by presenting a five-dollar bill at a bank and asking to trade it for lawful money. Of course, no one knows what lawful money is, and the story ends with the couple agreeing that they can still have fun even though they're married.

"Tattletale Tape" followed, in the March 4, 1955 issue of *Collier's*, and it marked the eleventh and last appearance of Finney's original young, married couple, Tim and Eve Ryan. The Ryans had not been heard from in print since September 1952; this time, they are staying at the apartment of Tim's boss, Al Webber, babysitting the Webbers' son, Alec.

After putting Alec to bed, Tim and Eve discuss the boy's parents in less-than-flattering terms. The boy secretly records their conversation and plays it back for them. Tim fears he'll lose his job if his boss hears the recording. Eve is worn out by Alec, who refuses to go to sleep, but Tim finally succeeds in putting the boy to bed with a sleeping pill.

At the story's end, Tim saves the day by revising the recording so that it contains only praise for the Webbers. This lighthearted story has nothing special to recommend it, but it does serve as a fitting end to the Tim and Eve Ryan series.

Jack Finney's next published story, "Of Missing Persons," finds him returning to the time travel theme that runs through much of his best work. In the magazine's table of contents, the editors write that

> For quite some years now, and we state this with conviction and without any attempt at false modesty, *Good Housekeeping* has been considered by the country's leading authors, as well as by the general public, to be the top magazine for short stories. Here's a case in point. Stories as good as this usually appear only *here* ["What's in this Issue"].

"Of Missing Persons" tells the story of Charley Ewell, a lonely bank teller in New York City who tells a travel agent, "'I'd like to — get away'" (144). He wants to escape, he says, "'From New York ... and cities in general. From worry. And fear. And the things I read in my newspapers.... From life itself— the way it is today, at least'" (144).

Charley is shown pictures of idyllic Verna, which he thinks looks like "the way America once looked when it was new" (145). The agent explains that Verna is light years away but easy to reach. For example, he mentions a family called the Bradens (an in-joke by Jack Finney, also known as Walter Braden Finney) and explains that people have been escaping to Verna for a long time — Ambrose Bierce and Judge Crater among them.

Charley decides to go, buys a ticket, and goes to a bus stop "on one of the narrow streets west of Broadway" (149), where he describes the bus: "It was precisely the sort of obscure little bus you see around there, ridden always by shabby, tired, silent people, going no one knows where" (149).

In this passage, as in the entire story, Finney's talent for setting fantastic events in the most mundane places is evident. Charley boards the bus and watches the "strained, harassed faces" (149) of drivers in passing cars as the bus takes him and its other passengers to a barn on Long Island, where they await transport to Verna.

Believing he's been tricked, Charley leaves the barn, but turns back as he does so. Like Lot's wife, this brief glance back is his undoing, as he sees — "for less than the blink of an eye" (150) — a vision of Verna, and the life he could have lived.

His one chance gone, he returns to his drab life, haunted by the knowledge that he has lost the opportunity to leave unhappiness behind and start anew. The story ends with his advice to the reader to make the trip to Verna if he ever gets the chance — because it won't come again.

"Of Missing Persons" is a story of longing to escape from the modern world, but this time the escape is to another world, where life is like it used to be, only better. Combining the best elements of today (work-saving technology) and yesterday (everything else), it offers a new start for the world-weary. Finney picks up the thread from "I'm Scared" and again offers a glimpse into a possible alternative to those tired of modern life.

As Gary K. Wolfe notes, "'Of Missing Persons' replaces time travel with space travel, but the theme of escape remains central" (253). Mike Resnick, writing in *The Magazine of Fantasy and Science Fiction* in 1997, adds that it is a "tremendously moving tale that elicits the emotional response John Campbell was trying for when he wrote the classic 'Twilight.'"

In a lighter vein was Finney's next story, "A Man of Confidence," which appeared in the August 1955 issue of *Good Housekeeping*. The confidence man of the title is registered in a Miami Beach hotel as Alfred G. Henkle, inventor, and he lures a mining engineer named Frank O. Lucca into wanting and finally buying a machine to counterfeit money.

The story ends with Henkle flying off by airplane and admiring the gold bar he received from Lucca in trade for the phony counterfeiting machine. However, Finney subtly suggests that the con man may himself have been conned by the mining engineer when he explains that the large gold bar was as heavy "as only two metals, gold — and lead — can be" (115). This twist is so subtle that one could almost miss it, but it leaves the reader wondering just who in this story is being conned.

Jack Finney returned to the subject of time travel in his next story, "Second Chance," one of his best tales. The story is told in first-person narration by an unnamed narrator who is a senior at Poynt College in Hylesburg, Illinois (a name quite similar to Finney's college town of Galesburg). He buys a beat-up Jordan Playboy, a classic car from the 1920s, spends all of his time restoring it, puts 1923 license plates on it, and then takes it out to pick up a girl for a date. Even though he beats a new 1956 sports car at a traffic light, his date is not interested in riding around all night in an old car, and won't go out in it.

The narrator drives off alone into the night, deciding to take the "old Cressville road" (191), which had been the only road to Cressville until a new highway had bypassed it fifteen years before. "I liked just drifting along the old road," he recalls, singing songs from the 1920s and "having a wonderful time" (192). In his mind, he begins to think he's really in the 1920s, and soon other vintage cars begin passing him.

"I've read some of the stuff about Time with a capital T," he tells the reader, and then briefly explains Einstein's comparison of time to a river. "I wonder if we aren't barred from the past by a thousand invisible chains," he continues, and concludes that — because everything was just right that night — "we were free on the surface of Time" and "simply *drifted* into the time my Jordan belonged in" (194).

Finney's narrator in "Second Chance" finds himself back in the 1920s after having put himself in a position to accept such a change. This marks a step forward from "The Third Level," where the narrator accidentally wanders into the past, toward the method that Si Morley in *Time and Again* would use fourteen years later, where he is able to create a situation and mentally will himself into the past.

The narrator in "Second Chance" drives back to Hylesburg and along Main Street, comparing what he sees to what he knows from the 1950s. Parking his car, he walks along Main Street, until a crowd comes out of the Orpheum movie theater and a young man hops into the narrator's car and begins to drive off. The narrator runs in front of the car and stops the driver momentarily before he drives off into the night. The narrator spends the night walking around 1923 Hylesburg and in the morning finds himself back in 1956.

Time passes and the narrator goes back to school, where he meets and falls in love with Helen McCauley, whose father just happens to have an old Jordan Playboy in his barn. Mr. McCauley gives the narrator the car, and he soon realizes that it's the same one that was stolen from him back in 1923. Mr. McCauley tells of a night in 1923 when he had almost been killed while racing a train in the Jordan Playboy, and the narrator realizes that he had jumped out in front of the car and stopped McCauley on Main Street for just enough time to prevent the man's death.

The story ends with a beautiful passage where the narrator explains that "it's an especial tragedy when a young couple's lives are cut off for no other reason than the sheer exuberance nature put into them" and that "when that old Jordan was restored" it went back to 1923 and gave them a second chance. The narrator confides to the reader that he will marry Helen McCauley and "we'll leave on our honeymoon in the Jordan Playboy" (199).

"Second Chance" is as good a story as Jack Finney ever wrote. Michael Beard called it "perhaps Finney's most successful realization of the mystique of artifacts from the past" and argues that it "suggests that there is a redemptive power in connections with the past" (184). Kim Newman called it a perfect short story (197), and Mike Resnick pointed out that it (and "The Third Level") "may well have been the precursors of Finney's wildly successful time travel novels."

Finney's next published work was the novella, "The House of Numbers," which will be discussed in the next chapter. His third story to see print in 1956 was the outstanding suspense tale, "Contents of the Dead Man's Pocket," which appeared in the October 26, 1956 issue of *Collier's*. This was to be Jack Finney's last story in *Collier's*, where his first published work had appeared in 1947. The magazine, which had been founded in 1888 and had reached a circulation of 2,500,000 during World War Two, had begun to decrease in popularity after the war and ceased publishing on December 16, 1956, less than two months after "Contents of the Dead Man's Pocket" was published ("Collier's Weekly" and "Crowell-Collier").

Unlike "Second Chance," "Contents of the Dead Man's Pocket" is narrated by a third person, omniscient narrator, who tells the story of Tom Benecke, a resident of an apartment on the eleventh floor of a building in New York City. His wife Clare leaves to go to the movies by herself as he stays home to type a memo for his job. A sheet of paper suddenly flies out the window and sticks onto the wall by the ledge outside. On the sheet is all of the research that Tom has done to support "his idea for a new grocery-store display method"; Tom thinks, "of all the papers on his desk, why did it have to be this one in particular!" (85).

Suspense begins to build as Tom climbs out onto the narrow ledge to retrieve the sheet of paper. He slides along, eleven stories above Lexington Avenue, panics when he looks down, and nearly falls, his body swaying "outward to the knife edge of balance" (86). After being frozen with fear, he begins to edge back along the ledge to his apartment window, but in the process of breaking another near fall he accidentally shuts the window.

Unable to break the glass and terrified by the knowledge that his wife will not be home for hours, he tries to send signals by dropping first flaming letters and then coins to the street below, but his attempts go unnoticed on the busy streets of New York. Finally, the only thing left in his pockets is the sheet of paper he had climbed out on the ledge to retrieve. He thinks of falling to his death and "[a]ll they'd find in his pockets would be the yellow sheet. *Contents of the dead man's pockets,* he thought, *one sheet of paper bearing penciled notations — incomprehensible*" (90).

Tom thus comes to realize that he has put his life in jeopardy for something worthless. He laments his wasted life, regretting all of the nights he stayed home working while his wife went out and all of the hours he'd spent alone. He resolves to make one final attempt to break the glass, knowing that if he fails the strength of the blow will cause him to fall to his death. As he puts his all into the blow, he speaks his wife's name and feels himself falling through the broken window into the safety of his apartment.

He puts the sheet of paper on his desk and opens the front door "to go find his wife." Blown by a draft from the hallway, the sheet flies out of the window again, but this time, "Tom Benecke burst into laughter and then closed the door behind him" (91). The door that closes at the end of "Contents of the Dead Man's Pocket" is clearly both a literal and a figurative one, representing the end of a wasted life and the beginning of one that promises to have more meaning. One can read into this a parallel to Jack Finney's decision in the late 1940s to leave behind his life as an advertising man in New York City and move to California to devote his time to writing.

Stephen King allegedly wrote his story "The Ledge" as an homage to Finney's "Contents of the Dead Man's Pocket" (Newman 197–98), and the latter stands as one of Jack Finney's most suspenseful short stories.

Jack Finney also published a one-act play in 1956 entitled *Telephone Roulette*, which is discussed in chapter seventeen.

Three short stories were published in *Good Housekeeping* in 1957; two were romantic comedies and none were chosen to be reprinted in either of Jack Finney's subsequent short story collections.

"Rainy Sunday" is the second story to feature Benjamin and Ruth Callandar, who had first appeared in "Legal and Tender," published in February 1955. The Callandars and their friends, June and Charley Howser, banter by telephone about who should leave their San Francisco apartment to visit whom on a rainy Sunday afternoon. They conclude by having a party by telephone. Like the Tim and Eve Ryan stories, this lighthearted tale mainly focuses on the relationship between the young couple at its center. Unlike the Ryans, who live in New York, the Callandars live in San Francisco.

"Expression of Love" again features the Callanders (now spelled with an "e"), who meet the Howsers at Union Square in San Francisco. Charley and Ben play pranks and drive Ruth and June to plan a few pranks of their own.

"Fast Buck" recalls "Stopover at Reno" as it tells the story of a young couple named Sam and Laurie, who regretfully realize that the $2500 they've saved over four years is only half the money they need for a down payment on a house. Sam suggests that they drive to Reno, Nevada, to spend the night, and Laurie agrees. They then drive through the mountains to Reno, where Sam plans to wager on dice to win the rest of the money they need.

Tension mounts in the casino as Sam bets their savings, winning and losing in turns but never getting very far ahead. At one point he loses all of his money, then begins to win it back on a desperation bet using a few dollars from his pocket. A winning streak brings him back to $2560; he and Laurie stop gambling, stay the night in Reno, and add $10 to the house fund.

This suspenseful tale mixes the domestic concerns of a young, married couple with the excitement of gambling at a casino.

Between 1947 and 1957, Jack Finney published thirty-eight short stories, two serialized novels that were later expanded into book form, and a novella. It was clearly time for some of his best stories to be collected in book form and, in 1957, his first collection of short stories, *The Third Level*, was published. It collected eleven stories that had been published before and added "A Dash of Spring," for which no prior publication source has been found.

The stories chosen for this collection were "The Third Level," "Such Interesting Neighbors," "I'm Scared," "Cousin Len's Wonderful Adjective Cellar," "Of Missing Persons," "Something in a Cloud," "There Is a Tide," "Behind the News," "Quit Zoomin' Those Hands Through the Air," "A Dash of Spring," "Second Chance," and "Contents of the Dead Man's Pocket." The back cover copy on the 1959 paperback edition of *The Third Level* sets forth the collection's theme: "Their subject is time... But time on a new level, a diverting, sometimes frightening level, where the Past, the Present, and the Future are all joined...." While not exactly true of all of the stories in *The Third Level,* this blurb shows that time travel tales were becoming a hallmark of Jack Finney's fiction.

The new story, "A Dash of Spring," is a bit of fluff where real life is contrasted with life as it is presented in magazines or movies. The resulting romance that blooms between Louise Huppfelt and Ralph Shultz is presented in a humorous fashion and the story reads like one that Finney might have written in the late 1940s.

Reviews at the time *The Third Level* was published were mostly favorable. The Kirkus Service called the book "amiable" and recommended it as "pleasant timepassing." John F. Moran, writing in the *Library Journal,* noted that "fantasy ... is the chief element" in the collection, but said that the theme of escape from the present "becomes fairly tiresome when it crops up time and again." P. Schuyler Miller wrote in *Astounding Science-Fiction* that "'if you want to know the kind of SF the general public wants, this [volume of short stories] is as good a sample as you're likely to get'" (quoted in Jones 75), and J. Sydney Jones commented that "all of these stories provide escapist reading in the most literal of its meanings: Finney's characters are escaping from their present predicaments" (75).

The magazine *Infinity Science Fiction* selected *The Third Level* as the year's best short-story collection (Beard 183–84), and Damon

Knight wrote that Finney re-invests the theme of time travel "'with all the strangeness and wonder that properly belong to it'" (quoted in Beard 184).

Later critics have viewed the collection as a classic. Stephen King wrote in 1981 that, in *The Third Level,* "Finney actually defined the boundaries of [Rod] Serling's *Twilight Zone*" (236), arguing that the well-known television series that premiered in 1959 owed much of its success to groundwork that had been laid by Jack Finney. Finally, Mike Resnick, writing in 1997 in *The Magazine of Fantasy and Science Fiction,* remarked that this collection was "the very best book [Finney] ever signed his name to."

With the short stories he published between 1955 and 1957, culminating in the collection, *The Third Level,* Jack Finney secured for himself an honored place in the ranks of twentieth-century writers of fantasy. His next novel, however, would return to the genre of crime fiction that he had explored in *5 Against the House.*

SIX

The House of Numbers

The cover of the July 1956 issue of *Cosmopolitan* magazine advertised "The House of Numbers" as a "complete novel by Jack Finney, so gripping and fascinating you can't put it down." Inside, the "complete suspense novel" spans the course of 26 pages. In May 1957, an expanded version of the story appeared as a paperback first edition (Dell First Edition A139), and the back cover told readers that it was "soon to be an M-G-M movie starring Jack Palance." The movie, retitled *House of Numbers,* was released that same year.

The House of Numbers is told in first-person narration by Benjamin Harrison Jarvis, a 26-year-old man whose brother, Arnie, is a prisoner at San Quentin Prison. The book opens as Ben and Ruth Gehlmann, Arnie's fiancée, view the prison from the vantage point of a small boat in the San Francisco Bay. They plan to help Arnie escape, and Ben tells Ruth to "'take a *good* look, because you're looking at the kind of place you'll end up in instead ... if anything at all goes wrong'" (7).

Ben and Ruth met and rented a house together in Marin County (where Jack Finney lived) in order to plan Arnie's escape. Ruth is beautiful and from a wealthy, old San Francisco family. Arnie bought her an expensive engagement ring but paid for it with bad checks and was sent to prison for fraud. She feels guilty and Ben explains that Arnie also talked him into dropping everything to plan for the escape. Even though they agree that "'it's impossible to get a man out of there,'"

50

(17), Ben suspects that they'll have to go through with the attempt at escape, and the thought frightens him.

Finney uses some narrative trickery in *The House of Numbers,* switching points of view between different narrators. The second and third chapters are narrated in the first person by Arnie Jarvis, who is brought before a San Quentin disciplinary committee that is investigating an attack on a guard. An ex-convict who has been paroled is being brought back to the prison to identify the guard's attacker and, though Arnie feigns disinterest at the hearing, he thinks that he must escape within the next four days to avoid being identified as the culprit.

In chapter three, Arnie grills fellow inmate Al about escape and Al recalls various failed attempts over the years. Arnie retires to his cell to think of a way out.

Chapters four through ten are narrated by Ben. After visiting Arnie in prison, Ben returns and explains the predicament to Ruth, who has already packed her bags to go back to San Francisco. Ben explains that Section 4500 of the California Penal Code prescribes the death penalty for an assault with a deadly weapon committed by a prisoner serving a life sentence. Arnie is facing death, and Ben has a plan to help him escape. Ruth agrees to stay and help.

In chapter five, Ben tells Ruth a good deal about Arnie's background, explaining some of the factors in his life that may have made him commit a crime. Ben explains that Arnie's identity is based largely on what other people think of him — "'he has no conviction inside himself about what he really is; it has to be supplied to him all the time'" (45). Arnie was greatly affected by his father's sudden unemployment when Arnie was in high school, and Arnie's repeated attempts to appear successful culminated with the fraudulent engagement ring purchase that landed him in San Quentin.

After this bit of background, Ben and Ruth split up to spend the afternoon buying supplies to carry out their plan. Finney does not reveal the details of the plan to the reader, just as in *5 Against the House* he held back details of the casino robbery plans in order to create suspense.

Problems begin to emerge in chapter six, when Mr. Nova, a neighbor, approaches Ben and Ruth. He's an aging guard at San Quentin who tells Ben that he saw him at the prison. Nova offers to help Arnie, but Ben declines the offer from the unsavory man and returns home with Ruth to continue preparing. At two a.m., they drive up Highway 101 to the San Rafael ferry near the prison wall. Ben and Ruth's time together has sparked an attraction between them, and they kiss before Ruth drops Ben off at a preselected place.

In chapter seven, Ben climbs over the prison wall and hides inside an empty furniture crate outside the building where the prisoners make furniture. He sleeps poorly and waits for morning, which arrives in chapter eight. The details of the escape plan begin to come clear at this point, when Arnie gives Ben his identification card and takes his place in the furniture crate. Ben is now Arnie, fading into the daily life of prisoners and living the life of a convict. After successfully making it through a search, Ben arrives at his lodging for the night: "I was locked in cell 1042 of San Quentin Prison" (83).

Details of prison life dominate the next two chapters, as Ben learns about the various checks and counts that the guards use to keep track of the inmates. The first count completed, Ben knows that he has successfully replaced Arnie and that his brother will not be missed. Ben then follows the rest of the convicts into the huge cafeteria for dinner. In this portion of the novel, Ben is the eyes and ears of the reader, experiencing first-hand what it is like to be an inmate of San Quentin and describing it all for us from the point of view of an innocent man.

Finney's point of view here is interesting, especially in light of the book's dedication: "To my friend, Harley O. Teets, Warden of the California State Prison, San Quentin" (4). Despite having committed a crime in order to help his guilty brother break out of prison and avoid paying for a violent crime, Ben is portrayed as an innocent man, and his prison experience is a mixture of fear and awe. The awe is rather odd, and reads as if Finney were writing a public relations piece for the benefit of the jail. As Ben looks around the cafeteria, he thinks:

> It was a cheerful room, it occurred to me, the floor a rich red, tables of light wood, beautifully made and varnished, the walls a soft green and painted with murals. And it was immaculately clean. *Not bad*, I thought, and leaned back a little on my stool, comfortably; ... [99].

Although this sense of peace does not last long and contrasts with what happens next, the reader gets the sense that Finney is laying it on a bit too thick here, as if trying to present a balanced point of view in order to please a friend.

Ben's problems begin as he absentmindedly lights a cigarette after dinner. With this act, he unknowingly breaks a prison rule, and a guard yells at him. His identification is checked and he sees his neighbor, Nova, watching him. Nova follows Ben back to his cell and Ben resolves to kill Nova to protect his own secret — yet Ben's conscience prevents him from carrying out the murder. "I was willing; I could justify it; I knew I had to do it... But I could not kill him... I was incapable of the act of murder..." (105). Ben is not Arnie; he has an intact superego in place to stop himself from carrying out the desires of his id.

Fortunately for Ben, Nova thinks he is Arnie, and the danger passes. Ben's life in prison continues, and he thinks "I truly understood how utterly anonymous and depersonalized a man became when he entered this place" (110). He thinks of his life outside and his address is of interest: 175 Loming Court, Mill Valley, California (110), in the same town where Jack Finney lived. Finney gives the prison system another plug, as Ben thinks: "The warden of this prison and the men around him at this particular moment in the prison's history, Arnie claimed, did their imaginative and resourceful best for the men California required them to confine" (111). Yet, as chapter ten ends, Ben worries that Arnie might betray him and leave him there, then chides himself for failing to trust his brother.

Chapter eleven returns to Arnie's point of view and he narrates the story of his preparations for escape, preparing a hole in the ground covered with plywood for some unexplained purpose and then returning to his hiding place in the furniture crate.

Ben narrates chapter twelve, in which the escape plans take an interesting twist — Ben takes Arnie's place in the crate and Arnie returns to his cell. That night, Ben climbs the prison wall and meets Ruth, who drives east into Nevada, toward Reno.

Arnie's escape begins in chapter thirteen, which he narrates, as he slips into the hole he had dug two nights before. "I'm in a grave" (130), he thinks, but as time passes and he realizes he will soon be reported as missing, his excitement grows. As Ben told Ruth earlier in the novel, Arnie's sense of self comes from what other people think of him. "You're nobody in prison —" he thinks, "*nothing*— just a pair of blue pants and a shirt. But once you're *missing* from Quentin, damn them all — you're somebody then!" (133). Arnie's thought provides a chilling conclusion to chapter thirteen, as the reader realizes that his need for outside confirmation of his identity was at least partly responsible for his need to escape and put his brother and his fiancée in danger.

The next three chapters alternate between Ben's and Arnie's points of view. Ben buys a gun in Reno, then returns home and carves a dummy revolver out of wood. He and Ruth hear a radio report telling them that Arnie has escaped, and they drive out to the Golden Gate Bridge, where Ruth throws the real gun into the bay.

Meanwhile, Arnie spends the day hiding underground, nearly going crazy in the heat and becoming consumed with jealousy as he thinks of Ben and Ruth together. Next day, Ruth drives Ben to a road near the prison and lets him out. Ben uses the dummy gun to kidnap a man driving alone in a car and force him to drive to a prearranged spot; Ben then steals the car and leaves the man by the side of the road.

The remainder of the book is narrated by Ben, ending the alternating points of view. Ben abandons his stolen car and Ruth picks him up. They express their love for each other and Ben proposes marriage. Despite some guilt feelings about Arnie, they make plans together and go home, only to find Nova waiting for them in their living room. He has figured out their role in Arnie's escape and suggests that a bribe will make him keep quiet. When he suggests that sex with Ruth be part of the bribe, Ben unsuccessfully attacks him.

Ben escapes (or so we think) and returns to San Quentin, climbing over the wall and back into the hole with Arnie. The brothers scale the wall to escape, only to find Nova waiting for them on the other side. They overpower the guard and take him home, where Arnie is crushed to learn that Ruth plans to marry Ben in his place.

Arnie's life has been ruined for nothing — he went to jail due to his plans to marry Ruth, and he escapes only to find that his worst fears have been realized and his own brother has stolen her affections. Arnie loses a fight with Ben and leaves; "my heart cried out for him, but there was nothing to say" (180–81), thinks Ben.

In the final chapter of *The House of Numbers,* Ben and Ruth are taken to see the warden (to whom the novel is dedicated), who tells them that a neighbor of theirs called anonymously to report that Ben had helped Arnie escape. The exchange between Ben and the warden is Finney's last bit of public relations, as the warden convinces Ben to turn in his brother to protect him from himself. The warden tells Ben:

"Listen, Mr. Jarvis, we spend our lives and careers here, scrounging second-hand ball bats and discarded television sets, begging free movie films, fighting for an extra five-cent-a-day food allowance per man, trying to drag this prison a single step closer to what it ought to be! We put in hours we're never paid for — we put in our lives — doing our damnedest with what we're given and what we can scrounge, trying to get these men through prison, and still keep some spark of humanity alive in them. And, yes! — sometimes we fail" [189–90].

This strange conclusion demonstrates the main reason that *The House of Numbers* does not totally succeed as a novel. In *5 Against the House,* Al Mercer explains that he dislikes casinos and thinks robbing one is ethically justified. At no point is the reader forced to consider that the casino is really a nice, honest place underneath it all, where basically good people run a business that benefits its customers.

In *The House of Numbers,* Jack Finney goes out of his way to try to defend the people who run San Quentin, and it weakens the novel, especially because the defense consists mostly of speeches or thoughts (by Ben Jarvis) about how the jail really is not such a bad place after all. Never mind the fact that it reduces its inmates to numbers; the warden is doing his best. Strangest of all is the character of Nova, the sadistic guard, who represents the only authority figure from San Quentin that seems realistic. Finney never explains how such a character functions in such an ideal setting.

Despite these shortcomings, the novel ends effectively, with Ben agonizing over the idea of betraying his brother to the warden. The last line is especially good: "And I was crying for my lost brother as he reached out for his phone" (192). Ben and Arnie are just the latest in a long line of conflicted brothers, going back to Cain and Abel, whose differences defy resolution. *The House of Numbers* was a true "paperback original" of the 1950s — not a great novel, but one with enough interesting twists and turns to be worth reading.

Comparing the 1957 novel with the 1956 novella reveals considerable internal evidence to suggest that Finney wrote the short version first and then expanded it to novel length. It is possible that the novel was written to coincide with the filmed version of the story that was released soon after the novel's publication, since the novel was published as a paperback original and the upcoming movie was advertised on its back cover.

The differences between the novella and the novel are not as significant as those revealed by a careful comparison of the two early versions of *The Body Snatchers*. The story in *The House of Numbers* is reworked in the expanded version but the changes are not significant. They mostly provide more character development among the three main characters, adding background and details to make their personalities more evident.

A possible flaw in proofreading occurs on page 95 of the short version, where Ben's cellmate Al tells him that "'A con got out last year, 1954.'" The story was published in the July 1956 issue of *Cosmopolitan,* and this line suggests that Finney may have written it in 1955. Two pages are added to the end of chapter ten in the book (110–11), where Finney has Ben thinking with admiration of how hard it is to run the prison and what a good job the warden does. This addition only serves to weaken the novel.

The other notable change comes at the novel's end. In chapter one, Ruth and Ben discuss the crime that sent Arnie to San Quentin — he committed fraud by cashing bad checks to pay for an engagement ring (15). This scene is absent from the original novella. Instead, we learn at the very end of the story that Arnie was jailed "'for driving while drunk, killing a man with his car'" (115). Changing Arnie's crime from a callous act of negligence (in the novella) to a foolish attempt to gain status (in the novel) is just part of Finney's effort to deepen the characterizations in the longer work. The plot is the same in both versions, however, as is the moving final line.

As a paperback original, *The House of Numbers* attracted little attention from reviewers at the time of its publication in 1957, and the lack of subsequent editions has resulted in its becoming one of Jack Finney's least known novels. More recent critics have discussed it briefly, most notably Marcia Muller in *1001 Midnights*. Calling it a "riveting tale" (Pronzini and Muller 247), she points out that Finney's view of San Quentin "is colored by his association with then-warden Harley O. Teets" but adds that "the method Finney devises for the escape is ingenious, and the characters are well drawn." She concludes that "the suspense, as with all Finney's works, is guaranteed to keep you turning the pages" (248).

Jon L. Breen, writing in 1999, remarks on Finney's "in-depth research" into San Quentin (30), and Fred Blosser, writing in that same year, calls the novel "an inventive return to crime fiction with the patented Finney touch of approaching a familiar genre ... in a new and different way" (51). Blosser calls the setting "impeccably researched," the characters "incisively drawn," and the "stratagems cleverly developed" (51). He also suggests that Ben's impersonation of his brother Arnie recalls the "chilling impostures of *The Body Snatchers*" (51), though in this case the identity switch is done for allegedly benevolent reasons and with full cooperation by the person whose identity is assumed.

The filmed version, retitled *House of Numbers,* is a surprise when viewed today. The screenplay is faithful to the novel, and the film is a gritty, black and white tale that holds up quite well. It is covered in detail in chapter nineteen. The novel on which it was based, however, is a letdown after the triumph of *The Body Snatchers.* Yet Finney would continue in the crime genre for his next novel, *Assault on a Queen,* before leaving caper novels behind for more than a decade.

SEVEN

"The U-19's Last Kill"
and *Assault on a Queen*

After the publication of *The House of Numbers* and *The Third Level* in 1957, Jack Finney published six more short stories in the 1950s (these will be discussed in chapter eight) and one more serialized novel. Entitled "The U-19's Last Kill," it ran in six consecutive weekly issues of *The Saturday Evening Post* from August 22, 1959, through September 26, 1959. It was reworked and expanded for book publication that same year as *Assault on a Queen*.

Part one of the serial begins as Frank Lauffnauer leaves a resort hotel on Fire Island, New York, clearly looking for something. He retraces a route and paddles out a mile into the Atlantic Ocean before diving ninety feet to the bottom and locating a sunken submarine from World War One. It is the German sub U-19, in which he rode as a 15-year-old sailor and abandoned near the end of the war. Lauffnauer thinks about bringing the sub back up and making her operational, and sets about enlisting a crew.

The narration then switches from the third person to the first person, as Hugh Brittain tells the reader, "I suppose there are unrecognized moments in everyone's life when enormous events begin with no least hint or indication of it" (40).

This opening line from Hugh recalls a similar thought of Al

Mercer's in *5 Against the House*; it is Jack Finney's way of establishing that the story is being told by a narrator who is reflecting back on past events. Hugh and Alice Muir have been dating but she breaks it off because she knows he is not ready to settle down. Hugh tells her: "'You have to *sell your life*— most of it, the best part if it!— simply in order to stay alive!'" (41).

Hugh and Alice both work for "one of the big broadcasting networks" (41) and Hugh is afraid he's wasting his youth. By breaking off his relationship with Alice, Hugh clears his mind and severs his ties, making him "ready — ripe — for what happened on Saturday morning" (44).

Hugh visits the luxury liner the *Queen Mary*, which is docked in New York Harbor, to see off a co-worker who has just retired. Hugh is exploring the ship when he meets Vic DeRossier, with whom he had served in the Navy. Vic leads Hugh on a tour of the ship, and Hugh thinks of how spacious it is compared to the submarine on which he once served. Vic and Hugh leave the ship and have lunch at a Manhattan drugstore, where Vic asks Hugh to join him and four others in a scheme that will net them "'a million and a half dollars'" (46).

Vic tempts Hugh by telling him that he'll have a good time, "'the kind you were made for'" (46), and Hugh agrees to think it over before meeting Vic again the next morning. Part one thus ends with several of the main characters and themes introduced and suspense beginning to build regarding the nature of the crime that Vic has in mind.

In part two, Vic takes Hugh to a cottage on Fire Island and introduces him to the other members of his team: Frank Lauffnauer, Rosa Lucchesi, Ed Moreno, and Lincoln Langley. Hugh notices that Frank speaks with a German accent and asks, "'Were you a Nazi?'" (74). Frank explains that, while he never joined the National Socialist Party of Germany, he did fight for Germany in the Second World War. After "'difficult'" times in the 1920s, he tells Hugh, Hitler rose to power and Frank's life improved. "'Hitler concerned me,'" he tells Hugh, "'for I truly do not like fanatics of any kind'" (74).

Lauffnauer explains that he was trained as a submarine commander but "'simply did not know of the terrible things Germans were doing in occupied Europe'" (74). The tension between Hugh and Frank is broken by Rosa, who remarks, "'You do not like Nazis, Mr. Brittain?

... Neither do I..."" (74) but points out that Langley, who is black, still does not have equal rights in supposedly freedom-loving America.

Another source of tension is Moreno, who had served in the Navy with Hugh. Moreno's rank was below that of Hugh, but now Moreno announces that he will be the captain on this mission. Frank explains the mission to Hugh, who is skeptical. According to Frank, a Nazi war criminal named Reinhold Kroll has been hiding in Argentina for thirteen years, "'waiting until the time is ripe ... for Germany to begin her climb back to glory'" (77). Kroll has a specially-made trunk that contains one and a half million American dollars and "'seventy-five thousand in Swiss currency'" (77). Frank plans to steal the trunk, but the reader is kept in suspense regarding just how this will be accomplished by raising the U-19.

Hugh decides to join Vic, Frank, and the others on their mission and, as part two ends, Frank succeeds in bringing the long-sunken submarine to the surface. Part three finds the group exploring the submarine and finding the bodies of dead seamen still aboard. Frank reads from the submarine's logbook, explaining that influenza struck the crew in 1918 and Frank had to abandon the ship.

Hugh returns to New York and takes care of his affairs, meeting with Alice Muir one last time to say goodbye. He returns to Fire Island and joins the others as they work to rehabilitate the sub. At the end of part three, Hugh thinks that the weeks spent working on the sub were "the best moments and days of my entire life" (81).

In part four of the serialized novel, work on the sub concludes and romance develops between Hugh and Rosa, setting up a conflict between Hugh and Ed Moreno, who also fancies the lone female in the group. In the meantime, Frank receives a letter from Argentina with recent photographs of the Nazi Reinhold Kroll, "'reading peacefully in the garden of his villa in a Buenos Aires suburb only a few days ago'" (106). The letter reports that Kroll will fly to New York in the next two days and leave almost immediately thereafter, carrying the trunk with him. Part four concludes with the members of the group going to bed early to get a good night's sleep before proceeding with their plan.

The plan is finally explained in part five, as Hugh, Frank, and the others board the U-19 and sail out into the Atlantic Ocean. They approach the *Queen Mary* at sea and Langley hails it, pretending to be on a British submarine conducting a secret mission. Permission to board the ocean liner is secured and Hugh accompanies Frank and Vic as they paddle a raft to the ship and climb aboard.

Once aboard, they tell the captain that they have a torpedo aimed at the ship and will sink it if he does not cooperate. The captain agrees to their terms and orders all of the ship's first-class passengers to assemble in the main lounge. Hugh addresses the passengers and tells them to line up, adding that "'We are looking for one person only, an escaped criminal'" (134). The passengers file by, and Hugh is surprised to see Alice Muir, his former girlfriend, among them.

They find Kroll, who appeals to Frank in German to let him go and continue his mission. Frank slaps the man, telling him that "'Germany has had enough of *Führers*... And so have I'" *(137)*. Hugh and Frank take Kroll to his cabin, where they find the trunk and over two million dollars hidden inside. The hidden compartment of the trunk is difficult to open, however, and they decide to bring the entire trunk with them as they escape the ship.

Hugh and Frank find Vic and hurry back to their raft, realizing that the crew of the *Queen Mary* had succeeded in quietly signaling to a destroyer nearby that they were in trouble. As Hugh climbs over the side, he hears Alice call to him, and part five ends on a suspenseful note.

The sixth and final part of "The U-19's Last Kill" finds Vic and Frank taking Alice hostage and bringing her back to the sub with them. While she is able to fit through the hatch easily, Kroll's trunk is not so fortunate, and Vic and Frank frantically try to break it apart without success. Finally, Hugh takes the trunk full of money and casts it into the ocean, where it sinks. Hugh boards the sub and they barely avoid capture by the Navy destroyer, escaping with their lives but without the Nazi fortune.

The experience brings Hugh and Alice closer together and they realize that they are in love; they leave together, and the reader is left with the suspicion that their story is only beginning.

"The U-19's Last Kill" is an exciting story that has never been reprinted. Readers of *The Saturday Evening Post* had a positive response if the letters column in the October 31, 1959 issue of the magazine gives an accurate reading of their opinions. George R. Seeley of Lakeland, Florida, wrote that "Never have I met so many pleasant characters" and that "My curiosity was aroused by the number of smiles and grins." Bryan Dove of Hamilton, Bermuda, was paying close attention to detail, and wrote to complain that Finney has a character refer to the "H.M.S. Submarine" when it should be the "H.M. Submarine." He also found fault with the method Finney described for one British officer's saluting another.

Not long after the publication of the serial, Simon & Schuster published *Assault on a Queen,* the novel version of the story. It is greatly expanded and revised from the serialized version, and the plot changes are more significant than in any other novel that Jack Finney expanded from a prior magazine version.

The changes begin in the early chapters of the book. Hugh's relationship with Alice is shown in more detail, and their walk through Manhattan recalls similar scenes in Finney's earlier short stories featuring Tim and Eve Ryan. A scene is added to the book where Hugh rebels against a traffic cop and receives a ticket; this act of civil disobedience prefigures similar acts in *The Night People,* a novel that has much in common with *Assault on a Queen.* When Hugh meets Vic in chapter two, the amount of money to be gained is also lessened—from "'a million and a half dollars'" to "'hundreds of thousands of dollars'" (36). This is important because the robbery in the book is utterly different than that of the serial.

Bigger changes begin to emerge in chapter three of the novel, where Frank Lauffnauer's Nazi past is mentioned only in passing. The section of the serial that Finney cut made Frank a more sympathetic character by having him explain his feelings about Hitler and the Nazi party. In the book, his past is less detailed and thus more suspect.

Even more surprising changes occur in chapter four, as Finney deletes the entire section of the plot that provided the motivation for the robbery. In *Assault on a Queen,* there is no trunk with money hidden inside, nor is there a Nazi war criminal named Kroll who plans to travel from Argentina to Germany to restore the Third Reich. Instead, Frank and his team have no motivation other than greed, and the story suffers as a result.

In chapter eleven, Lincoln Langley still hails the *Queen Mary* by identifying the submarine as the "'H.M.S. Submarine Trident'" (137), demonstrating that Finney probably did not see the letter in *The Saturday Evening Post* correcting this salutation before the novel was published. Vic's incorrect salute to the captain of the *Queen Mary* is also unchanged from the serial. The novel veers off into uncharted waters in chapters eleven and twelve, where the robbery takes place.

While "The U-19's Last Kill" has Frank and Hugh identify and rob the Nazi Kroll, *Assault on a Queen* takes a different approach. Without a person on board the ship to look for, and without a trunk full of money to find, Finney must come up with something else. Instead, Frank orders the ship's purser to unlock the passengers' safe deposit boxes, which he promptly empties into mail sacks. He then takes all of the money from the ship's bank. Whereas Hugh, in part five of the serial, tells the passengers, "'We are looking for one person only, an escaped criminal,'" in the novel he tells them, "'We want your money, nothing else'" (155).

The passengers then file by and Hugh, Frank, and Vic collect their money. This change in the novel is its central flaw, and Finney returns to the same ethical problem he tried to confront in *5 Against the House*—that of attempting to justify having a likeable character stealing from presumably innocent people for no good reason. In *Assault on a Queen*, Hugh wrestles with his conscience in an interior monologue as he systematically robs the ship's passengers. Regarding the money, he thinks "I felt sorry for the people who had lost it" (160) and he realizes that "we were pirates" (161). The "fear and strain" begins to wear on him, as does "the occasional look of pure contempt that looked out at me from the eyes" of those he robs (161).

Hugh recalls Frank and Ed Moreno telling him that "these people ... were rich or close to it" and that "we'd be taking only the cash they had on them, and they could all afford that." Hugh realizes that "in robbing some of these people, I could be doing them a terrible harm." He adds that "I suddenly understood that I was stealing. I suddenly understood that I was a thief." Hugh concludes that "there is a difference between knowing that stealing is wrong, and actually doing it; and the difference is enormous" (163).

Hugh reaches an understanding about what he has done, but it is too little and too late. He cannot back out; he can only escape. In changing the story and the motivations for the robbery in this way, Jack Finney removed a believable plot device and substituted an incredible one. The scenes on the *Queen Mary* in *Assault on a Queen* are forced, and Hugh's interior monologue makes him sound incredibly foolish. The Nazi subplot of "The U-19's Last Kill" may have been the stuff of pulp fiction, but it was more believable than the novel's passengers who rather docilely hand over their wealth.

The other big change from serial to novel involves Alice Muir, who is central to the climax of "The U-19's Last Kill" but who is absent from the concluding chapters of *Assault on a Queen.* In the novel, Hugh never sees her on board the ship, nor is she taken hostage and brought on the submarine. While it may be a coincidence in the serial, it gives a welcome closure to the relationship that was developed at the start of the story. The novel suffers because of the change.

In the novel, Hugh simply pushes the boat launch away from the sub, leaving it with sacks full of money to drift at sea. As readers, we are supposed to see this as the result of Hugh's ethical dilemma about robbing the ship's passengers, but again it seems forced and unbelievable. The oversized trunk of the serial is more satisfying.

The novel ends with Hugh walking off alone, intending to continue a courtship with fellow thief Rosa that had been developed in the course of the book. Alice Muir is forgotten, to the book's detriment. Unfortunately, *Assault on a Queen* is an example of a novel that was expanded from a serial less than successfully. Perhaps Jack Finney thought that the Nazi subplot was too far-fetched; whatever the reason for the changes he made, they do not result in a better story.

Regardless of its merits, *Assault on a Queen* appears to have been a very successful novel. After two paperback originals in a row (*The Body Snatchers* and *The House of Numbers*), this novel was published in hardcover by Simon & Schuster. A book club edition followed, and the story was adapted for the movie screen in 1966. The film, which starred Frank Sinatra, is examined in detail in chapter nineteen.

At the time of its publication, *Assault on a Queen* was widely reviewed, unlike Finney's prior novels. The Kirkus Service wrote that "the magnitude of the plot's conception is in no way supported by the scope of Jack Finney's imagination. And so despite infinite detail on the technical problems involved in such a venture, the assault seems to be on the reader's credulousness." Bennett Epstein, writing in the *New York Herald Tribune,* disagreed, remarking on the novel's "ingenious and utterly fantastic plot" and called it "an engrossing story from the prologue to the last page."

A reviewer in *The New Yorker* agreed that "the plot is fine" (192) but complained that "its execution, in the literary sense, is something less than dexterous, and, in the physical sense, is deplorable, because the men have nothing of the brigand about them, and nothing of the pirate." He points out that the characters "move in torpor, rancor, and apprehension, and end up about as they began" (193). Sergeant Cuff, however, wrote in the *Saturday Review* that the novel was a "beautifully detailed yarn."

Since its initial publication, *Assault on a Queen* has received little critical attention. Both Michael Beard and J. Sydney Jones noticed that the thieves in this caper novel are an older group than those in *5 Against the House,* and Stephen King described Rod Serling's script for the film adaptation of the novel as "a work which can most humanely be characterized as unfortunate" (237). More recently, Jon Breen pointed out that, in this book, "Once again, Finney's amateur criminals try to show they aren't really evil people by offering justification for an *almost* victimless crime" (30), and Fred Blosser praised Finney's "talent for exploring an arcane subject in fascinating detail" (52).

Finney would not write another crime novel until *The Night People,* which he published in 1977. In the meantime, he would write the last of his short stories, pen several novels that blended comedy, fantasy, and time travel, and even write a play that would close before it got to Broadway. With *Assault on a Queen,* the early part of Jack Finney's career as a novelist came to an end.

EIGHT

Later Short Fiction
and a Play (1958–1966)

After publishing *The Third Level* in 1957, Jack Finney continued to write and publish short stories in popular magazines, albeit at a slower clip than he had been doing in the early part of the 1950s. From June 1958, when "Vive La Différence!" appeared in *Good Housekeeping*, through April 1965, when "Double Take" appeared in *Playboy*, Finney published a total of 17 short stories, some of which were collected in 1963's *I Love Galesburg in the Springtime*. "Double Take" was to be the last short story he ever published and, after the play *This Winter's Hobby* was performed in 1966, he would confine his fiction to novels for the final 29 years of his life and career.

"Vive La Différence" is another of the light, domestic comedies that Finney had specialized in with such characters as Tim and Eve Ryan and Ben and Ruth Callandar. This time, Hank and Hilda Jessup argue about a dream Hilda has had; she is mad at Hank for his behavior in the dream and the confusion escalates to a humorous conclusion.

This rather forgettable story was followed by a much better one, "Seven Days to Live." This tale, which was later reprinted as "Prison Legend," returns to the prison setting of *The House of Numbers* and again features a sympathetic warden. As the story begins, he reads requests from condemned men and comes across one from Mexican

Luis Perez, who asks for paint supplies. Perez is set to die in seven days and wants to paint a mural on the wall of his cell. The warden approves the request, the paint is delivered, and Perez begins to paint.

Suspense builds as Finney's third-person narrator describes the painting. A pattern of boards begins to form, and onlookers realize that Perez is painting a door. Word spreads fast through the prison and the warden visits the cell; the door is amazing in its detail and looks real. The warden, fighting the impulse to have the paint removed, allows the project to continue, even as Perez puts up a blanket and paints behind it on the day before his execution.

Behind the makeshift curtain, the warden sees that Perez has painted a likeness of the door to his home in Mexico, and the warden can see into the house through the painted cracks and knotholes in the door. On the morning of the execution, the warden comes for Perez, who emerges with the words, "'It is finished'" (62), echoing the words of Jesus at the crucifixion. As he leaves the cell, the creaking of old door hinges is heard. Just before Perez is killed, the governor calls with a stay, explaining that another man has confessed to the murder for which Perez had been convicted.

Back in his cell, Perez shows the warden the completed painting. The door now stands open, and in it is Perez's wife, "her face contorted in an agony of joy, and she was running toward the open doorway, her arms outflung, as though it had just opened, and someone she loved were stepping through it" (62). Perez tells the warden that this is what he will soon see; the story ends with the warden wondering how Perez had made the impossible come true.

"Seven Days to Live" is a moving story, where a prisoner succeeds in cheating death by means of an inexplicable talent. Finney tells a fantastic tale in a realistic setting where, as Stephen King wrote, he can "create the fantasy ... *and then not apologize for it or explain it*" (236). The reader is simply grateful that the impossible occurred and the tale is well told.

"Bedtime Story" is yet another light comedy about a young, urban couple. Mike and Iris Cutler are much like the Ryans or the Callandars; they spend the story playing practical jokes on each other in the middle of the night and it ends with them about to take the first step toward having a baby.

One of the main characters in Finney's next story, "All My Clients

Are Innocent," is engaged, but his business partner tries desperately to prevent him from getting married and following the path of so many of Finney's other young characters. In this entertaining story, Al Michaels is a lawyer in his mid-twenties who works with famous attorney Max Wollheim. The story's title refers to Max's oft-repeated claim, which he explains refers to the fact that everyone is innocent until proven guilty.

Mr. Balderson, accused of robbing seven shops, hires Max and Al. He has fired his lawyer and wants Max to defend him at his trial, which is scheduled to start the next day. Unfortunately for Al, he is supposed to get married tonight, but that does not stop Max from pulling out all the stops to convince him and his fiancée to postpone the wedding so that Al can prepare the case.

The trial goes well for the defense the next day and Max wins the case. Balderson confesses after the verdict that he really was guilty, and Al's fiancée is furious that she gave up her wedding to help him defend a guilty man. She storms off, leaving Max and Al to celebrate their victory and Al's baptism of fire as a lawyer.

"All My Clients Are Innocent" is funny and a good read, but Jack Finney never returned to these characters again. The story was adapted for television in 1962, as discussed in chapter eighteen.

Finney's next story was one of his best time travel tales, "The Love Letter." In it, Jake Belknap, a 24-year-old bachelor, tells the reader, "I live in Brooklyn to save money and work in Manhattan to make it" (16). He recently bought a desk at a second-hand store; the desk had come from "one of the last of the big old mid-Victorian houses in Brooklyn; they were tearing it down..." (16).

Jake is dating Roberta Haig but does not really care if he sees her again. Alone in his apartment he explores the old desk, and Finney describes its nooks and crannies in loving detail. In a drawer, Jake finds an envelope, and in the envelope a letter dated May 14, 1882. The letter is written in the style of the 1880s and is signed by Helen Elizabeth Worley of Brooklyn, who expresses her love for her sweetheart, the intended recipient. Jake decides to write an answer, and thinks: "I am trying to explain why I answered that letter. There in the silence of a timeless spring night it seemed natural enough..." (48). The important word here is "timeless," for in writing this letter Jake takes the first step in a romance for which time is no barrier.

Using an 1869 stamp he finds in his childhood stamp collection, Jake prepares the letter for delivery and walks to the house from whence the desk had come. He copies down the address and mails the letter at a post office that had been built soon after the Civil War. Like Si Morley in *Time and Again,* Jake Belknap carefully recreates the past in order to transcend time and mail his letter.

The next week, Jake finds himself in the New York Public Library perusing a "big one-volume pictorial history of New York" and sees a photograph of "a street less than a quarter mile from Brock Place... I knew that Helen Worley must often have walked along this very sidewalk." He thinks of Varney Street as he knows it and compares it to Varney Street as pictured in 1881; today, it is "a non-descript joyless street, and it's impossible to believe that there has ever been a tree on its entire length." Jake looks at the picture and thinks about how people in 1881 had time, time "to build huge wide porches on which families sat on summer evenings with palm-leaf fans" (52).

Jake Belknap yearns for a simpler time, as characters in many of Jack Finney's best stories often do, from Tim Ryan in "Manhattan Idyl" to Si Morley in *From Time to Time.* He thinks

> Maybe I live in what is for me the wrong time, and I was filled now with the most desperate yearning to be there, on that peaceful street — to walk off, past the edges of the scene on the printed page before me, into the old and beautiful Brooklyn of long ago [52].

"The Love Letter" is a clear precursor to *Time and Again,* but in this short story the narrator never succeeds in traveling back to the 1880s. Instead, he finds in the old desk a second letter from Helen Worley, replying to his own and full of desire to meet him. Much like the narrator in "Second Chance," Jake thinks, "late at night ... the boundary between here and then wavers" (52). He writes back to Helen, explaining that it is 1959 and, although they can never meet, he has fallen in love with her.

She replies a week later with a photograph of herself. Across the bottom is written the message, "'I will never forget'" (54). Jake knows she will not be able to write to him again, since he has used up all of the drawers in the desk. The story ends as Jake locates Helen's grave, with her message to him engraved on the headstone.

"The Love Letter" is a brilliant story that stands with Finney's best short work. Writing in 1996, Kim Newman called it one of Finney's "perfect short stories" (197), along with "The Third Level" and "Second Chance." The story was adapted for a television movie that aired on February 1, 1998; the tale is greatly expanded and updated, but Finney's themes remain at its core. The movie is well worth watching and garnered good reviews (Steven W. Schuldt called it a "near-classic"), and it is discussed in detail in chapter eighteen.

Jack Finney followed "The Love Letter" with the six-part serial, "The U-19's Last Kill," which began three weeks later in the same magazine (see chapter seven). His final short story to be published in the 1950s was "Take One Rainy Night...," which marked the fourth and last appearance of Ben and Ruth Callander (again with an "e"), who had previously appeared in *Good Housekeeping* in 1955 and 1957. This time, the Callanders and their friends the Howsers play pranks on each other involving a trip to the movies on a night of bad weather.

"The Other Wife" followed in the January 30, 1960 issue of *The Saturday Evening Post;* this story was the basis for the novel, *The Woodrow Wilson Dime,* and will be discussed in chapter ten.

The first of Jack Finney's last ten short stories to be published was "Crazy Sunday." Told in the third person by an unnamed narrator, it features another young New Yorker, Victor Talburt. Talburt is married with a young son; he enjoys his first moments of freedom in years as his wife and child leave for the weekend to visit her mother. On a whim, he takes an overnight flight to Paris, where he roams the city and recalls his time there in the Army. He sees his former girlfriend, Suzanne, but does not approach her, realizing that they have both grown in the five years since they have last seen each other. In a surprising twist for a Jack Finney character, Talburt understands "that his youth wasn't still here waiting to be returned to" (246). He returns home to New York and his family, having bought the French bread his wife had requested.

"Crazy Sunday" is a charming story with a happy protagonist; unlike the main characters in so many of Finney's tales, Victor Talburt is satisfied with his life and with the present and does not try very hard to recapture a time of past happiness.

The same thing cannot be said for the narrator of Finney's next story, "I Love Galesburg in the Springtime." Oscar Manheim is a reporter for the *Register-Mail* who learns of several unusual events in the town of Galesburg, Illinois. The first involves E.V. Marsh, who has changed his mind about building a factory on Broad Street near the city limits. After a meeting with the town leaders, Marsh had walked the streets of Galesburg and liked them; Manheim agrees, recalling how he fell in love with the town the first time he saw it as a child. Manheim remarks that many of the houses "have the half comically ugly, half charming look, made of spaciousness, dignity, foolishness, and conspicuous waste, that belongs to another time" (183).

Marsh tells Manheim that he was nearly run over by a streetcar at the end of his walk. He describes hearing the sound of an old phonograph being wound and seeing the old-fashioned outfit and grooming of the motorman. Yet when he told people about his near miss he was arrested for being drunk and disorderly and learned that the streetcar tracks had been torn up in the 1930s. The embarrassment of the incident made him change his mind about building the new factory in Galesburg.

Manheim tells the reader that he never put the unusual details in Marsh's story when he wrote it up for the newspaper; he begins to think of Galesburg as a person, adding that it "laughs at me a little" and "once expected big things of me" (184). He explains that he turned down a scholarship at Harvard to stay in Galesburg and attend Knox College, because he has always been in love with the town.

A second incident related to Manheim involves an old house that was saved from burning to the ground by a horse-drawn, steam-powered fire engine operated by men from the past. The third and final incident described by the narrator involves a man who changed his mind about selling his farm to developers after he received a telephone call on an old, disconnected phone from a boyhood friend who had been killed in France in 1918.

Oscar writes, "I'm glad about that ... because here in Galesburg, and everywhere else, of course, they're trying — endlessly — to destroy the beauty we inherit from the past. They keep trying, and when they succeed, they replace it — not always, but all too often — with drabness and worse." He continues: "we're doing these things, to ourselves ... as though any feeling for beauty or grace or a sense of the past were a kind of sentimental weakness to be jeered down" (190).

Manheim explains the strange events of the story by arguing that "Galesburg's past is fighting back ... when the need becomes desperate enough..." (190). The story ends with another example of the fight, as the past once more penetrates into the present to prevent the destruction of beautiful old trees.

In "I Love Galesburg in the Springtime," Jack Finney plays around with the theme of time travel again, with the town where he attended college serving as the traveler. The people in the story do not long for the past; in fact, most of them are trying to eradicate it. Instead, the town itself becomes a force of preservation, perhaps because there are no people left to do the job in its place. This is a cautionary tale, one in which man's insensitivity to aspects of a place and its history eventually causes rebellion by the place itself. Unlike *The Body Snatchers,* where the deterioration of a town is due to alien apathy, this story puts the blame squarely on the residents of Galesburg, Illinois.

"An Old Tune" is a gentle tale of a man who does not escape through time, exactly, but does use an old-fashioned method to float above the times in which he lives. The story begins with the mysterious line, "On the sixth day he was home alone, Charley Burke walked out onto the patio...." Recalling Genesis, Charley is portrayed as godlike, alone on the sixth day. Why is he alone? Has his wife left him? Finney does not tell us. Charley works in San Francisco and "was conscious of the emptiness of the suburban house" (113). Seeing a hawk, he wants to fly, too, and reads an article about the use of hot air balloons in the nineteenth century. "Men understood the things they used then; they were masters of the machines that served them." In contrast, Charley thinks that men of today are "no longer masters of very much at all" (230).

Charley builds a hot air balloon and floats up in it, hanging above Marin County, where Jack Finney also lived. The next night, he is joined by a neighbor, Mrs. Lanidas, and they sing the old tune of the title, "Come, Josephine, in my flying machine," as they see San Quentin Prison and narrowly avoid the Golden Gate Bridge, each of which serves as a setting in novels by Jack Finney. "Charley felt godlike" (233) and bestows blessings on the community below.

The ride over, Charley's wife and daughter return, although we are never told why they were gone or where they went. Charley sees Mrs. Lanidas at a P.T.A. meeting six months later, and they share a secret as the story ends with her saying "'Call me Josephine'" and him whistling the "old, old tune" on his way home (233).

"An Old Tune" is a charming, wistful story that features many of Jack Finney's signature touches but never veers into outright fantasy.

The title characters of "Where the Cluetts Are" find an even more effective way than Charley Burke did to escape into the nineteenth century. The story is told by an architect named Harry, whose clients, the Cluetts, commission him to design and build a house just as it would have been done in the 1880s. As the laborious process goes on, Harry tells Ellie Cluett that "'we're looking at a vanished sight. This is a commonplace sight of a world long gone, and we've reached back and brought it to life again.'" The house is finished and the Cluetts begin living a Victorian lifestyle — guests arrive by carriage and the house is lit by gaslight. "It was a scene lost to the world," Harry thinks, "a glimpse of another time and manner of living" (112).

Eventually, the Cluetts retreat further into the past, having fewer visitors and recalling events from long ago that they should have no way of knowing. By the end of the story, the Cluetts live as if it is the 1880s, "as though the house existed in some other year." Harry concludes that the house is haunted by "its old self" and that its "ghost has captured the Cluetts — rather easily, for I think they were glad to surrender" (113).

"Where the Cluetts Are" recalls "I Love Galesburg in the Springtime" in the way inanimate objects and locations work to recapture the past; this time, it is just one house instead of an entire town.

Fantasy takes over in the weak story, "The Man with the Magic Glasses." In it, a New York office worker named Ted buys a pair of glasses in a joke shop that allow him to see through women's clothes. He ends up in love with frumpy co-worker Freida, who bought a love potion from the same shop. Finney's interest in the nineteenth century peeks through when Ted compares Freida's hair to that worn by "someone in an 1895 out-of-focus tintype" (94) but, other than that, there is little to recommend this story. Jack Finney appears to have realized its flaws as well, because he reworked it considerably before including it in his collection *I Love Galesburg in the Springtime* as "Love, Your Magic Spell Is Everywhere." It was reprinted in the collection *About Time* under a third title, "Lunch-Hour Magic."

"Old Enough for Love" followed, in the May 1962 issue of *McCall's*. This is a clever and engaging comedy set in San Francisco, in which a young couple (like the Ryans or the Callandars) know Fred, a much older man who changes his appearance, name, and job in order to date a beautiful young woman. After marrying her, the older man tires of the act, but all is well when he admits the truth to his wife.

Jack Finney's "Hey, Look at Me!" is a ghostly tale about writers and critics. Narrated by Peter Marks, a book editor at a San Francisco newspaper who lives in Mill Valley, it concerns the late Max Kingery, a writer with whom Marks had coffee every day. Max had been a young and serious man who had planned to be a famous writer. He died of pneumonia and nobody noticed. Six months later, he returns, and Peter sees him. Others in town see him, too, and Peter finds evidence in the writer's house that he had been using great effort to try to write but had failed.

Marks surmises that Max was still trying to gain attention as a writer, even after death, like a child shouting "'Hey, look at me!'" by writing his initials on a rock by the side of the road. In the end, Max has the last laugh when he has "MAXWELL KINGERY, AUTHOR" carved in big letters on his own tombstone and the bill is given to Marks, who is, after all, "'just a critic'" (74).

Like Fred, who pretends to be younger in "Old Enough for Love," the title characters in "The Sunny Side of the Street" represent an example of Finney's young, urban marrieds beginning to mature. David and Fran have two children and he ponders their sudden loss of freedom as parents. He and his wife hire a babysitter and set off across the Golden Gate Bridge and into San Francisco, where they register under assumed names at a hotel. Despite their seeming freedom, neither can stop thinking about their children, and each secretly calls home to check up on them. They head for home as the story ends, agreeing that children are worth the lack of freedom that they cause.

This charming story foreshadows the restless couples of Finney's later novel, *The Night People,* as well as its San Francisco setting. Like Fred, in "Old Enough for Love," David fantasizes about being younger and having more control over his life. Unlike Fred, however, he realizes that he is satisfied with his situation without having to go to extremes.

Jack Finney's last short story in this period was "Time Has No Boundaries," which appeared in the October 13, 1962 issue of the *Saturday Evening Post.* Narrated by Professor Bernard Weygand and set in San Francisco, this tale marks the author's return to stories about time travel, as Inspector Martin Ihren discovers that criminals are escaping back in time to avoid capture. He tries to convince Professor Weygand to bring the criminals back but the professor says he cannot; Ihren settles for sending incriminating letters back through time to a police chief in 1885. The professor gets the last laugh, however, and sends the policeman himself back to 1893.

Once again, Jack Finney's characters do not respect authority figures. This theme will recur in *Time and Again* and will be central to *The Night People*. The time travel in "Time Has No Boundaries" is not really the wistful sort of so many of Finney's stories, though — this time, criminals retreat from the present to avoid capture.

In 1962, Jack Finney published his second short story collection, *I Love Galesburg in the Springtime*. Like *The Third Level*, it featured mostly stories with fantastic themes, omitting the urban comedies in Finney's catalogue and thus consigning them to the dustbin of history. The stories in this collection included "I Love Galesburg in the Springtime," "The Man with the Magic Glasses" (retitled "Love, Your Magic Spell Is Everywhere"), "Where the Cluetts Are," "Hey, Look at Me!" "Tiger Tamer" (retitled "A Possible Candidate for the Presidency"), "Seven Days to Live" (retitled "Prison Legend"), "Time Has No Boundaries" (retitled "The Face in the Photo"), "An Old Tune" (retitled "The Intrepid Aeronaut"), "The Other Wife" (retitled "The Coin Collector"), and "The Love Letter." In addition to giving new titles to six of the ten stories, Finney updated most of them, added to "Time Has No Boundaries," and partially rewrote "The Man with the Magic Glasses."

This outstanding collection has been out of print for decades, although several of the stories were collected in the 1986 volume *About Time*. Reviews of the 1965 British reprint of *I Love Galesburg in the Springtime* focused on its theme of nostalgia, which one writer found to be "a more attractive ingredient in these stories than the fantasy" (Young). Another writer, reviewing the book for the *Times Literary Supplement,* added that "Jack Finney certainly has a style of his own, but it is a cosy one, more after de la Mare than H.G. Wells, and he toys delicately with time-shift fantasies, haunted by an addiction to mid-nineteenth-century American provincial architecture."

Finney published one more short story in his lifetime. Titled

"Double Take," it appeared in the April 1965 issue of *Playboy*. The editor's introduction praised the author's "gentle touch with fantasy not quite like any other storyteller around" (293) and 26-year-old Jake Pelman, the dialogue director of a movie being made in New York, tells the story itself. He is taking the train from Hollywood to New York with beautiful starlet Jessica Maxwell, and his job is to help her prepare to film her last scenes, which are set in the 1920s. She is too immature at 20 to master the emotions of a broken heart, however, and his expectations for her performance are not high as they arrive in New York on a spring night.

Regular readers of Jack Finney's work will suspect what is about to happen when the narrator states that lower Fifth Avenue had not changed much since the 1920s and they are filming with a vintage bus that still has its 1926 license plates. The cast and crew get into costume to take the bus for a test drive and various people board the bus as it has clearly been transported back to the flapper era. One of the new riders is a handsome young man who falls in love with Jessica at first sight — he speaks to her but she dismisses him coldly.

The next day, Jessica has trouble getting the right emotion while filming her big scene until the actor playing an older man utters a phrase that causes her to realize he is the handsome young man from the bus, now years older. Jake suddenly understands that the bus had traveled back in time the night before, and Jessica delivers an Oscar-caliber performance once she realizes that she had broken the man's heart long ago.

The story ends with Jessica crying with the knowledge that "love will not wait" (313). She asks Jake to accompany her back to Hollywood, again by train, and he thinks that his chance at love is at hand.

"Double Take" is a lovely, nostalgic tale in which another trip back in time occurs when the setting is just right. New York is the place, the 1920s the time, and lessons are learned about seizing the day when love comes to call.

After "Double Take," Jack Finney wrote full-length books almost exclusively for the rest of his life, with one exception. In the spring of 1966, *This Winter's Hobby* premiered in Philadelphia, after having had a tryout in New Haven, Connecticut. It was a full-length play by Jack Finney, and it was headed for Broadway. It never got there, as will be explained in chapter seventeen.

For the rest of his career as a writer, Jack Finney was mainly a novelist, and he never published another short story or had another play performed after 1966. In fact, his fifth novel, which had been published in 1963, was a marked departure from the novels that had come before it.

NINE

Good Neighbor Sam

In 1963, Jack Finney published *Good Neighbor Sam,* his fifth novel. It was his first novel not to be serialized or based on a prior magazine work; however, it shares so much with his prior work and foreshadows aspects of his subsequent work that it fits perfectly into the middle of his writing career.

In a 1966 interview, Finney commented that "'when I write a book I really am thinking about a movie. With "Good Neighbor Sam," I had Jack Lemmon in mind from the very beginning'" (Wilson). The filmed version of this novel was released in 1964 and starred Jack Lemmon; nevertheless, the novel is much more than a blueprint for the movie, and it bears close examination in relation to the author's other works.

The story begins with a takeoff on the famous opening line of *Moby-Dick;* here, the narrator tells the reader, "Call me Sam" (7). He is 29-year-old advertising man Samuel L. Bissell, married to 25-year-old Minerva Bissell and living in Sausalito, California, in the heart of Marin County, also home to Jack Finney. He works at the Burke and Hare advertising agency in San Francisco. Burke and Hare were grave robbers who rose to infamy in nineteenth-century Scotland by stealing corpses to sell to doctors for medical research, much as Bissell and his colleagues use bits and pieces of ideas to create their advertising campaigns.

Sam has a hobby that involves building a mobile from junk on his patio; again, creating something out of the garbage he finds around him. Sam also has a distraction named Janet Ebbett, a beautiful young woman who lives alone in the house next door and who stands to inherit eleven million dollars when her grandfather dies. The catch is that she has to be married at the time he dies, something complicated by the fact that she is now divorced and without prospects.

In chapter two, Janet's lawyer informs her that she may still be married, since her final divorce papers have not yet come through. Sam's amorous daydreams of Janet are interrupted in chapter three by the arrival of Janet's greedy cousins, Irene Krupp and her brother, Jack Bailey. Finney makes a wry comment on a name shared by himself and the intended star of the movie version of the novel when he has Sam think: "any guy calls himself Jack as though it were a name and not a nickname couldn't be trusted not to steal a wet cigar butt" (32).

The comedy of identities begins as Janet introduces Sam as her husband, Howard Ebbett, to her suspicious cousins. Sam is forced to go home with Janet and continue the charade until the cousins leave. A private detective then takes up surveillance outside the house in a poorly disguised truck, and Sam spends the early morning hours sleeping uncomfortably on Janet's sofa so that he can leave for work that morning from her house, as would her husband.

Sam's problems mount in the fourth chapter, when Janet drives him to work and his boss, Mr. Burke, thinks she is his wife. The silly ad campaign that Sam works on — "'When liver bile doesn't flow just right, BELS for the belly make the world seem bright!'" (52) — suggests that Jack Finney knew the ins and outs of the world of advertising well, since he worked in a similar agency in New York in the 1940s before turning his hand to writing fiction. Another account, for Nesfresh eggs, is Sam's particular specialty, and a funny scene ensues in which Sam convinces his colleagues that the best way to advertise Nesfresh is to use the tried and true method of testimonials. Speaking of the photographs of "real" people to be used on the billboards, Sam remarks, "'Fake them up to look honest and real'" (61).

That night, Sam becomes even more confused by his attraction to Janet, but when he kisses her after a dance she is grateful for his kindness rather than seduced by his charms. He sleeps in his own bed but awakens at dawn and is smuggled back to Janet's house in a laundry basket. Sam goes to work and hears from Min, his wife, who has discovered evidence in the hills above their house that they are, in fact, being watched by a private detective. Min met the man as he was trying to break into Jan's house; he told her that he knows that Jan is not married. Min convinces Sam that he must stay at Jan's house again that night to prolong the charade — he is tired of being tempted, and thinks that "I was beginning to feel like a guy standing around with his mouth open for hours wondering whether to bite into a wax apple" (86).

After dinner, Sam watches television and Finney slips in a humorous reference to his own novel, *The Body Snatchers:* "if I ever heard nostalgia for what is now on the air, I'd know the mutants had taken over and we were no longer human" (87). Sam then falls asleep, his wife goes home, and he is again left alone with his desirable neighbor. Sam's imagination runs away with him in chapter seven as he and Jan get ready for bed, but when he hears her breathing down the hall and knows she is fast asleep rather than waiting for him to burst into her bedroom, he realizes that "obviously she wasn't the least worried about me or herself" (97).

A new character joins the story in chapter eight to confuse matters even more, as Jan's husband Howie enters through the back door in the middle of the night, only to be tackled by the suddenly protective Sam. In chapter nine, Howie tells Jan that he still loves her and she realizes that she cannot throw him out because it would arouse suspicion in the private detective who is watching the house. Howie is jealous of Sam, who has done nothing to cause him to be jealous, and both men eventually realize that Howie will need to sneak next door to Sam's house and leave in the morning as if he were Sam.

Sam then grows jealous of Howie when Min pays extra attention to her new husband. That evening, the confusion of identities grows ever greater as the two couples play bridge and Sam makes another connection that recalls *The Body Snatchers:*

> the Germans have an interesting legend about what they call *Doppelgangers;* literally, *doublegoers.* Under certain circumstances, that is, a precise physical duplicate of a man is evoked, each one capable of being in separate places... [123].

Sam is still trying to think of a way to have his cake and eat it, too, but the suggestion of *doppelgangers* also recalls the duplicate bodies in Finney's earlier novel.

In chapter eleven, Sam finally meets the private detective who has been watching his neighborhood. The man's name is Reinhold Shiffner (recall that the Nazi in "The U-19's Last Kill" had been named Reinhold Kroll) and he, like everyone else in the novel, is mixed up about who is who. Instead of realizing the truth about the relationship between Sam and Janet, he is convinced that the two are actually married and that Sam is sneaking next door to have an affair with Min. He also suspects that Howie and Sam are trading wives, and he wants $10,000 in blackmail to prevent him from showing photographic proof to Sam's neighbors.

A very funny scene ensues as Sam drives through San Francisco with Shiffner and sees for the first time a billboard connected with the ad campaign he had been working on earlier in the book for the Nesfresh account. Surprisingly, Sam and Janet's picture has been used on huge billboards all over the city and they are identified as "Mr. and Mrs. Sam Bissell" (136). Sam then drives frantically around the city, swerving whenever another billboard comes into sight, desperate to prevent Shiffner from seeing the billboards and learning the truth (though even that is wrong, as Sam's wife in the picture is Janet) that will cost Janet her inheritance.

Jack Finney provides some insight into his own move from the East Coast to the West Coast in chapter thirteen when Sam thinks

> I began to feel embarrassed, a dirty San Francisco slacker who had to
> be pressured into working late. In New York they obviously *like* to work
> late, they enjoy it. It's different in San Francisco; we like to *stop* work.
> Or better yet, don't start [145].

Sam finally decides to give in to temptation and sleep with Janet. That night, he drives home and climbs into Janet's bed under cover of darkness, only to find Min waiting there. Sam makes the mistake of saying, "'Oh, Janet, Janet, *Janet,* I've wanted this for a long, long time'" (152) and Min runs off, furious, to Howie.

Janet feels sorry for Sam and agrees to sleep with him, but before this occurs he remembers that there are billboards all over town that have to be vandalized, and he and Janet set out with paint supplies. Sam is truly a good neighbor — despite his lustful ideas, he always ends up doing the right thing.

Chapter fifteen, in which Sam and Janet paint over the names and change the faces on billboards, links *Good Neighbor Sam* to Jack Finney's earlier crime novels. As in those books, Sam and Janet have a plan and gather various supplies to carry it out, but the details of the plan are withheld from the reader.

Since this is a comic novel, the plan is mounted on a much smaller scale, but to readers of Jack Finney's works the pattern is familiar. Sam also paints an epithet on top of a police car when he and Janet are surprised but not discovered by patrolmen. Sam thinks, "The fact is that I don't like cops" (172), and he is thus a precursor to the characters in Finney's later caper novel, *The Night People,* who expend a great deal of effort in the San Francisco area to demonstrate their dislike of the police.

In a sense, all of *Good Neighbor Sam* can be read as a satire on Finney's earlier novels; here, the impossible task for Sam is to pretend to be Janet's husband while keeping his own marriage intact. As the novel comes to an end, Sam and Janet paint the last of the billboards, and each paints messages to their spouses begging forgiveness. Min forgives Sam and explains that Janet will not inherit the eleven million dollars, after all. Her grandfather, it seems, wrote another will and left all of his money to the Communist Party, "'on condition that they divvy it up and disband ... it'll drag through the courts for a hundred years'" (189). Sam's efforts have been for naught, but the novel provides good fun for the reader.

Good Neighbor Sam was quickly turned into a movie starring Jack Lemmon. As always, Jack Finney had nothing to do with the film. According to screenwriter Everett Greenbaum, "Finney was a mystery. We never heard from him nor could we learn anything about his personal life." The film is very funny and sticks closely to its source. It is discussed in detail in chapter nineteen.

The novel itself received very little attention. In 1999, Jon Breen wrote "Finney handles the farcical events ... with a flawless comic touch and along the way presents some pointed satire on his former profession of advertising" (31). That same year, Fred Blosser remarked that, while the novel deals with a marital crisis, "don't expect the suburban angst of John Updike or John Cheever" (52).

Good Neighbor Sam is a pivotal book in Jack Finney's catalogue. It was his first novel not to be serialized or adapted from a shorter work, and it was his last novel for over twenty years to be made into a movie. With *Good Neighbor Sam,* Finney synthesized elements from his earlier short fiction, featuring young, urban married couples in humorous situations, with elements from his big caper novels, and the result is a satisfying comedic work.

TEN

"The Other Wife" and
The Woodrow Wilson Dime

After the publication of *Good Neighbor Sam* in 1963, Jack Finney's productivity as a writer slowed considerably. He was not involved in the film adaptation of *Good Neighbor Sam* that was released in 1964. He published one short story, his last, in 1965, and he was not involved in the film adaptation of *Assault on a Queen* that was released in 1966. His play, *This Winter's Hobby*, had a brief run that year, and he published nothing at all in 1967.

In 1968, his sixth novel, *The Woodrow Wilson Dime*, was published. It was expanded from the short story, "The Other Wife," which had appeared in the January 30, 1960 issue of the *Saturday Evening Post* and which had been reprinted with very minor changes as "The Coin Collector" in *I Love Galesburg in the Springtime*.

"The Other Wife" is narrated by 26-year-old New Yorker Alfred Pullen. His wife, 24-year-old Marion, complains that he does not pay enough attention to her, and he tells her that "'we've been married four years. Of course the honeymoon's over!'" (54). Al's poor choice of words ensures that he spends the night on the living room sofa.

Al and Marion are the unhappy version of Tim and Eve Ryan — young, urban marrieds whose life together has lost its spark. In this story, Finney gives the old theme a new twist by means of an unusual coin. At the beginning of the story, Al checks his pocket change and sees a Woodrow Wilson dime, thinking it is simply "'a new kind of dime'" (54). After his uncomfortable night on the sofa, he walks to work the next morning and unconsciously pays for a newspaper with the unusual dime. This simple act catapults him into a parallel universe immediately, without fanfare. He sees a sign advertising "Coco-Coola" and thinks it is just a sign painter's mistake. Yet he soon realizes that the world around him has changed. Cars look different, the Empire State Building is shorter, and the newspaper under his arm is the defunct *New York Sun*.

Finney presents all of this in his best raconteur narrative style, with Al telling the reader what he sees and punctuating his tale with comments such as, "Do you understand now?" and "maybe you've figured it out too" (54). Al thinks about the big changes that could have been brought on by small alterations in the course of history (something every science fiction reader familiar with Ray Bradbury's short story, "A Sound of Thunder," has considered), and concludes that "There is every conceivable kind of world" and it is possible that "these other possible worlds actually exist; all of them, side by side and simultaneously with the one we happen to be familiar with" (56). This proposition had been explored in Fredric Brown's humorous 1949 novel, *What Mad Universe*. In Jack Finney's hands, though, the idea is used to turn the institution of marriage upside down.

As Al begins to understand that he has memories from his life in both worlds, he finds himself able to exist in this new world without much difficulty. He goes home to his apartment and is greeted passionately by his wife, a beautiful brunette with whom he had broken up years before in his other world. After a brief moment of worry that he is cheating on his wife Marion, he succumbs to his situation and realizes that, in this world, he is married to Vera and it is perfectly appropriate for him to enjoy life with her. "What a wonderful time Vera and I had in the months that followed" (56).

He delights in the subtle differences he finds in this new world, such as an additional book by his favorite author, Mark Twain, who (in this world) lived eight years longer and "died in 1918 in Mill Valley, California" (56), where Jack Finney lived. Al also enjoys other books, including "*The Third Level*, a collection of short stories by someone or other I never heard of, but not too bad" (56, 58).

Unfortunately, Al's personality in this world is the same as it was in the other, and after four or five months the novelty wears off and he is bored again. He deduces that the alternate worlds intersect at a certain point, "at a corner newsstand, for example, on Third Avenue in New York" (58), and occasionally something from one world will slip into another, as did the Woodrow Wilson dime. Al looks for and finally finds a Roosevelt dime; spending it, he returns to his original world and his wife, Marion, thrilled to see her again.

As the story ends, Al tells the reader that "sometimes I'm a little tired at night lately" and that he has found another Woodrow Wilson dime. He has it "safely tucked away" (58) and plans to use it to return to Vera's world when the time is right.

In "The Other Wife," Al Pullen advocates a form of bigamy that is only possible in a science fiction story. Like many of Jack Finney's forays into fantasy, the impossible elements of the tale are used to facilitate wry commentary on the everyday lives of his characters. When Al suddenly travels into an alternate world, he does not become involved in an exciting adventure, nor does he attempt to use his special knowledge for gain. Instead, he proceeds to live the same sort of mundane, workaday life that he lived in his prior world, going to work every day and returning home to his wife at night. For Al, boredom is the enemy and the solution is to make a simple variation in his surroundings. One finishes the story secure in the knowledge that Al will live out his life going from world to world every few months to recharge his emotional batteries.

"The Other Wife" spans four pages in the *Saturday Evening Post;* eight years after its publication, Finney published a greatly expanded version as the novel, *The Woodrow Wilson Dime.* In the meantime, he had published *Good Neighbor Sam,* another novel that uses humor to examine a man's desire for two beautiful women. In the midst of the sexual revolution, Jack Finney wrote two novels (his only two of the decade) that were essentially sexual farces featuring protagonists whose lives were firmly rooted in the establishment.

In the novel, Alfred Pullen becomes 29-year-old Benjamin Bennell, and his wife is now named Hetty. Bennell is a surname that Jack Finney used several times (recall Miles Bennell in *The Body Snatchers* and Ben Bennell in "Husband at Home" and "Stopover at Reno") and Ben, like Al in "The Other Wife," is stuck in an unhappy marriage and a boring job. He works for a company called Saf-T Products and thinks, "So that's what we do at my office; we fool around with paper while trying to hold insanity, raging and snapping at the edges of vision and mind, at bay..." (7).

Finney expands the story to novel length by exploring Ben's marriage and work life in detail, all narrated ironically by Ben himself. Ben speaks to the mirror in his bathroom and it talks back; a hand even emerges from the ceiling to stamp "FAILURE" on his forehead (3). Ben thinks about his old girlfriend Tessie (Vera in the short story) and is described as an unhappy, unpleasant person who (fortunately for the reader) is an entertaining narrator.

A new character is introduced in chapter three; he is Nate Rockoski, a friend of Ben's who is always trying to invent something to make him rich. One Saturday morning, Ben and Nate fool around with a 360-degree camera that takes pictures of people from all sides. Two of the stretched-out photographs are reproduced in the midst of the text, making this the first example of the technique that Finney would use so extensively in his next novel, *Time and Again*, using photographs and other illustrations to complement the text.

In chapter four, Ben spends the Woodrow Wilson dime and is thrown into the alternate world; the novel takes four chapters to accomplish what happens on the second page of the short story. Ben realizes right away what has happened and tells the newsagent that he needs a Roosevelt dime to get back to his own world through the intersection point at the newsstand (32–33).

Ben takes a ride in a taxi cab and the driver tells him something that suggests that this world is more in keeping with one that author Jack Finney might prefer: "'I don't know where you come from, but in New York we don't believe in getting rid of everything the minute it gets a little old'" (34).

Ben goes home to Tessie and his life becomes more exciting. He's an executive at the advertising agency at which he works, and Finney again satirizes this industry (as he did in *Good Neighbor Sam*) by describing products such as Navel-O-No, a wax plug used to cover unsightly navels (46). Finney has some fun with the changes in this new world, and even the voice from Ben's bathroom mirror congratulates him.

It does not take long for Ben to get bored, however, and he visits friend Nate Rockoski, in this world a famous inventor. Ben realizes that zippers are unknown here and decides to invent and patent them. He visits Custer Huppfelt, another character not in the short story. He had known Custer since childhood in the other world; here, Custer is a patent attorney. Finney complicates matters by having Custer bring his girlfriend Hetty (Ben's wife in the other world) along for a game of bridge with Ben and Tess. Ben becomes jealous and his happy life turns somber as he struggles with his feelings about Hetty and Tess.

Custer and Hetty are engaged, and although Ben tries to stop their wedding, he fails. Custer sends Ben a message that a manufacturer wants to buy his zipper for $250,000, but Ben is so morose about Hetty's marriage to Custer that he spends a Roosevelt dime and returns to his original world, where he rushes back to his wife.

By this point in the novel, the story has diverged completely from that of the short story. Ben's return to his first world is an unhappy one when he discovers that he and Hetty have divorced and she is now engaged to none other than Custer Huppfelt. Ben then engages in a series of humorous acts in an attempt to win Hetty back. These include having his face printed on postage stamps, something Jack Finney himself had done way back in 1947 when his first short story had been published in *Collier's* (see discussion of "Manhattan Idyl" in chapter one).

All of Ben's tricks are for naught until he offers Custer the sum of $250,000 to call off the wedding. Custer agrees, validating Ben's belief that he is a cad, and Ben spends another Woodrow Wilson dime and returns to the alternate world, only to find that Custer has stolen his patent for the zipper. Ben then tries other schemes to get rich quick, but nothing works. Finally, he plans to steal the money from Custer, and a scene follows that rivals the conclusion of *Good Neighbor Sam* for pure slapstick fun.

Ben visits Custer's home in New Jersey and drugs his St. Bernard, then dons a St. Bernard suit that features mechanical controls for barking, tail wagging, and so on. Disguised as a dog, Ben gets inside Custer's house with Custer and, after some funny mistakes with the dog suit's controls, Ben grabs a clipboard, sheet of paper, and pen, and dives into Custer's backyard pool. Custer follows, and Ben handcuffs him to the underwater ladder. Ben, having brought a breathing tube with him, then negotiates with Custer by writing notes and finally gets the combination to Custer's safe. Ben gives Custer the breathing tube, leaves him handcuffed under water, and emerges to remove the money from the safe without Custer ever knowing who robbed him.

In the novel's final chapter, Ben finds a Roosevelt dime and returns to his own world. He gives Custer the money, but Custer remains true to form and tries to go ahead with the wedding to Hetty anyway. He is stopped at the last minute by a lawman who arrests him for using counterfeit money: it seems the paper money from the alternate world has President George C. Coopernagel's picture on it.

In the end, Ben and Hetty reconcile but, as in the short story, Ben concludes by telling the reader that he still switches worlds and wives whenever he gets bored.

The Woodrow Wilson Dime was widely reviewed at the time of its publication. The Kirkus Service remarked that "Finney is a funny far-out man. The *Dime* is worth the price." Barbara Bannon, writing in *Publishers Weekly,* called it a "breezy, flippant novel" but complained that, by the end of the novel, "things start to go to pieces and the humor wears thin." Schuyler L. Mott wrote that it was "perhaps not the best-written fantasy, but it is a lot of fun," and Martin Levin of the *New York Times* added that "Mr. Finney's slick fantasy moves too swiftly to encourage examination."

Since 1968, the novel has received slight critical attention. Michael Beard, in his 1981 survey of Jack Finney's work, compared *The Woodrow Wilson Dime* to "The Love Letter" but noted that, instead of an "erotic link" with the past, this novel achieves a similar link "not by going back in time but by shunting laterally from one possible world to another" (184–85). Beard continues by noting that, often in Finney's works, "the artifact of one setting draws humans to its source" (185) and commenting that "the construction of the alternate world is one of Finney's most innovative creations" (185). He concludes, however, that

[t]he weakness of *The Woodrow Wilson Dime* emerges from the conflict between the strangeness of the alternate world and the gratuitous hallucinatory style with which the narrator comically describes both worlds.... Such a style may have seemed innovative in 1968, but the two kinds of strangeness — hallucinatory narrative style and alternate world — conflict with one another and ultimately blur the novel's effect [185].

The novel was slightly updated and revised for publication in the 1987 compilation volume, *Three by Finney;* for the most part, the changes had to do with updating popular culture references to make them familiar to readers of the late 1980s.

In 1996, Kim Newman wrote that Finney's "recurrent theme is of a lost past or alternate now where life and love are somehow better than in his tartly-characterized, body-snatched American present," and added that "*Time and Again* and *The Woodrow Wilson Dime* are vastly more complex versions of the theme" than were the author's earlier short stories (197).

The Woodrow Wilson Dime was Jack Finney's first novel not to be made into a movie, but a copy of the book offered for sale in 2003 included a "letter from well known Hollywood production company to studio head" (Advertisement), so it is likely that Finney's agent tried to sell the film rights. Perhaps Hollywood in 1968 was no longer the place for this sort of slapstick. In any case, the novel was only reprinted in the three-novel collection *Three By Finney,* nineteen years later.

In the meantime, Finney was working on his masterpiece, the novel that would develop a cult following after its publication in 1970, *Time and Again.*

ELEVEN

Time and Again

In 1970, at almost exactly the midpoint of his career as a writer, Jack Finney published his masterpiece, *Time and Again*. An illustrated novel, it has developed a cult following in the three decades since it appeared, receiving more critical and popular attention than any of Finney's prior or subsequent works.

The story is told in the first person by narrator Simon Morley, an artist in a New York City advertising agency. As the novel begins, Morley meets Ruben Prien, from the U.S. Army, who asks Si (as Morley is called) to join a secret government project. Si had been in the Army before but does not relish the idea of re-enlisting; he is twenty-eight years old and two years' divorced. Rube (Prien's nickname) knows many personal details about Si, including that he is "'bored and dissatisfied ... and time is passing'" (15). Like Hugh Brittain in *Assault on a Queen*, Si is open to the idea of adventure and excitement, and Rube capitalizes on this trait.

Also like Brittain in the earlier novel, Si has a girlfriend, Kate. She owns an antique shop on New York's Third Avenue, where Si likes to poke around and look at stereoscopic views of times past.

In discussing his relationship with Kate, Si tells the reader, "I don't like to and I could not reveal everything about myself.... So if now and then you think you can read between the lines, you may be right; or may not" (21). It is tempting to see a parallel with the author

Jack Finney in these lines, since he shied away from publicity during his entire career.

After a pleasant weekend with Kate, Si surprises himself by quitting his job on Monday and calling Rube Prien. Si is told to go to an address that Thursday, which he does, only to find a moving and storage warehouse. He fills out forms and undergoes some tests, meeting Dr. Oscar Rossoff, who hypnotizes him. Si then meets the director of the project, E.E. Danziger, an engaging 68-year-old man, and mentions that he enjoyed *Huckleberry Finn,* recalling the narrator of Finney's prior novel, *The Woodrow Wilson Dime,* who was elated when he discovered more books by Mark Twain in a parallel world.

The nature of the project begins to be revealed in chapter three of the novel, as Si sees various rooms in the warehouse where people engage in acts from past eras: a U.S. soldier fights a World War One German soldier, a woman dances the Charleston, etc. From a vantage point above, Si sees a mockup of a street from a small town in the 1920s, where a man named MacNaughton sits on a porch, enjoying an uneventful afternoon.

Professor Danziger begins to explain Einstein's theories of time to Si in chapter four. Danziger extends the idea of time being a river in his own way and tells Si "'that a man ought somehow to be able to step out of that boat onto the shore. And walk back to one of the bends behind us'" (52). He argues that our knowledge of the present stems from an accumulation of many tiny details that tie us to it, an idea that Finney had explored before, as in the story "Second Chance," where the driver of an antique car moves into the past when the conditions are right.

Danziger takes Si to the building's roof and they survey the Manhattan skyline; the professor reminds Si that there are fragments of earlier times scattered throughout the city. He and Si walk to the Dakota Building, which Danziger remarks "'is close to being a kind of miracle'" (56). At this point, *Time and Again* becomes an illustrated novel, as Jack Finney adds photographs to illustrate the text. Chapter four features six photographs of the Dakota Building and its surrounding area, and they add a new dimension to the story. Finney had experimented with photographs in *The Woodrow Wilson Dime,* but in *Time and Again* they become central to the book's success.

Back at Danziger's office, the professor explains to Si that there are rooms in the Dakota that have views of Manhattan that have remained unchanged since the 1800s. Danziger wants to experiment with time travel "'just for the hell of it'" (64), and explains that all of the scenes Si has observed at the warehouse are merely preparation for the real thing — each of the participants will go to the real places and try to travel back in time. Although Danziger asks Si to travel back to 1901 San Francisco, Si replies that he would prefer to go back to New York City in January 1882 to watch a man mail a letter.

In chapter five, Si explains the reason for his strange request. His girlfriend Kate was adopted as a child by the Carmody family. Her stepfather Ira was the son of Andrew Carmody, a financier and advisor to President Grover Cleveland. Andrew Carmody killed himself, according to Si, after moving his family to Gillis, Montana, in 1898. After his death, his wife erected an odd gravestone with a nine-pointed star in a circle. Ira Carmody photographed the stone and Kate shows it to Si, along with a letter postmarked January 23, 1882.

The letter sets up the central mystery of the novel. It appears to have been partially burned and missing words, but it refers to a meeting at the courthouse and the "'Destruction by Fire of the entire World'" (73). The letter, the suicide, the gravestone — all fascinate Si, and he tells Danziger that he wants to be present when the letter is mailed so that he can try to unravel the mystery. In the tradition of all of the great time travel stories, Danziger warns Si that "'there cannot be the least intervention of any kind in events of the past'" (73), at which point the reader knows that Si will have to do exactly that before the book is through.

Danziger also tells Si that his own parents met on February 6, 1882, at Wallack's theater and that he would love a sketch of their meeting. Finney has thus set up the story in the first five chapters of *Time and Again;* Si is another of the author's young, urban characters whose life is about to change because of an opportunity that arises at a time when he is dissatisfied with his life.

In chapter six, the time travel experiment begins. Si meets everyone in the Project (as it is called) and immerses himself in the details of life in the 1880s. Kate is also introduced to the Project and helps Si, who moves into a room at the Dakota that is just as it would have been on January 5, 1882. In this chapter and the next, Jack Finney slowly adds details of the past to enrich Si's experience, such as having him read the *New-York Evening Sun* and *Frank Leslie's Illustrated Newspaper*. Si grows accustomed to looking down at Central Park and thinking it is the year 1882; he is gradually getting used to the idea, even though he knows he is still in the twentieth century. Another photograph is used here, of a snowy Central Park, and it is difficult to figure out if it is from 1882 or 1970.

Si finds himself drifting mentally into 1882 when Dr. Rossoff arrives and hypnotizes him once again. Si goes outside for a walk in 1882 and sees a horse-drawn sleigh being pulled through the snow. In chapter eight, Si returns to the site of the Project and is probed to see if he really traveled back in time. One of his memories recalls an earlier Jack Finney novel: "'the *Queen Mary*— the ship, I mean — was sold to a town in southern California'" (105). Soon after, Kate joins Si and they both travel back to January 23, 1882, by means of self-hypnosis. In chapter nine, Finney begins to give the reader a tour of old New York, as Si and Kate board a bus that takes them down Fifth Avenue. An old photograph illustrates the scene outside the bus, while a sketch by Si himself shows what the people inside the bus looked like. The tour continues in chapter ten, as Si and Kate get off the bus and observe the mysterious letter being mailed at the post office. The mystery deepens as they follow the man who mailed the letter and see that his boot leaves an imprint in the snow that is the same design as that on Andrew Carmody's tombstone. After returning to the Dakota, they agree that they are back in 1970 and confirm it by looking out of a window at the modern world below.

The narrative of *Time and Again* cleverly draws the reader into the past bit by bit. In the early chapters, we learn that Si is not happy with his life in the present. He is presented with an offer to return to the past and shown tantalizing glimpses of different times that have gone before. A method of time travel is suggested to him and he is put in a place where he can attempt to accomplish it. He at first travels back only briefly, then for a longer time in the company of Kate. The stage is now set, ten chapters into the novel, for Si to do something more, and in chapter eleven the people at the Project ask him to go back to 1882 and follow the man who mailed the letter to see what he can learn. This ends the first part of *Time and Again;* though the book is not formally broken into parts, Si's return in chapter twelve to 1882 New York begins a much more extensive visit to the past.

In chapter twelve, Si begins to get involved in the lives of the people he meets. He is intrigued by Julia Charbonneau, who shows him to his room in a boardinghouse, and immediately dislikes her fiancé, Jacob Pickering, who is also the man whom he had watched mail the letter during his last trip through time. Another important character introduced in this chapter is Felix Grier, a young man with a new camera. Though Grier has little to do with the story, his camera allows Jack Finney to include numerous photographs of characters in the book, including Julia, Pickering, and even Si Morley himself, groomed in a fashion to fit the times. In all, chapter twelve features two sketches and eight photographs, all of which add immeasurably to the reader's enjoyment of the tale.

In chapter thirteen, Si and Julia get to know each other and tour New York City on foot. Later events in the novel are foreshadowed as the pair sees the arm of the Statue of Liberty, which had not yet been assembled. Finney also looks forward to the novel's sequel, *From Time to Time* (though he surely did not realize it), when Si remarks on the absence of "a still-nonexisting Flatiron Building" (176). This chapter features seven sketches, allegedly done by Si Morley, that depict various sights he sees on his way around the city.

The mystery begins to be solved in chapter fourteen, as Si hides behind a statue in City Hall Park and listens in on a conversation between Pickering and Andrew Carmody where Pickering attempts to blackmail the wealthy man with knowledge of fraudulent business practices. Chapter fifteen finds Si trying unsuccessfully to break into Pickering's office. He tells Julia that he has been called away suddenly, and this trip to the past ends with Pickering bursting in to the boarding house to display his new tattoo — Julia's name is etched across his chest. This chapter features a full-page sketch by Si of Julia, looking remarkably like Katharine Hepburn.

The story briefly returns to the present in chapter sixteen, as Si now begins to compare the world he knows with the world he has begun to explore. "*Today's faces are different,*" he thinks, and adds that "there was also an *excitement* in the streets of New York in 1882 that is gone" (218).

Back at the Project, Si learns that others have also succeeded in time travel, but that the world was slightly different upon their return — one man can no longer find any trace of an old college friend from

"Knox College in Galesburg, Illinois" (222), Jack Finney's alma mater. There is a dispute about whether the experiments should continue, and Professor Danziger resigns from the Project when the others decide that the work will go on. Si readies himself to return to the past, which he does in chapter seventeen.

A woodcut, a watercolor, and four photographs appear in this chapter, which mostly details Si's enjoyment of a snowfall in 1882 and his delight at the way the people of that time behave in the snow. Pickering reveals that he and Julia are engaged to be married, and Si decides to try to interfere, even though it may change the future. He rationalizes his decision by thinking that "there were always consequences to *any* future of every act in the past ... the future which was my own time was going to have to take its chances" (255).

In chapter eighteen, Si borrows housemate Felix's camera and walks all over Manhattan, taking pictures that are then reproduced in the book. Finney uses twelve photographs of old New York sights in this delightful section, in which plot takes a backseat to period detail. Si walks across a catwalk above the Brooklyn Bridge, anticipating a similar stunt that occurs in *The Night People,* and tells Julia that he is a private detective investigating her fiancé. The novel's climax occurs in chapter nineteen, which runs for forty-five pages, over ten percent of the novel's length.

Si and Julia break into Pickering's office, only to be forced to hide there when Pickering and Carmody arrive. From their hiding place, Si and Julia witness Carmody paying blackmail money to Pickering and then tying the man to a chair before searching his office. This continues all night and into the next morning, ending as Carmody sets fire to Pickering's papers. The fire quickly gets out of control in the old building, and Si and Julia must make a harrowing escape along the building's ledge (recalling Finney's earlier story of a man on a ledge, "Contents of the Dead Man's Pocket"). A huge fire ensues and Si heroically rescues a woman trapped on a high floor.

Part of the mystery is solved when Si learns that the building that burned used to house the newspaper, the *New York World.* He finally understands Carmody's suicide note ("*That the sending of this ... should cause the Destruction by Fire of the entire World—'Building'* was the missing word" [317]). Si also comprehends that his actions did not cause the fire and did not change history. The rest of the mystery is solved when Si sees Carmody's boot print in the snow and realizes that it matches the figure on Carmody's tombstone.

Besides being well written and very exciting to read, chapter nineteen of *Time and Again* features two pages of reproductions from the February 11, 1882 issue of *Frank Leslie's Illustrated Newspaper,* showing sketches of the fire and of Si's daring ladder rescue. Clearly, Jack Finney was intrigued by this event and by its coverage in the paper, and his novel was at least partially plotted around this real, historical event.

Si and Julia are then taken to the police station, and from there to Carmody's mansion, where they meet Mrs. Carmody and a horribly burned Andrew Carmody, who identifies them as having started the fire. Finney's dislike of the police surfaces here, as it would again in *The Night People,* when Si wonders, "why, *why* do cops habitually and meaninglessly act nastily, as though it were a kind of instinct?" (332). The couple manage to escape and, after a chase through Manhattan, hide in the Statue of Liberty's arm, where Si reveals the truth of his background to Julia before willing them both back to the present. Two photographs are featured in this chapter, but they add little to the narrative.

Back in Si's world, the tables are turned, as Julia is now the one to experience life in another time. Finney's words are enough to describe New York this time, and once again, Jack Finney has a character think about why the modern world is so bad:

> No, I won't let you stay here. Julia, we're a people who pollute the very air we breathe. And our rivers. We're destroying the Great Lakes; Erie is already gone, and now we've begun on the oceans. We filled our atmosphere with radioactive fallout that put poison into our children's bones, and we knew it. We've made bombs that can wipe out humanity in minutes, and they are aimed and ready to fire. We ended polio, and then the United States Army bred new strains of germs that can cause fatal, incurable disease. We had a chance to do justice to our Negroes, and when they asked it, we refused. In Asia we burned people alive, we really did. We allow children to grow up malnourished in the United States. We allow people to make money by using our television channels to persuade our own children to smoke, knowing what it is going to do to them. This is a time when it becomes harder and harder to continue telling yourself that we are still good people. We hate each other. And we're used to it [378–79].

Si Morley decides not to tell Julia any of this, but the fact that he thinks it shows that he is a product of his times. When *Time and Again* was published in 1970, anti-establishment sentiment was widespread. Si Morley fits into the line of Finney characters who long for escape from the world in which they live; his description of what is wrong with that world is rather different than that provided by Miles Bennell in *The Body Snatchers,* but the feeling of dissatisfaction is the same.

The mystery gets a twist in the tail in chapter twenty-one, as Julia deduces that the burned man she and Si met at Carmody's mansion was not Carmody at all, but rather Pickering, who would spend the rest of his life impersonating the man he had tried to blackmail. Julia walks back into the past, using the unchanging Brooklyn Bridge as her location for time travel.

The final chapter of *Time and Again* finds Si back at the Project, resisting all efforts to have him continue with the time travel experiment. He says goodbye to Kate and writes *Time and Again* as a journal of his experiences, hiding it in the New York Public Library where it will be found by "a friend, a writer ... the only man ever to look through a great decaying stack of ancient religious pamphlets in the rare-book section" (393). That writer, of course, is Jack Finney, who spent years researching New York history to write this novel.

The final pages of the book tie up the last thread left dangling, as Si promises Professor Danziger that he will stop the project. He returns to 1882 and prevents Danziger's parents from meeting, thus erasing the future scientist and his work from the course of history. As the novel ends, Si heads for 19 Gramercy Park, and Julia.

The book concludes with a page-long footnote in which Jack Finney addresses the reader. "I've tried to be factually accurate in this story," he begins, but "I haven't let accuracy interfere with the story" (399). Most interesting are his admission that the Dakota Building was not built until 1885 (thus removing Si Morley's main spot for time travel) and that the photographs used in the book "couldn't all be strictly of the eighteen-eighties. Before 1900 things didn't change so fast as now — one more reason why Si so wisely decided to stay back there."

In an advance review published in the March 9, 1970 issue of *Publishers Weekly,* Barbara A. Bannon wrote that the novel is "delightful, clever and imaginative" and correctly pointed out that "the actual blackmail plot is almost incidental. The real fascination of the book lies in

Morley's discovery of the New York of that period...." She added that "Finney has the gift of making his time travel perfectly believable, largely through the smooth use of authentic details."

The week before, *Kirkus Reviews* had called the novel "a fully illustrated fascinator" and remarked that "the time transitions are seamless." The novel was published by Simon & Schuster in May 1970, and subsequent reviews were mostly positive. The *Washington Post* called *Time and Again* "one of the most original, readable, and engaging novels to have come along in a long time" (Blackburn). Thomas Lask wrote a long piece about the book for the *New York Times* on July 25, 1970, and W. G. Rogers followed this with another long review in that same newspaper on August 2, 1970, calling the novel "a most ingenious confection of time now and time then." This glowing review set the tone for reviews that followed, in numerous magazines and journals.

Yet *Time and Again* sold only modestly upon first publication (Hirschfeld 13). Finney appears to have been captivated by the subject matter, though, because he wrote four lighthearted articles for the *New York Times* during the next year. The first was titled, "Where Has Old-Fashioned Fun Gone?" and described a Christmas celebration on the floor of the New York Stock Exchange in 1882. Finney ends the article with these wistful remarks: "Maybe, just maybe, New York has begun reaching back toward a day when it would have been possible to say 'Fun City' without sneering."

Next came "Off to the Golden West," which relates a coast-to-coast trip by train circa 1890, and ends with the following editorial comment: "Jack Finney, author of 'Time and Again,' is in love with yesterday." Finney's third *New York Times* piece was titled "St. Nicholas Monthly's Xmas List" and reproduced sketches and advertising copy from an 1875 periodical. Finally, he published "When Felony Had Style," which featured mug shots and information about criminals from the late nineteenth century. Some of the information came from "the testimony of Thomas Byrnes, famous nineteenth-century head of the New York cops" and a character in *Time and Again*.

In the decades that followed, Jack Finney's novel attracted a "cult following" (Hirschfeld 13) and was the subject of a considerable amount of critical discussion. After the initial flurry of reviews, the first writer to look seriously at *Time and Again* was Richard Gid Powers, in his introduction to the 1976 Gregg Press edition of *The Body Snatchers*.

Powers calls *Time and Again* Finney's "most important novel" and comments on the author's "acute and aching sense of what was lost when the world grew up and became 'modern.' Finney's heroes are romantic traditionalists so much in love with the past that they are able to wrench themselves *into* it by an overwhelming act of will" (vi).

In a 1977 discussion of the novel, Quentin Gehle points out numerous instances of Finney's use of irony, "which at some times is far more subtle than at others" (7645) and comments that "even though the novel suffers from disunity, that disunity does make available the appeal of a detective story, a love story, and a science-fiction tale" (7646). Two years later, Anne Carolyn Raymer's piece on the book explained, in comparing the hero of *Time and Again* to that of Edward Bellamy's *Looking Backward,* that "Morley can appreciate that era because, unlike Bellamy's hero who escapes from it, he is not a Utopian but an ordinary man capable of enjoying the simple delights of a less hectic and complicated era." She adds that "Finney's handling of character ranks among his most important contributions" (2285). Unlike Jack Finney's other novels (save *The Body Snatchers* which, it can be argued, received attention because of the popularity of the films it inspired), *Time and Again* rather quickly became a novel of interest to literary critics.

By February 1979, the *English Journal* was publishing suggestions for activities to help teach the novel to students (Haagen 46). A *New York Times* article on July 6, 1986, reported that Columbia University history professor Kenneth T. Jackson was using *Time and Again* in his college courses, calling it an excellent introduction to Victorian New York City (Fleming). Michael Beard called it a "minor cult book among New York enthusiasts" in his 1981 survey of Finney's career, and wrote that "*Time and Again* is the most solid and consequential of Finney's novels and the one in which his characteristic stratagems and complex turns of plot work out in the most satisfying manner" (185).

A study of the novel by Brooks Landon correctly notes that it "returns to a common theme in his short fiction, and represents in several ways the distillation of his central concerns as a writer: his fierce championing of individuality and his dissatisfaction with the complicated, dulled, and polluted contours of modern life" (1938). He writes that "more than three million copies have been printed" and concludes that, "in *Time and Again,* there is no fantasy that can equal the allure of the past, no tomorrow as safe and desirable as yesterday" (1942).

Time and Again was listed as one of the entries in David Pringle's 1989 volume, *Modern Fantasy: The Hundred Best Novels,* and regular reprints of the book kept it in the public eye as the new millennium approached. Curiously, though, no film had been adapted from the novel in the twenty years since its publication. An interview with Jack Finney published in the May 25, 1990 issue of the *New York Times* reported that Universal Pictures had bought the rights to film the novel around the time it was published but that no film had ever been made. "My agent tells me he no longer bothers to tell me how many inquiries he gets," said Finney of interest in filming the novel. As of 1990, Finney and his agent, Don Congdon, planned to try to reacquire the television rights to the novel, but no television adaptation was ever made. Finney also remarked that he was "350 pages into a sequel, with 150 to 200 pages to go" (Van Gelder). The sequel would not be published for another five years, right before the author's death.

Time and Again's reputation continued to grow in the 1990s. A 1994 article in the *New York Times* reported that "over the years, the novel ... has captivated and entranced some of the biggest names in the film business" (Hirschfeld 13) and has attracted "a vast cult following" among readers. Movie star Robert Redford "said he plans to produce, direct and probably star in a film version for Universal Pictures." The article adds that Jack Finney "started the novel in the late 1950's, inspired by a lifelong fascination with old photos, prints and newspaper articles" but that he "became so blocked that, at one point, he abandoned the effort, then started 'Time and Again' over again with a completely retooled plot."

The article (basically a history of the novel's success since its publication), states that *Time and Again* sold "27,000 copies in hardcover" and "200,000 copies as a large-sized trade paperback" (13, 20), something less than the more than three million copies that were earlier said to have been printed. It also noted that walking tours around Manhattan of sites from the novel were "still popular" (20) and that an elaborate banquet had been held earlier that year at Columbia University, reproducing the atmosphere of 1882.

Finally, a "Broadway musical based on the book" was said to be in the works (20). More than two decades after its publication, *Time and Again* was more popular than ever. In 1995, the *New York Times* listed it as one of the ten best books about New York (Roberts 14), and the sequel, *From Time to Time,* was published early that year.

Jack Finney died in November 1995, but interest in his 1970 novel did not wane. Advertisements for "The Jack Finney 'Time and Again' Tour" around Manhattan continued to run in the *New York Times* as late as 2001, and the growing popularity of the internet in the late 1990s allowed fans of the novel to publish their own reviews for each other to read.

The musical version of *Time and Again* is discussed in chapter seventeen. As of January 2002, Robert Redford was still considering filming the novel (Kobel), which was in the running that same year when a New York City committee met to select a single book to recommend to all New Yorkers.

Why, then, is *Time and Again* so enduringly popular? Why has it remained in print since 1970 and attracted such a cult following? I think that the main reason is because it is such an entertaining novel. Finney uses melodrama skillfully and his wistful recreation of 1882 New York touches something in readers who, like Si Morley, often grow tired of the modern world. The novel is also very well written, and the characters are appealing. In his excellent 1999 survey of Finney's work, Jon L. Breen wrote that *Time and Again* is "Finney's finest achievement" (32) and explained that, while the illustrations are nice, "the magic of the writing does most of the work" (33). That same year, Fred Blosser called the novel "perhaps the most impressive historical novel ever written about everyday urban life in nineteenth-century America" (53).

In short, *Time and Again* is the central book in Jack Finney's oeuvre. In it, one finds themes that ran through his work from his first short story to his last novel, and its main character is one of his most memorable. *Time and Again* is Jack Finney's masterpiece.

TWELVE

Marion's Wall

In *Marion's Wall,* published in 1973, the formula of *Time and Again* is turned upside down. This time, a character from the past travels to the present and wreaks havoc on the life of the narrator, 30 year old Nick Cheney Jr.

The story begins with a letter, written to Nick Jr. by his father, Nick Sr. Nick Sr. recommends an old Victorian house at 114 Divisadero Street in San Francisco, California, where he once lived in the bottom apartment.

As the story proper opens, the reader realizes that the letter is an old one, and that Nick Jr. and his wife Jan have already bought the house in question and are in the process of remodeling it. While stripping wallpaper, they uncover a message, written in red lipstick and covering the large, living room wall: "Marion Marsh lived here, June 14, 1926. Read it and weep!" (18). They do not know who Marion Marsh was, but, when Nick brings his visiting father home from the airport, they are surprised to learn that he knew Marsh quite well and was present at age twenty when she wrote the message.

She had been an aspiring actress in the 1920s, Nick Sr. explains, and she wrote the message for future generations to read after she had become famous. She died in a car crash, however, before making it to Hollywood. Nick Sr. tells Nick Jr. and Jan that Marion had a small part in only one movie —*Flaming Flappers*— and that Joan Crawford inherited the next part she was hired to play and became a star in her place.

The writing on the wall becomes the showpiece of the house at a party that the Cheyneys throw after renovations are completed in chapter two. Time passes and winter turns to spring, then to summer in San Francisco. Jack Finney's theme of the destruction caused by progress surfaces as Nick Jr. walks home from the bus stop and looks out over the bay: "The money-makers were destroying the city as fast as they could go, blocking off the old views with higher and higher buildings ... and the destruction of the Bay itself with fill and pollution continued" (30–31). Yet the destruction is not complete, and transplanted Midwesterner Finney's voice may be heard through the thoughts of his character in this passage: "But there was still an awful lot of beauty to destroy before they finally Manhattanized or Milwaukeeized San Francisco, a lot still left that was good to look at meanwhile. As a Midwesterner, a flatlander, I appreciated this place, and had been here long enough to feel a part of it" (31). The author of this passage was born in Milwaukee and lived in Manhattan before moving to California, so when Nick Jr. thinks these thoughts it's likely they were shared by his creator.

Like so many of Jack Finney's young, urban protagonists, Nick Jr. worries about getting stuck in a rut, and something happens that will change his life. *Flaming Flappers* is being shown on television that night, and he and Jan sit down to watch, looking for a glimpse of the starlet who wrote the message on their wall.

Silent films were enjoying a revival of interest as both nostalgia and history in the early 1970s, and Jack Finney taps into that trend in *Marion's Wall.* Yet Nick cannot stay interested in the film, which seems remote to him, and he instead plays with his dog, Al, joking that he's really a person in a dog suit and thus recalling the climactic scene in *The Woodrow Wilson Dime.*

Jan calls to Nick and they watch Marion Marsh's scene in the movie; Nick thinks that "unlike every other figure in the absurd scene, this one tiny gray-and-white figure was alive" (39). After the movie ends and Jan goes to bed, Marion's ghost appears and speaks to Nick, thinking he is his father. She had resurfaced in order to see her own movie for the first time, and she appears, brief and transparent, at Nick's request. After she disappears, Nick goes to bed and is surprised that Jan awakens to make love. Nick then falls asleep, pleased that whatever had been interfering with his and Jan's happiness had suddenly disappeared with her unexpected behavior.

In chapter three, Nick learns that Marion had possessed Jan's body when they made love the night before. Jan's strange behavior continues at a party the next night, where Marion takes over and, using Jan's body, behaves in a manner much like that of a 1920s flapper. Afterwards, she and Nick speed through the night in his old Packard on a wild, drunken ride ("I was so confused," thinks Nick [57]). He reveals that it's not the Roaring Twenties anymore and that he's the son of her old lover. She seduces him and, when they make love, this time Nick knows it is not really Jan.

The next morning, Jan is ashamed of her behavior the night before, but Marion soon takes over her body again and drags Nick further down into her world of debauchery. They make love and drink again, spending the day drinking champagne, playing 78 RPM records, and dancing like Eddie Cantor. Marion drives Nick to the train depot and is sad to see the decline of the formerly grand passenger trains.

Marion tells Nick about seeing Douglas Fairbanks and Mary Pickford leaving for Hollywood on the *Lark,* and Jack Finney has Nick think this evocative description of another lost American institution:

> She looked slowly around at the worn empty benches; at the long row of ticket windows nearly all permanently boarded over with raw plywood; at the dusty-windowed restaurant in a corner of the waiting room, the big handles of its entrance doors chained together and padlocked; at the great overhead blackboard labeled ARRIVALS — DEPARTURES, its green-ruled spaces empty; at the dismantled lunch counter, its row of metal stool supports still bolted to the floor, the stool tops gone [78–79].

Long-time readers of Jack Finney might compare this railroad station to the Grand Central Station of "The Third Level": in the 1950 story, a visitor to the still busy station could use it as a gateway to the past. By 1973, Finney seems to say, even this method of time travel has been closed off, and Marion Marsh can only recall the distant past through memory.

Further disappointment awaits Marion when she and Nick drive to the site of the old Alcazar Theater, which is now an ugly motel. "'It's a different world, Marion,'" Nick tells her. "'The Alcazar's gone. So is the

Lark. So will the SP station before long. And the world is filling up with motels. *Flaming Flappers* was long, long ago. And I'm not my father'" (81).

Marion decides that she is tired and gives up on recovering the past. She claims she is leaving forever, and Jan awakens, in control of her body again. She sees the chaos that Marion's visit has left in their house and deduces that she has been possessed by the flapper's ghost. The knowledge that Nick made love to her knowing that Marion was in control angers her, and she tears Marion's dress to shreds, a sign that Nick's marriage is in trouble.

In chapter five, Nick and Jan's relationship grows as she forgives him and admits that being possessed was both "'frightening'" and "'interesting'" (89). Nick discusses the 1920s with his father, who recalls them in a way that is consistent with similar passages in so much of Jack Finney's fiction. While Nick Sr. admits that "'we tend to remember what was good in the past and forget what was bad,'" he insists that "'It was just a grand and glorious time to be alive and young in'" (91). "'The people were different ... nicer.... I don't remember the hatred there is now.... It was just a better time'" (91).

Nick Jr. and Jan then go to bed together, after an awkward passage in which Nick uses the word "'fuck'" and then explains how he had to train his proper wife to use "'bad words'" (92). This passage (and similar ones in Finney's next novel, *The Night People*) show the author trying to be modern but sounding like an aging writer (Finney turned 62 in 1973, the year that *Marion's Wall* was published) trying to keep up with the times. Jack Finney's fiction is most enjoyable when he and his characters are longing for the past.

At the end of this chapter, Marion Marsh returns to take control of Jan's body again, delighted to see a modern movie and excited by the advent of sound and color. The movie experience makes Marion change her mind about going away and leaving Nick alone. The next morning, he awakens to find her again possessing Jan's body and determined to pick up the pieces of her aborted movie career. She wants to visit Hugo Dahl, who worked as a prop boy on her only film, *Flaming Flappers*. His name is still in the telephone book. Marion entices Nick by telling him about an old friend who collected films. Nick explains to Marion the mania that infects collectors and reveals that his "'impossible dream'" is to find "'all forty-two incredible reels of Erich von Stroheim's lost masterpiece... *Greed*'" (107).

Nick soon gets to experience ghostly possession, when he accompanies Marion to a screening of the silent film, *The Four Horsemen of the Apocalypse*. During the show, he is possessed by the ghost of Rudolph Valentino, the film's star, and feels "the hopeless yearning for what might have been" (111). This incident, coupled with Marion's insistence, convinces Nick to talk to Jan about letting Marion travel to Hollywood in Jan's body to try to break into the movie business.

In chapter seven, Jan agrees and gives Nick and Marion two weeks to succeed. They drive to Hollywood (with Valentino briefly taking over Nick's body during the trip) and Nick convinces Jan to live up to her promise, despite her immediate dislike of the movie town. They go to a movie studio and meet Hugo Dahl, who believes Jan when she tells him that she is Marion Marsh's granddaughter and agrees to give her an audition. In a humorous passage, Nick is possessed by Rodolpho Guglielmi (the real name of Rudolph Valentino) and awakens in the middle of a dangerous stunt on the wing of a biplane flying above Los Angeles. The scene is quite a contrast to another scene, in Finney's short story, "An Old Tune," where the narrator calmly travels above Marin County in a hot air balloon.

Both Nick's stunt work and Jan's audition are masterful, yet they and the spirits inhabiting their bodies are crestfallen when they see the footage used in television commercials advertising bottles of catsup. In the meantime, they locate the mansion where aged film collector Ted Bollinghurst lives, and Marion succeeds in landing a bit part in one of Dahl's films.

In the conclusion of *Marion's Wall*, Jan/Marion finally gets her chance to shine in a movie. Marion lights up the room in her scene, which occurs at a party, but when the character disrobes, Marion soon becomes disgusted and tells the onlookers that "'this isn't the MOVIES at all'" (153). Her brief career at an end, she stalks off of the set and takes Nick to visit Ted Bollinghurst. Now in his eighties, Bollinghurst lives in an opulent Hollywood mansion built in the heady 1920s and named Graustark. Nick and Jan/Marion get a tour of the house, which is home to an impressive collection of rare movie memorabilia. This sits in stark contrast to the portrayal of Hollywood of the 1970s that they saw at the studio. Here in the mansion, where time has stood still, the glory days of silent film live on. Bollinghurst, Nick thinks, is "a movie fan, an old-film buff, of which there are a lot of us — but with the money to take it just as far as he wanted to go" (165).

Bollinghurst's film collection is equally impressive and even includes the complete *Greed*. In his private screening room, furnished like a 1920s movie palace with an organ that Ted plays in accompaniment to the silent films he shows, they watch *Daughters of Jazz,* the film that Marion would have starred in had she not died. Ted admits to having been in love with her, having replaced all of Joan Crawford's scenes in his copy of the movie with clips of Marion.

As the film begins, Jack Finney provides an in joke to long-time readers as the screen credits read, "From the novel by Walter Braden" (177), Finney's legal name. The novel's climax occurs as the film catches fire and burns down the mansion, with Ted Bollinghurst remaining at the pipe organ, playing like Lon Chaney in *The Phantom of the Opera*. Nick rescues Jan, but Marion's ghost stays behind, sitting in the front row of the theater as the house burns to the ground.

The novel ends with Nick and Jan changed by their experience. They earn residuals from the commercials they made while in Hollywood, and Nick uses the money to buy some old movies. The one thing that does not change is the wall: "That hasn't changed, and never will as long as we're in this house. *Marion Marsh lived here,* it still says in that enormous, free-swinging scrawl of lipsticked letters across it, *Read it and weep*" (187).

Reviews at the time of publication were positive. *Kirkus* called *Marion's Wall* "a pleasantly ensorceling story of a time that was down nostalgia alley at the corner of Sunset and Vine" and the *Library Journal* called it "a slick ghost tale with a humorous gimmick" (McCormick). *Publishers Weekly* added that the novel was "entertaining and suspenseful fantasy, especially for old-time film buffs" (Bannon). *The Booklist* remarked that *Marion's Wall* was "unusually agreeable" with "an appropriate conclusion."

Subsequent critics have not had much to say about the novel. Michael Beard's 1981 survey article compared Marion Marsh's appropriation of Jan Cheyney's body to the actions of an earlier class of Finney villains but explained that, this time, "the body snatching is benign: she stays only long enough to realize that she does not want a movie career in the film industry of the 1970s" (185). In her 1996 article, Kim Newman pointed out the novel's debt to Thorne Smith (author of *Topper*) and wrote that "*Marion's Wall* is as concerned with evoking the minutiae (and slang) of the past as *Time and Again* with a strong undercurrent of dissatisfaction with a plasticized present" (197).

More recently, Jon Breen has pointed out that the setting of *Marion's Wall* "returns to the young, married suburban ambience of *Good Neighbor Sam*" (34) and, by extension, to the many early stories Finney wrote featuring characters like Tim and Eve Ryan.

Finney followed *Marion's Wall* with three more short articles in the *New York Times,* all published in 1973 and following the pattern of the four earlier pieces he had published on that newspaper's editorial pages in 1970. "Getting It Right This Time" describes an 1871 plan to build an elevated railway above New York's Park Avenue. "Man's First Flight: Over Manhattan, 1876" relates an 1876 newspaper story of a successful test of a flying machine and asks a modern engineer if it is plausible. Finally, "Esprit de Postal Corp." describes the 1875 relocation of New York's post office from an abandoned church to a new building. Finney quotes favorite author Mark Twain's 1876 remarks about the inefficiencies of the postal service. Clearly, in the wake of *Marion's Wall,* Finney was still captivated by the subject of his prior novel, *Time and Again.*

Marion's Wall has not achieved the success of *Time and Again,* although it was reprinted in a slightly updated form in the 1987 collection, *Three By Finney.* In 1985, the film adaptation of the novel, *Maxie,* was released, making it the first of Finney's novels to be filmed since *Good Neighbor Sam. Maxie* takes liberties with *Marion's Wall,* making Jan the main character and updating the story to the mid-1980s. Still, it is an entertaining film, and the gist of Finney's story remains. It is discussed in detail in chapter nineteen.

Marion's Wall is an entertaining novel that touches on Jack Finney's interest in the past and continues to explore some of the themes he had written about in *Time and Again.* His next novel, *The Night People,* would mark a return to the type of novel he had not written since *Assault on a Queen.*

THIRTEEN

The Night People

Jack Finney's 1977 novel *The Night People* marks his return to the caper story, which he had used successfully early in his career but which he had not explored since 1959's *Assault on a Queen*. *The Night People* is similar to *Five Against the House* in a number of ways, since each book tells the story of a group of bored young people who decide to turn to crime to spice up their otherwise dull lives. Instead of the college students of the earlier book, however, the main characters in the 1977 novel are working adults.

The novel opens with a prologue, much like a teaser opening for a television show. In it, Lew Joliffe and his friend Harry are climbing up the cables of San Francisco's Golden Gate Bridge. Their excitement is mixed with fear, and Lew thinks back to how they began as the Night People. The story is told by Lew in third person narration, and this odd prologue serves as an introduction to the majority of the book, which thus becomes an elongated flashback. Oddly enough, the pages from the prologue are not repeated in chapter ten, in which the actual event takes place.

One may speculate that Finney's publisher forced this opening onto the novel, perhaps thinking it needed a grabber to hook the reader's interest. It is not like the beginning of any other of his books and it is followed by chapter one, in which the story really begins. Of all of Jack Finney's novels, *The Night People* suffers most from dating, as many of the situations and attitudes expressed by its characters seem locked in the hedonistic 1970s era it portrays. Its events occur in Mill Valley, California (Finney's home at the time), and in surrounding Marin County. Lew Joliffe is a lawyer in his late twenties who shares an apartment with his lover, Josephine "Jo" Dunne, an architect. The story takes place in 1976, and Lew dictates a cassette tape for listeners 100 years in the future. Finney uses this method to provide expository details about the two characters. Lew is having trouble sleeping and dons a ski mask to go outside for a walk in the empty, suburban streets. Finney's running in-joke with his legal name appears again as Lew calls to one house, "'Hey, Walter Braden! Come on out, and play!'" (259).

Lew comes to a ballfield and pretends he is batting in the World Series, then sits on a porch swing and dares himself to complete six swings in the loud contraption. This awakens the resident of the home on whose porch the swing hangs, and Lew hides when the man comes out to investigate. Chapter one ends with Lew returning home, having completed his first nighttime act of rebellion.

In chapter two, Lew drives to work with neighbor Harry Levy, and they share their boredom with their mundane lives and jobs. Before leaving home, Jo asks Lew why he is in a bad mood. He answers with sarcasm: "'Nothing. Nothing that isn't bothering everybody. The national debt. Corruption in high and low places. Decline in moral values. Blatant sexuality'" (266). But these modern, 1970s-era concerns are not really the problem. Instead, Lew and neighbor Harry are both examples of young, urban, successful men in Jack Finney's fiction who are bored with their lives and yearn for adventure. Lew says to Harry, "'I just mean is it okay with you if this turns out to be all you ever do?'" and, later, "'sometimes it bothers me that this could be more or less it from now on'" (269). Like Si Morley in *Time and Again*, like Hugh Brittain in "The U-19's Last Kill" and *Assault on a Queen*, like Tim Ryan in so many early short stories, the two men in *The Night People* appear to have good lives but are bored by their material success. Si Morley has his problem solved when he is offered a chance to travel back in time. Hugh Brittain escapes boredom by joining with his friend Vic DeRossier to rob the *Queen Mary*. Tim Ryan good-naturedly seems to find things to liven up his days. Lew Joliffe and Harry Levy continue this trend in the swinging seventies in *The Night People*, in which they experiment with sex and vandalism to manufacture entertainment.

The use of casual obscenities that began in *Marion's Wall* continues in this novel, as Harry tells wife Shirley that she doesn't "'give a fuck'" and she replies that she does not "'like casual, pointless dirty talk'" (273). This leads to a discussion of wife-swapping, a 1970s phenomenon that truly serves to date the novel.

In chapter three, Lew goes for another lonely walk late at night and is surprised to see that the freeway, which is crowded every morning, is completely deserted at night. Finney uses a very slow exposition in *The Night People,* and the story drags a bit as a result. The reader knows from the opening scene on the Golden Gate Bridge that something is going to happen, but the story of two self-absorbed young couples verges on being no more than a tale about spoiled adult brats. Lew tells Jo a colorful story of an event from his childhood that she immediately knows is untrue; she realizes that his trait of "occasionally spinning out a fantasy to her or others, making it as believable as he could" (283) is a sign of his uneasiness. Lew is also considering running for city council, which would not only make his place in the community even more stable, it would be another signal that he is growing up and becoming an adult. Finney implies that Lew's antics in *The Night People* are a reaction to this fear of maturity, something that many members of his generation were experiencing at the time.

Lew's slow metamorphosis into a risk taker continues in the novel's fourth chapter, as he goes for his third nighttime walk. This time, he walks out onto the empty freeway and lies down in the middle of the road. Harry's wife Shirley is out walking her dog at the same time and joins Lew in the road. They kiss and he admits that he desires her. They then try to scare a passing car before going home. Lew's sexual fantasy is dashed when Shirley excitedly tells him that she wants Harry and Jo to join them on their next outing; she coins the term "'the Night People'" (291) and Lew feels a pang of sorrow at the realization that "the solitariness of his night-time walks" (291) is gone.

In chapter five, Lew tells Jo about his nighttime walks, and admits that he has "'always liked the notion of some secret way to walk off into another world'" (293), recalling the actions of the narrator in Finney's early story, "The Third Level." Living in California, he misses the snowy winters of his Illinois childhood and tells Jo that one Christmas he flew back to Chicago and went to see his parents' house. It looked different than he had remembered, however, and even though he did not go in, he was satisfied at having seen it (293–94). This attempt to return to the past puts Lew even more squarely in the line of Jack Finney's fictional characters who have done (or tried to do) the same thing; the incident also recalls a similar one in the short story "Crazy Sunday," where a young father travels to Paris on a whim and learns "that his youth wasn't still here waiting to be returned to" (246). For her part, Jo also shares an affection with many of Finney's characters in that she "'always liked the idea of a summerhouse ... the little lath and scrollwork places you'd go off to by yourself on a long 1890 kind of summer afternoon'" (294).

That night, the foursome goes for their first nighttime walk together. They end up frolicking on the freeway until a police car passes. They are concerned that he may have seen them and they observe him park at a nearby service station and get coffee. In true 1970s fashion, Harry is angry at the power the police wield over innocent citizens — "'answer questions; produce *identification,* for crysake. All that shit — I hate it'" (302). To give Jack Finney credit, though, the anti-police expressions and acts of the characters in *The Night People,* while they may seem dated and pandering to popular feelings of the 1970s, are actually extensions of behavior common to Finney's characters as far back as Tim Ryan (see "Sounds in the Night," a 1951 short story).

Although Harry fantasizes about vandalizing the police car, nothing is done and the Night People go home peacefully. Starting the next day, everyone goes back to their normal lives. Chapter six includes another scene reminiscent of an early Finney story; this time, Lew and Harry refuse to get up and visit each other on a rainy Monday night, so their wives facilitate a party by telephone. In 1957, Finney had published the story "Rainy Sunday," in which the same thing happens between two other couples, the Callandars and the Howsers. A comparison of the scene in *The Night People* with the earlier short story makes it clear that Finney had the story in hand when he wrote the novel; the entire scene is rewritten and updated, but the events and many of the words are repeated verbatim. Of interest to Finney's readers is the change that occurs when Lew sings his high school song. In "Rainy Sunday," Ben and Charley sing "'Revere old Courtland, dear old Courtland,'" which earns this reply: "'their high-school song,' June murmured to Ruth. 'Can you tie that?'" (307). In *The Night People,* it is changed to "'On Proviso, on Proviso,/Fling your colors high!'" to which this reply is given: "'Their high school song,' Shirley murmured. 'Can you tie that?'" (312). The change is interesting because Jack Finney attended Proviso High School.

A close examination of *The Night People* reveals that it is an amalgam of many things that Jack Finney had done before in his fiction, with a rather clumsy attempt to update its events to the 1970s by means of casual obscenities, radical attitudes, and frank discussions of sexuality. Another Night People outing occurs in chapter six, and this time it is wilder than the last. While dancing in an empty shopping center parking lot and drinking champagne, the two couples are surprised by Floyd Pearley, the same policeman they had seen on their last outing. Pearley is portrayed as a reactionary, his behavior and speech a caricature of an ignorant policeman in contrast with the smooth, well-spoken Lew Joliffe. Harry is belligerent and lectures the policeman about his behavior, but Lew calms Harry down and they almost walk away before Harry's childish behavior forces a confrontation. The couples are forced to run away and escape after Pearley pulls his gun and threatens them.

To add insult to injury, the couples then go home, get high on marijuana, and take nude Polaroid pictures of each other. Unfortunately, chapter six of *The Night People* is one of the more embarrassing examples of Jack Finney's fiction, and it demonstrates why he was a much better writer when he was not trying to pander to the fashions of the times.

In chapter seven, Harry's childish behavior continues. He reveals to Lew that he printed an enlarged photograph of Lew, Jo, and Shirley in the nude and hid it in a book in the Mill Valley Library. Lew must recover the photograph before the library opens the next morning and a student discovers it. The crime is planned, and that night Lew and Jo enter the library through an unlocked back door and begin searching for the book. Accidental exposure of Lew's flashlight leads to an investigation by the police, and of course one of them is Floyd Pearley, the target of Harry and Lew's invective on their last adventure.

Lew and Jo hide from the police in a suspenseful scene and, as they escape to Harry's getaway car, Harry reveals that he has stolen the ignition keys from the police car. He tosses them out of the window into the road and a car chase ensues, but again the couples evade the police and retire to bed.

Two thirds of the way through *The Night People,* its central problems are already clear. First of all, the characters are not particularly engaging or likeable. Lew is a spoiled adult, Jo is sketchily drawn, Shirley is essentially an object for Lew's lustful thoughts, and Harry is a childish boor. Secondly, there is no real motive for their actions, other than boredom or nastiness. One gets the feeling that these are not people that one would like to meet, and the cardboard manner in which their encounters with the police occur does not engender reader sympathy. However, the novel's big set piece is yet to occur, despite the fact that it was given away in the prologue.

In chapter eight, Lew suggests climbing to the top of the Golden Gate Bridge. Before this is planned, however, there is another encounter with Officer Pearley, whose dialogue is embarrassing: "'You was the guy at the liberry,'" he tells Lew. "'You flang the keys!'" (369). Though Harry and Lew walk away, the policeman arrests Shirley, leading to Harry's punching the policeman and stealing his gun. Though the couples think they have escaped and reached home safely, the police successfully track them down and Harry and Shirley are forced to evacuate their apartment and move in with Lew and Jo. Everyone decides that they will have to leave California and start life anew, but Lew and Harry vow revenge on Office Pearley and discuss Lew's plan about climbing the bridge.

In chapter nine of *The Night People,* Pearley gets closer to finding Harry and Lew as they evade his search and plan their last and greatest prank. The preparation and gathering of materials recalls similar scenes in earlier Finney novels, such as *5 Against the House* and *Assault on a Queen,* but by this point in the novel the situation has grown so ridiculous that it is hard to care about the fates of these characters.

The novel concludes in chapter ten, where the scene in the prologue finally makes sense. The two couples drive to the Golden Gate Bridge, where Harry and Lew begin their climb to the top. Oddly enough, the suspenseful pages from the prologue are not repeated, which diffuses the sense of fear that the earlier section of the novel had begun to create. The men make it to the top and then descend like mountain climbers; Jo and Shirley send up supplies by rope. Their job complete, they rejoin the women and drive to the service station where they had first seen Officer Pearley. They do things to annoy him, such as jamming the coin slots on his favorite coffee machine, then steal his police car when he arrives.

They drive to the Civic Center and use a ramp to park the police car on the building's roof, taking a Bonnie and Clyde style photograph together before leaving. The stunt makes the TV news, and the embarrassment of Officer Pearley continues as the Chief of Police makes fun of the situation, telling a reporter that Pearley "'was in hot pursuit. Of a stolen hang glider. Had him cornered up there on the roof'" (403). The comment recalls Finney's earlier story, "An Old Tune," but *The Night People* contains little of the lyricism of that earlier tale of a man reaching the top of the Golden Gate Bridge by balloon.

As the day ends, the Night People's final prank gets underway. Lew, Harry, and Shirley use three vehicles to block all four lanes of traffic on the Golden Gate Bridge. Harry hooks up a power source and Jo and Shirley pull on ropes to let down a huge white sheet that will serve as a screen. Harry then projects their life story onto the screen, to the enthrallment of those stalled in traffic on the bridge. The final shot is the one of Lew, Shirley, and Jo naked, and as the novel ends, Lew and Jo drive toward Santa Fe; she had almost decided to leave him but she has chosen to stay with him to see what will happen next.

The Night People is a dated novel, filled with characters and situations of the mid-1970s that seem quaint and unpleasant today. It represents Jack Finney's most awkward attempt to keep up with the times, and it would be his last, since he would not publish another novel for 18 years.

Upon publication in 1977, *The Night People* was not widely reviewed. *Kirkus Reviews* commented that "this scenario would work better as a Finney short story or as a frisky film; given too many pauses between bon mots and escapades, it's easy to find the night games resistible — to become disenchanted with the second-childhooding, suspicious of motives, and impatient for Finney to probe beneath the high spirits." A *Publishers Weekly* review called the novel, "nice jaunty escapism" (Bannon), and a *Booklist* writer referred to it as a "humorous novel attractive both as snappy entertainment and social commentary," but the novel faded quickly from view after a paperback reprinting and was never filmed.

Critics writing in the decades since the novel's publication have barely mentioned it, but Finney himself referred to it in a 1995 interview, when he mentioned that he had not ever read to anyone at the Mill Valley Public Library, "not too surprising, when you consider that in 'Night People,' his 1977 novel, he explained how the average citizen could burglarize the place. 'I was concerned,' says Thelma Percy, 75, who was the head librarian then. 'The instructions were explicit. We didn't want to encourage that sort of thing'" (Ickes 36). In 1999, Jon Breen wrote that "these characters ... are less endearing than the author's usual. It may be that Finney's decision (otherwise unprecedented in the novels) to write in the third person damaged the kind of tenuous reader identification needed to render his central characters likeable" (35). Fred Blosser was more impressed with the novel, writing that "*The Night People* may be most remarkable as a parable of anomie and angst in the comfortable white-collar middle class during the Ford and Carter era, comparable to the free-flowing, absurdist seventies movies of Paul Mazursky and Robert Altman" (55).

Jack Finney was 65 years old when *The Night People* was published in 1977. He had not published a short story since 1965, and he would not publish another. Despite his impressive early record for having his novels made into films, his last four novels had failed to interest Hollywood, and no film adaptation of his work had been released since *Assault on a Queen* in 1966. He would not publish another book for six years, and one may safely assume that, after *The Night People*, he was in semi-retirement.

FOURTEEN

Forgotten News:
The Crime of the Century
and Other Lost Stories

As the 1980s began, American society was changing. The 1970s had been a time of upheaval, and Jack Finney's attempt to reflect the prevailing spirit had resulted in *The Night People*. The popular filmed remake of *Invasion of the Body Snatchers*, released in 1978, changed the tone of the original story so completely that it looked like Jack Finney's best work was out of step with the times. Yet his love of traditional values and his interest in America's past began to coincide with the return to the past being promoted by new president Ronald Reagan, and nostalgia was once again in vogue. Finney's 1970 novel *Time and Again* had continued to sell for a decade, and was well on its way to achieving cult status and popularity beyond anything else he had written. It is not surprising that his next published work would be *Forgotten News: The Crime of the Century and Other Lost Stories,* a book that hearkens back to the era explored in *Time and Again*.

Forgotten News was published in 1983 and is Jack Finney's only non-fiction book. It begins with a short essay entitled, "What Is This Book?" (vii-xiv). The essay immediately reminds readers of *Time and Again* because it includes 14 vintage illustrations from *Frank Leslie's*

Illustrated Newspaper, interspersed with Finney's tale about how he researched New York City history when writing *Time and Again.* It is interesting to note that the process Finney went through is exactly the same process that Si Morley goes through in the 1970 novel when he immerses himself in the details of an earlier age in order to prepare for his time travel.

Finney explains that, years after *Time and Again* was published, he went back to *Leslie's,* thinking of doing a book of short news items from the late 1800s. He had published an item on the op-ed page of the *New York Times* about an 1876 report of a helicopter prototype ("Man's First Flight: Over Manhattan, 1876"), and this led him to dig further into the old news sources. He discovered the stories that he would retell in *Forgotten News,* and the research and writing of the book took three years. Referring to the paper stock used in the old newspapers, he comments, "They generally used good material in the century before the world went bad" (xii).

The first thirteen chapters (and 186 pages) of *Forgotten News* are devoted to telling the story of Harvey Burdell, a dentist who lived at 31 Bond Street in New York City in 1856 and 1857. Finney uses copies of illustrations from the *New York Times* and *Tribune,* as well as from *Frank Leslie's Illustrated Newspaper* and *Harper's Weekly,* to enrich the tale. He also includes contemporary photographs of locations that occur in the narrative. Finney introduces Emma Cunningham, a widow with five children who works her way into Burdell's home and life. In a wry nod to his own work, Finney writes that "There has been some ridiculous fiction written about people traveling back in time to earlier days, but absurd though such books are, I wish they were true" (9).

By using the news sources of the time, Finney tells of the events leading up to Dr. Burdell's murder, and of the murder itself, on January 30, 1857. Finney writes that he recalls a childhood memory of seeing "gaslight on new snow" near a railroad station in the Chicago suburbs while with his parents. Finney calls it "a nineteenth-century sight reaching out into the twentieth to take hold of me forever" (47).

As the tale unfolds, the murder is discovered and the investigation begins with a coroner's inquest and the doctor's funeral described in detail. Finney surmises that faces then were different than they are now (in 1983): "Faces different because the people are different" (102). "I think that's why movies and television of other days are so often unpersuasive. They get the clothes right, sometimes, but the faces of the people wearing them are today's" (102).

The inquest is followed by an indictment and then a gripping murder trial, told by Finney in a captivating style, with comments on everything as it unfolds. Finney has read every word of the old news stories and uses many tricks of fiction to keep the tale interesting — summarizing, quoting, developing characters, and foreshadowing. In *Forgotten News,* Jack Finney successfully takes 100 year old newspaper stories and breathes life into them, fashioning a novel of sorts. Most interesting is the end of the story, where Emma is acquitted of Dr. Burdell's murder and yet does not inherit his wealth when her pregnancy is discovered to be a hoax. Finney's greatest regret is that, when the story was no longer newsworthy, the papers stopped reporting it, so "I can't tell you what happened to these people" (185) afterward.

Forgotten News then includes a fourteen-page "Intermission," in which Finney briefly presents several short bits of unusual news from the late 1800s, including a revised version of his earlier article, "Esprit de Postal Corp." (199–200). The next five chapters (and 74 pages) include the book's second long story, this time about the 1857 wreck of the *Central America,* victim of a storm off the coast of Georgia. As with the murder of Dr. Burdell, Finney uses illustrations and details from the 1857 news sources to bring to life this long forgotten story that was big news at the time it occurred.

Forgotten News concludes with another thirteen-page section of shorter news bits from the 1800s, including more details on the 1876 helicopter (282–84). This is a revision of the earlier *New York Times* piece, "Man's First Flight: Over Manhattan, 1876." Two other articles are also presented in revised form: "Where Has Old-Fashioned Fun Gone?" (278–81) and "Getting It Right This Time" (285). Most interesting to Jack Finney's readers, however, is the final story in the book, told in its last five pages. Finney reveals that a February 1882 story from *Leslie's* was a source for one of the key scenes in *Time and Again.* The story in question, illustrated by a full page woodcut on the cover of *Frank Leslie's Illustrated Newspaper,* detailed the heroic rescue of a woman named Ida Small by an anonymous man from the burning offices of the *New York World.* This incident, central to unraveling the mystery that drives *Time and Again,* turns out to have been a real one.

Even better, he reveals that Ida Small's son had read *Time and*

Again and had written to Jack Finney with the real story of his mother's rescue. In reality, the artist who drew the cover for *Leslie's* had invented the bearded man seen saving Ms. Small; she had told her son that there was no such man and that she was actually rescued by a fireman. Her son went on to share details of the rest of Ms. Small's life, providing the author with the rest of the story for at least one of the subjects of his research.

Forgotten News is a delightful book, where Jack Finney the raconteur uses his considerable skill to tell stories culled from long-neglected sources with a perspective that can be enjoyed by modern readers.

The book was widely reviewed and praised. *Kirkus Reviews* called it "offbeat, vivid, and entertaining," and Barbara A. Bannon of *Publishers Weekly* noted that it was "all most enjoyable, the period illustrations and Finney's asides being a decided plus." Gwendolyn Elliot, writing in the *Library Journal,* deemed it "a delightful nonfiction book," and Phoebe-Lou Adams, writing in *The Atlantic Monthly,* remarked that the book was "a wonder of orotund and inventive journalism" and called it "a grab bag of engaging Americana." A negative review appeared in the *Los Angeles Times Book Review,* where John Ned Mendelssohn complained about Finney's style and wrote that "his prose, littered with unrelated phrases stuck together with plenty of semicolons and wishful thinking, reads like the former half of a before-and-after advertisement for a correspondence course called Five Weeks Toward More Comprehensible Syntax."

The growing popularity of *Time and Again* led Simon & Schuster to issue a trade paperback entitled *About Time* in 1986. This book collected twelve short stories that had been collected previously in *The Third Level* and *I Love Galesburg in the Springtime.* The cover proclaimed "more time travel stories from the author of the beloved classic *Time and Again,*" and the following stories were collected: "The Third Level," "I Love Galesburg in the Springtime," "Such Interesting Neighbors," "The Coin Collector," "Of Missing Persons," "Lunch-Hour Magic," "Where the Cluetts Are," "The Face in the Photo," "I'm Scared," "Home Alone," "Second Chance," and "Hey, Look at Me!" "Lunch-Hour Magic" was the new title of "Love, Your Magic Spell Is Everywhere," which in turn had been reworked from the earlier "The Man with the Magic Glasses." "Home Alone" was the new title of "The Intrepid Aeronaut," which itself was a retitling of "An Old Tune."

About Time is an entertaining short story collection that unfortunately does not include any commentary by the author at all.

Reviews of the collection were positive, with most critics echoing the comment in the *Washington Post Book World:* "within their range, these stories are perfect." In a 1996 article about this collection, Kelly Rothenberg praised "the conversational way Finney invites the reader into his scenario and lets [him] explore along with the protagonist." She added that "Finney's writing is not stylish like Faulkner's or as distinctive as Hemingway's. It's very nondescript, conversational, sharing more in common with America's other most underrated writer, Rod Serling, than with anyone else (other than perhaps Stephen King ...)."

Simon & Schuster followed *About Time* with another collection, publishing *Three By Finney* in 1987. This trade paperback reprinted the novels *The Woodrow Wilson Dime, Marion's Wall,* and *The Night People,* with minor revisions. Gone from *Marion's Wall* was the dedication page in which Finney listed a long series of Hollywood personalities. Finney also changed several of the dates in this novel in a clumsy attempt to update the story to the 1980s—1973 becomes 1985, making Marion Marsh 80 years old instead of 68 (1973: 60; 1987: 154). Hugo Dahl is now in his seventies, not his sixties (1973: 100; 1987: 183); Ted Bollinghurst becomes ten years younger in 1926 (1973: 105; 1987: 187), and is well into his nineties, rather than his eighties, when the story takes place (1973: 156; 1987: 223). As Jon Breen later pointed out, the updates make "total nonsense of the chronology and the film-collecting references" (34). Reviews were once again positive, though; the *Washington Post Book World's* reviewer wrote that "each story is expertly written and well-made, told in a winning narrative voice, with moments of screwball comedy."

In 1987, Jack Finney won the Life Achievement Award at the annual World Fantasy Convention held in Nashville, Tennessee. However, the World Fantasy Convention's list of guests at that convention does not include Finney's name, which suggests that the publicity-shy author did not attend to collect his award in person ("History of the World Fantasy Conventions"). His career was nearing its end, and he did not publish any new fiction between 1977 and 1995. He had one more novel left to publish, and it would not appear until just before his death in 1995.

FIFTEEN

From Time to Time

Jack Finney was 78 years old when an article entitled "At the Movies" by Lawrence Van Gelder was published in the May 25, 1990, edition of the *New York Times*. While the article was chiefly about attempts to film the author's 1970 novel, *Time and Again,* it also contained a brief note explaining that, according to Finney, he was working on a sequel to that novel. He provided some details of the plot and the article added that the book was expected to be finished "sometime in the next year."

However, the sequel to *Time and Again* did not appear in 1990 or 1991. In 1993, the third filmed version of *The Body Snatchers* was released under the title *Body Snatchers,* and in 1994 the French translation of *Time and Again* (*Le Voyage de Simon Morley*) was awarded the Grand Prix de l'Imaginaire as best translated novel of the year ("The Locus Index to SF Awards"). Another *New York Times* article, "Is the Time Finally Ripe for 'Time and Again'?" reported, on March 20, 1994, that "Mr. Finney has completed a sequel, tentatively titled 'Time and Time Again,' which Simon & Schuster plans to publish next fall" (Hirschfeld 20).

According to another article by Van Gelder ("Some Time Later, a Sequel to 'Time and Again'"), Finney had begun "thinking about a sequel set in 1912" six or seven years before and had been doing research for the novel, yet, as his agent Don Congdon explained, "At least five times he stopped writing." The novel, finally titled *From Time to Time*, was eventually published in early 1995.

The novel begins with an "Author's Note," in which Finney briefly summarizes the plot of *Time and Again* and adds that "this book is the story of what happens when Si — out of simple curiosity — returns to the present just to see what's going on" (11). An epigraph follows, quoted from Allen Churchill's *Remember When*, and it sets the stage for Finney's last exploration of the good old days: "Historians say so: The years between 1910 and 1915 were the pleasantest this country has ever known..." (13).

The novel itself begins with a prologue, told by a third-person omniscient narrator. This narrative style, which Finney had used only once before in a novel (*The Night People*), alternates in the thirty chapters of *From Time to Time* with Si Morley's first-person narration. The prologue is a fascinating story about a meeting of top-level officials who gather to discuss instances of what appear to be changes in the historical record. John F. Kennedy's second term is recalled, as is the arrival of the *Titanic* in New York. The group exists to catalog events that suggest "that occasionally two versions of the same stretch of time seem to exist. Or to have existed, one of them replacing the other" (22). The odd part of it is, people tend to have memories of both time streams concurrently.

Si Morley's narrative takes over in chapter one, as he tells the reader about the Project (from *Time and Again*) and how he came to live in 1887. He is happily married to Julia, but she remarks that he has been singing strange songs from the 1900s. They discuss the possibility of his traveling back to the twentieth century, and he feels some guilt over preventing Dr. Danziger's birth with his action to change the future.

The story switches back to third-person narration for chapters two through four, as we are re-introduced to Ruben Prien, whose memory has been changed by the alteration in history but who has a strange feeling that something is missing. He is inexplicably drawn to a moving and storage company (the reader knows that this was the headquarters of the Project), and he receives a call from Oscar Rossoff, who has heard from John McNaughton. Prien and Rossoff both have memories that they can't explain.

Prien visits McNaughton in Vermont and learns that McNaughton has not forgotten anything, since he traveled through time to the 1920s and managed to retain his memory. Prien realizes that Si Morley wiped out Danziger and the Project by changing the past, and he and McNaughton decide to send the latter back to look for Si. In chapter five, McNaughton goes back to the day when Si had prevented Danziger's parents from meeting. McNaughton knocks Si down a flight of stairs, thus allowing Danziger's parents to meet and the prior series of historical events — culminating in the Project — to be reestablished. In the middle of chapter five, the narrative voice switches back to the first-person, as Si expresses his relief over what has occurred. McNaughton buys a one-way ticket to Winfield, Vermont, content to remain in the nineteenth century and never to be heard from again.

In chapter six, Finney includes a photograph and an illustration, which only serve to remind the reader how much this novel differs from *Time and Again,* which featured so many well-placed illustrations. In the first seventy-five pages of *From Time to Time,* there are only two photos and one drawing, and two of the three appear in chapter six. Si appears to let fate decide his path here, as he follows the choice of a bird held by the Bird Lady, whose bird will pluck from a box an answer to a question for the price of a nickel. Si decides to go forward in time, and withdraws an advance on his weekly salary. Finney makes an in-joke by having one of the bills drawn on the First National Bank of Galesburg, Illinois — Galesburg was Finney's college town and had figured in earlier stories, including "I Love Galesburg in the Springtime."

Si returns to the twentieth century in chapter eight, but this time he does not go to his old room in the Dakota Building, since it has been rented. Instead, he walks to the newly-built Brooklyn Bridge (an excuse for another illustration), where he sits on a bench and lets his mind fill with thoughts of the century to come. As in *Time and Again,* this method is successful, and Si returns to the Plaza Hotel, where he looks up Dr. Danziger's number in a telephone book.

Chapters eight through eleven return to the third-person narration of the novel's earlier chapters and pick up the story thread involving Ruben Prien. Prien brings Danziger back to the site of the now-abandoned Project and tries to convince him to restart it. When confronted with the evidence of changes in history that the reader saw in the novel's prologue, Danziger reasons that something must have happened around the year 1912 to cause the alterations. They discuss Si Morley's "published account, his book" (96), which included the erasure of Dr. Danziger from the face of the earth. Even though Danziger realizes that something must have been done to make him exist again, he does not want to alter historical events.

In chapter nine, Prien demonstrates to Danziger that there was an alternate historical world where the First World War never happened. Ruben wants to change history to eliminate the war in his reality, yet Danziger still resists. In chapter ten, Ruben tracks down Si and tries to convince him of the wisdom of eliminating the Great War. They meet in Central Park in the eleventh chapter and discuss a plan that had been developed by Presidents Theodore Roosevelt and William Howard Taft; they had wanted peace and had sent an operative known only as Z to Europe to try to broker a deal with heads of state. Z did not return from Europe and was never heard from again, and the Great War occurred. Prien has researched his identity and learned that Roosevelt's daughter, Alice, knew the man. He and Si figure out the approximate day he left for Europe and Si agrees to return to 1912 to look for Z and try to prevent the First World War.

The first section of *From Time to Time* is the setup, which comprises chapters one through eleven. Finney seems to have been trying to do many things at once here, because he takes a long time to get to the main part of the story and uses two distinct narrative techniques (first-person narration by Si Morley and third-person narration by an omniscient narrator) to tell the tale. The novel really gets going in chapter twelve, which returns to Si's first-person narration to explain how he prepares himself to return to 1912. He reads a 1912 newspaper at the New York Public Library in order to "look for what the people of 1912 had to tell me about themselves" (123). He then reads novels of the time, including "*Truxton King: A Story of Graustark*" (124), the title of which recalls the name of the elaborate Hollywood mansion that figured in the conclusion of Finney's earlier novel, *Marion's Wall*. Si watches old films at the Museum of Modern Art, looks at stereo views at the Museum of the City of New York, and sees models of clothing worn at the time. The process of soaking up details of life in 1912 appears to parallel the research process that Jack Finney must have gone through in preparing to write *Time and Again* and *From Time to Time*. Si Morley is a fantasy projection of the author; in the novels, his research allows him to do what Jack Finney (and his readers) can only dream of—travel back in time.

In chapter thirteen, Si enters Central Park at dusk and, sitting down on a bench, slips back into 1912. The next twelve chapters (fourteen through twenty-five) depict Si's adventures in 1912, as he experiences another time period and tries to solve the mystery of Z. Si quickly learns that he "had come into a time worth protecting" (140) and, as he did in *Time and Again,* he buys a camera and uses it to take photographs of what he sees. Finney includes these photographs in the book, but this time, unlike in the earlier novel, much of it seems like filler or travelogue, and it does not serve to move the story along. Si meets Helen Metzner, whom he thinks of as the Jotta Girl, after a dance she was doing when they met. They watch Roy Knabenshue ascend above Central Park in a homemade blimp, and Si gets a ride in a hydro-aeroplane with Frank Coffyn above the city. This allows him to discover that the building shaped like a ship, where Z was to meet "that man whom of all the world I most admire" at eleven o'clock at night to receive "The Papers" (117), was in fact the famous Flatiron Building, which still sits at the point where Broadway intersects Fifth Avenue at 23rd Street in Manhattan. To readers familiar with New York City and its landmarks, this is a rather obvious mystery, since Z's letter refers to the building as looking as if "one might sail her up Broadway or the Fifth Avenue" (117). Certainly, it pales in comparison to the mystery in *Time and Again* involving the "Destruction by Fire of the entire World" (73).

Si's trip in the hydro-aeroplane above Manhattan recalls similar trips by other Finney protagonists — most notably, that of the wistful narrator of "An Old Tune," who flies his balloon over Marin County, California, and returns to Earth with a new perspective. In *From Time to Time,* Si's search for Z is delayed when he and the Jotta Girl attend a play, which gives the author an excuse to include more 1912 photographs and details of the time. In chapter twenty, Si goes to the Flatiron Building at the appointed time and climbs onto a ledge above the street. From this vantage point, he observes Z meet Teddy Roosevelt, but he cannot see Z's face.

A subplot that runs through *From Time to Time* involves Si's search for the vaudeville act Tessie and Ted; the search concludes in chapter twenty-two. It turns out that Ted is Si's father, who would later become a drunk and die in his forties, before Si's second birthday. Si feels uncomfortable watching their act and is happy when it ends. This sub-plot parallels that of *Time and Again,* where Si searches for informa-tion about Kate's adopted family, but in the earlier novel this all works to move the main story along. It is interesting to consider Si's search for Ted in light of the fact that Jack Finney was born in 1911 and that his own father died when the boy was two years old.

The story takes a nice twist when Si learns that Archie, friend to Helen and acquaintance to Si, is actually Z, and Archie manages to escape Si and sail for Europe on the *Mauretania.* Si meets Helen again and realizes that the song she had been singing — the one that caused him to think of her as the Jotta Girl — was from the 1920s, and she thus could not be who she says she is. She admits that she was part of the Project as well and that Dr. Danziger had sent her back to 1912 to stop Si from taking action that would prevent World War One. In short, all of Si's careful research failed to let him recognize an anom-aly — the girl he spent all of his time with in 1912 was singing a song that had not been written yet! It is ironic that a mistake in research becomes a significant detail in a novel whose main character uses his-torical research as a method of achieving travel through time.

Back in the present, Si visits Ruben Prien and regales him with tales of the past. Rube wants Si to try again to change history, and con-vinces him to return to 1911 to attempt to prevent the sinking of the *Titanic.* It seems Si's son by Julia was fated to die in the First World War, and Rube theorizes that the *Titanic* disaster somehow led to the Great War's being fought. The story moves very quickly here, and logic is not central to its success. Instead, Prien comes up with a way to get Si to travel through time again, and Si returns in chapter twenty-seven to May 1911, where he sails from New York City to Ireland on the *Mau-retania.* He finds the *Titanic,* docked in Belfast and ready to set sail.

The final section of *From Time to Time* suggests that Finney had some difficulty getting the novel to work as a unit. From the long ini-tial section, which switches back and forth between first- and third-person narration, through the long middle section, which details Si's adventures in 1912, to the brief final section, which tells the story of Si's attempts to prevent the *Titanic* from sinking, the novel seems dis-jointed, resembling Finney's non-fiction work, *Forgotten News,* more than anything else. It reads as if the author had several ideas but never quite figured out how to meld them together (or edit them down) to make a coherent whole.

In any case, Si spends months walking the length of Ireland, killing time until spring 1912 (making one wonder why he did not just target a later date for this trip back in time); he books passage on the great ship and is taken aboard. He finds Archie in the lounge, and tries to warn him of impending doom, but Archie argues that he would never try to save himself at the expense of women and children and denies knowledge of any secret government papers. The Jotta Girl appears, telling Si that she had come through time to see if he would succeed in his latest mission. She tries to change the course of the ship by distracting its driver with a smile and a scarf over his face, but the ship hits the iceberg and begins to sink, leading to the question of whether her efforts caused a change in course that led to the collision. Si awaits the sinking of the ship.

From Time to Time ends with a brief thirtieth chapter, in which Si writes: "I'm home now. For good" and he means back in 1888 with Julia and their son. He thinks of old Mr. Bostick, who has just died, and how he had been born in 1799, "the year George Washington died.... Now he's gone, a thread to the past broken. But they break every day, don't they, the past ever receding, growing stiller and stiller in our minds" (302).

Jack Finney's last published work ends with this lament about the way that links to the past are disappearing constantly, just as he, too, would soon disappear. The novel was published in early 1995, the year he died, and it was greeted with more publicity and interest than any of his prior writings, probably because by then *Time and Again* had become a favorite among readers and critics alike.

The first review of *From Time to Time* appeared in *Publishers Weekly* on November 28, 1994. In it, Sybil Steinberg wrote that the novel "lacks the magic and urgency of its predecessor but is diverting nonetheless." An unsigned review in *Kirkus Reviews* agreed that the novel "fails to live up to the original" and called it "zestless." The publicity barrage for the book began in February 1995, around the time of its publication. Reviews appeared in the *Wall Street Journal* (February 1), the *Washington Post Book World* (February 12), the *Library Journal* (February 15), the *New York Times* (February 19), and the *Christian Science Monitor* (February 28). The reviews were often lengthy and, while praising Jack Finney's writing and recalling his long career, they invariably criticized some aspect of his new novel. Michael Dirda wrote that "structurally the novel is ramshackle," and Suzanne MacLachlan added that it "doesn't quite measure up" to *Time and Again*. Most enthusiastic was Frank Rich, who argued that the pleasures of the novel's evocation of old New York outweighed the fact that "Mr. Finney barely pretends to meet the obligations of fiction, science or otherwise...."

Even more surprising than the numerous and lengthy book reviews were the interviews and photographs that appeared in various newspapers and magazines, allowing readers a glimpse into Finney's life that he had studiously avoided providing, with few exceptions, for decades. *Vanity Fair* published a two-page article about the novel with a picture of the author in its February 1995 issue. *Entertainment Weekly* published a two-page spread in its February 24, 1995 issue, with a photograph of the author, concluding that "You just wish the novelist in him had occasionally throttled the popular historian" (De Haven 109). Bob Ickes published a four-page article in the *New York Times* on March 19, 1995, in which he interviewed both Jack Finney and his wife and summarized prior interviews. Finney tells Ickes, "'I wish people would stop assuming I want to live in the past. I don't! It would be a lousy place to live'" (37).

Another brief interview with Finney appeared in the April 10, 1995 *People* magazine, along with a review of *From Time to Time*. The writer admitted to having had problems writing the novel, but "after persistent prodding from his agent, he decided to 'struggle through and finish it'" (Sheff-Cahan 32). While he told Bob Ickes in March 1995 that he would not want to live in the past, he admits here that a visit would be nice: "'it would be fun to walk down Manhattan's West 74th in the 19th century ... and see if Edith Wharton would walk out of her house'" (32).

A new trend in book publishing led to *Time and Again* and *From Time to Time* being issued in abridged versions on cassette, with each novel read by actor Campbell Scott. A May 1995 review by Jean Palmer in *Kliatt* remarked that the abridgements concentrated on plot and left out "much of Finney's expertly detailed (and realistic) evocation of time and place."

Critical attention to the novel began with a long article by Robert

J. Killheffer in September 1995. In short, he recommends the book based on the pleasure it brings, noting that it may not qualify as "serious literature" but that it is "serious fun" (23). Cynthia Breslin Beres compared the two Si Morley novels in an essay that appeared in *Magill's Guide to Science Fiction and Fantasy Literature* in 1996; she concludes that the themes of the earlier novel are "somewhat blurred" in the later novel "by the generally thin plot." In 1999, Fred Blosser suggested that the novel's ending was Finney's way of "saying his own farewell to a full career of exploring the mundane and the marvellous" (56).

On November 14, 1995, Jack Finney died of pneumonia at Marin General Hospital in Greenbrae, California. He had turned 84 on October 2, and obituaries appeared in newspapers across America and abroad. He was survived by his wife, Marguerite, his son, Kenneth, his daughter, Marguerite, and his granddaughter, Annelise, to whom his final novel had been dedicated. According to the *Dayton Daily News,* "the family said no funeral service would be held" (*"Body Snatchers* Author Dies at 84"").

Since his death, Jack Finney's books and stories have continued to serve as the basis for adaptations in other media, including the television movie "The Love Letter" and the Broadway musical, *Time and Again.* His best novels — *The Body Snatchers* and *Time and Again* — are also his most popular, and both have remained easy to find in libraries and bookstores. His short stories, which comprised such a large part of his career, have not been as fortunate. The original two collections (*The Third Level* and *I Love Galesburg in the Springtime*) have been out of print for years, and *About Time* is now almost twenty years old.

Jack Finney never made pretensions to serious literature, and he can best be remembered as a popular author. From his earliest stories to his last novel, he wrote about Americans and their place in history; often, his most evocative work dealt with characters that either succeeded or wished they could succeed in traveling back to an earlier time. Hopefully, his short stories will again become available to readers in the near future; his lesser known novels also deserve reprinting. In short, Jack Finney's work stands as an example for readers of the sort of lives Americans led in the middle part of the twentieth century, as well as of their longings and dreams of a simpler time in a world that grew increasingly more complicated and confusing.

SIXTEEN

The Galesburg Letters

In the early 1930s, Jack Finney attended Knox College in Galesburg, Illinois. The yearbook issued in conjunction with his senior year, *The 1935 Gale,* includes a photo of a serious young man with glasses next to the following entry:

WALTER BRADEN FINNEY, A.B.

Forest Park

Tau Kappa Epsilon; R.O.T.C. 1,2;
Student staff 1, 2, 3; intramural swimming 1, 2, 3, 4; varsity swimming 4 [18].

Another photograph of the graduating senior was included in the yearbook's page of members of the fraternity to which Finney belonged, *Tau Kappa Epsilon* (103).

Over the next two decades, Finney married, divorced, and married again, worked in radio and advertising, and began his career as a writer. He became well known for his short stories and wrote several novels. One story and three novels were even adapted for television and film. In late 1959, he was working on a new story entitled "I Love Galesburg in the Springtime," which would eventually see publication in the April 1960 issue of *McCall's* magazine. As part of his research into the story's setting, he wrote a letter to the president of Knox College requesting information about Galesburg. This letter began a correspondence that would last, on and off, for almost twenty-five years, with some lengthy breaks in between. The letters to and from Finney have been preserved in the Knox College archives, and they show a side of the publicity-shy author that has been hidden from public view.

The President
Knox College
Galesburg, Illinois   November 14, 1959
Dear Sir:

I wonder if I could ask a favor of someone at Knox College; I don't know to whom I should address this.

I am a professional writer, and have just written a short story about Galesburg. I'm the author of a good many stories, which have appeared over the past ten years in *Good Housekeeping, Collier's, McCall's, The Saturday Evening Post, Cosmopolitan*, etc.; and of four novels, the last of which was just recently published, by Simon & Schuster [*Assault on a Queen*]. During these ten years I've written about Galesburg in my stories every once in a while.

But this newest story is entirely about Galesburg, and is full of references to the town, both contemporary and in the past. Trouble is that I haven't been in Galesburg since the late 30s, and I'm sure some of my references are inaccurate, out of date, or wrong for some other reason. This story will be published by *McCall's* magazine, and I told them when I sent it to them what I said above; that it undoubtedly is not accurate as it now stands.

McCall's wants me to go to Galesburg, to research my factual references, and I am delighted at the chance to come to Galesburg again, and will do so as soon as I can arrange a time for my visit.

It would help me enormously, though, if someone at Knox who knows Galesburg, past and present, might be willing to read my story in advance of my visit. Is there anyone at the college, do you think, who might be willing to do this? I ask, because of course my story (I was graduated from Knox in 1934, and am listed in your records under my real but seldom-used name of Walter B. Finney), contains references to Knox which I've got to check, too.

I have written to the editor of the *Galesburg Register-Mail*, asking him if he will, to read my story, and tell me where I've gone wrong. So there would be no need for whoever at Knox might be willing to read my story to correspond with me about it. All I'd like, if that's possible, is to have someone at Knox with whom I could talk when I get to Galesburg, who has read my story in advance of my visit.

It may very well be that this is a request which cannot be met; and I will certainly understand it if this is so. Please don't hesitate to let me know if it's impossible. I've enclosed a stamped addressed envelope for your convenience in letting me know about this, if you will.

Sincerely yours,

Jack Finney
223 Ricardo Road
Mill Valley, Calif.

The letter appears to have been well-received, for a reply was written by M.M. Goodsill, director of public relations for Knox College, on November 16, 1959, only two days after Finney's letter was written. He replied:

Dear Mr. Finney:

Acknowledging your letter of November 14, I'll be glad to read your story and search for errors. I used to be on *The Mail.*

I note you have written the editor of the *Register-Mail,* who is Chuck Morrow, and if he or Mac Eddy, associate editor, read the story also, I'm sure we'll catch anything that might be wrong. Or we'll know who to check with.

Kellogg McClelland at Knox is an encyclopedia of facts about the town and college also and we can refer unknown questions to him.

I presume you've read Earnest Calkins' "They Broke The Prairie."

We'll be glad to see you when you come.

Sincerely,

M.M. Goodsill

Handwritten notes at the bottom of the letter add that, on November 17, 1959, the college sent Finney copies of "Places of Interest in Galesburg" and another pamphlet or book whose name is illegible, and that on November 23, 1959, they sent him something called "Galesburg's Mighty Horse Market."

Finney must have visited Knox College in early December 1959, for he wrote the following letter to Goodsill:

December 14, 1959

Dear Mr. Goodsill:

Thank you again for your great courtesy, and helpfulness, to me when I visited Galesburg early this month. It was very kind of you to take the time and trouble to show me around Knox as you did; I would never have realized or seen the many interesting changes since I was in school which you pointed out to me.

Thanks to you and to Mr. Morrow of the *Register-Mail,* I was able to get all the material I needed, quickly and easily, for the story I am working on. All in all it was a successful and enjoyable trip, and I'm very happy to have had the pleasure of meeting you.

Finney added a postscript:

I've learned, incidentally, that the story which brought me to Galesburg is tentatively scheduled to appear in the April issue of *McCall's* magazine.

Goodsill replied on December 18, 1959:

Thanks for your letter of December 14. I'll watch for *McCall's* in April.

The snapshot I inflicted on you turned out all right, so I plan to run it in *The Alumnus.* Could you find time to send me a list of books and articles from your pen? Also, biographical material up to date?

Happy holidays to you!

Subsequent letters, including the letter with the list of writing, appear to have been lost. However, handwritten notes on the December 18 letter report that "letter with list given to Helen for files 12–18" and "snapshot to Helen 3–8–60 (used in *Alumnus* winter)." Another "snap to Helen 3–22–60 used & ret'd by R. mail" followed.

The Knox Alumnus issue of winter 1960 included a photograph of Finney under the heading, "Walter B. Finney, '34," and a brief biography. Of interest is the following paragraph:

Finney worked twelve years in advertising agencies in Chicago and New York after finishing Knox. Then moved to Mill Valley, Calif., where he now lives and writes at 223 Ricardo Road. "As my bit in furthering good-neighbor policy," he writes, "am married to a beautiful Canadian. Have daughter nine, named Marguerite after mother; son Kenneth, six, named after Secretary of Agriculture in Millard Fillmore's cabinet; dog Duke, named after English sea hero; have hamster named Harry, after Light-Horse Harry Lee; plus five guppies, unnamed. Very fond of Knox College."

Four more letters were exchanged between Goodsill and Finney in the early months of 1960. On March 22, Goodsill wrote: "The plan to circulate 5,000 extra copies of *McCall's* worked out. Just to make sure that you receive clips, I enclose two from *Register-Mail* March 21." The *Register-Mail* article essentially reprints the piece from the winter 1960 *Knox Alumnus* and adds some pertinent quotations from the story, "I Love Galesburg in the Springtime."

Finney replied on March 26, 1960:

Many thanks for the clippings you sent me on my Galesburg story in the current *McCall's*; I was pleased to see them, and I appreciate your thoughtfulness in sending them.

I often think of the fine tour of the college you took me on; it was a wonderfully pleasant experience which I hope to repeat with my family, perhaps this summer.

Goodsill replied on April 22, 1960:

Your letter of March 26 says you may bring your family to Galesburg "perhaps this summer."

When this happens I would like to get a group together to meet them — perhaps a dinner or garden party, provided your plans permit.

Finney's shyness is reflected in his reply of April 27, 1960:

Thank you very much indeed for your wonderfully kind idea to have a dinner or garden party for us if my family and I should come to Galesburg this summer.

We do hope to be there — I expect to have business in New York late this spring, or in the early summer, and my wife would like to see her parents in Toronto — and I have, lately, got my family all pepped up about seeing Galesburg. So we may very well be staying overnight in Galesburg before too long, spending parts of the preceding and following days. None of this is yet certain, though.

We'd very much like to see you then, but please don't even think of arranging a dinner, garden party, or anything of the sort. We'd be a little pressed for time, for one thing; I don't meet people in large groups very easily, frankly; we'd have two children along, restless after a long trip; and you must not go to any such trouble, anyway. We would love to have lunch with you, or something of that sort.

I had a very nice note from Earnest Elmo Calkins about my story about Galesburg recently.

Again thanks for your nice note, and very kind plans; if we come to Galesburg, you'll surely be hearing from me.

Earnest Elmo Calkins's book, *They Broke the Prairie,* had been mentioned by Goodsill in his November 16, 1959 letter to Finney. This was a book of local history, "first published in 1937 in honor of the Galesburg and Knox College Centenary" ("They Broke the Prairie"). Calkins died in 1964 and, after a six-year lull, the correspondence between Finney and Goodsill resumed. Goodsill wrote to Finney on September 1, 1966:

> *Knox Alumnus* ran a series, "Knox As I Knew It," by Earnest Calkins. There has been a lapse since his death.
>
> I'd like to publish similar articles in different age brackets. For example, the 1930s, by Jack Finney.
>
> Will you please consider doing a page or two for the *Alumnus?* Just to put you in the mood I enclose copy of a 1913-er's recollections.

Finney replied on September 8, 1966:

> Please believe, because it's true, that I gave your request to write something about Knox in the 1930s the most earnest consideration. I feel in your debt for past favors, and do not say no, as I have to, lightly. I thought about as hard as I'm able, to find out whether I might possibly have something to say about Knox in the 30s, and all I can tell you, finally, after mulling it over off and on for several days, is that I do not.
>
> It just isn't true, of course, that a writer can turn his hand to any field; and the field of reminiscence and interesting anecdote is one I don't belong in. There are many people, and not necessarily writers, by any means, whose minds retain a wealth of anecdote, and of interesting bits and snips from earlier times. But not me. I wouldn't know what to say, Max; I mean it. I can't think of anything that made the Knox of the thirties different from today's. I'm sure it was very different, but I don't even know what today's Knox is like. Believe me, you have a lot better people for this job than I, and they probably live in Galesburg, and know both the Knox of the Thirties and of the Sixties both.
>
> I'm sorry not to oblige; I would if I could.

Max Goodsill must have ceased being the Knox College director of public relations soon after this letter was received, for the following, lengthy letter was written to Finney on November 3, 1966, by the new director of public relations, William J. Kilkenny:

> The *Saturday Evening Post,* I should think, might be interested in taking A New Look at Old Siwash. It was the *Post,* after all, that helped to start

the whole Siwash business 58 years ago. Are you, I hope, interested in doing an updating piece for the *Post*?

In discussing the possibilities for such an article with Max Goodsill and a couple of other alumni, I came to realize that you would be the ideal author of it. Not only are you a well-established writer, but also you have an affiliation with Knox that would give you personal insights which might escape other authors.

A New Look at Old Siwash would be more than a publicity piece of considerable value to Knox; it would be an opportunity for a kind of rehabilitation of the term "Siwash" itself. As most dictionaries of slang, and some plain old dictionaries as well, have it, "Siwash" is a less than complimentary word. Knox seems to be inextricably committed to "Siwash" as a nickname, and although this is fine with the alumni, or at least some of the alumni, there are certain members of the faculty who consider "Siwash" a very heavy millstone around their scholarly necks. I feel that I am not telling you anything new here, but the debate over the propriety of such a nickname for a first-rate college, while it could hardly be the central point of a whole *Post* article, might provide a peg for a story. Another peg would be the fact that 1967 will be the 70th anniversary of George Fitch's graduation from Knox.

This is a matter that neither I nor anyone else with whom I have talked has discussed with anybody at the *Post*. We thought it would be best to have the idea suggested to the *Post* by an established author.

We have accumulated some material that might be of use to you if you are interested in undertaking this project, and we can gather up a great deal more if you wish. It is a matter that you might like to talk over with me on the telephone some day soon.

The letter concluded with a note that the writer was enclosing a number of booklets to help stimulate Finney's interest in the project, booklets such as "Knox Catalog" and "Calendar of Public Events." Kilkenny got no further than Goodsill had, however, as Jack Finney replied by letter of November 7, 1966:

Thank you for the compliment of thinking of me as a possible author of a *Saturday Evening Post* article on Knox. I appreciate it, but am obliged to say no because I am not an article writer. I write only fiction, and have never in my life written an article.

The two kinds of writing seem to be very different. There may be — no doubt are — writers who have done both, but I think they're rare. I've never known a writer of fiction who had ever written an article, or vice versa.

I wouldn't even know how to begin, and since my last knowledgeable look at Old Siwash was in 1934, with only one brief visit since, some seven or eight years ago, I don't think I'm your man on any count.

"Siwash" is defined by Merriam-Webster as "a small usually inland college that is notably provincial in outlook" ("Merriam-Webster"). The word was coined in stories by George Fitch, a writer who was graduated from Knox College in 1897. Fictional Siwash College was said to bear some similarity to Knox College ("George H. Fitch Papers").

This letter ended the correspondence between Jack Finney and the staff of Knox College for another twelve years.

On December 13, 1978, the exchange began again with this very interesting letter, written to Jack Finney by Robert Kosin from the city of Galesburg's planning department:

> The optimism in the ending of *I Love Galesburg in the Springtime* was misplaced. In the eighteen years since that short story appeared, Galesburg has lost its physical heritage to progress. A shopping mall on North Henderson has vacated much of Main Street. Squat apartments have been built among the homes on Broad, Kellogg, Cherry and Prairie Streets. Knox College has demolished Beecher Chapel, and intends to do the same with Whiting and Alumni Hall.
>
> I am in Galesburg to record its historical and architectural heritage. In 1976 over 180 acres of the central city was placed on the National Register of Historic Places. Yet, demolition of the Schlitz Sample Room on South Prairie occurred this month for the expansion of the First Galesburg National Bank. I have enclosed copies of the articles on the building which appeared on the front page of the *Register-Mail*. Progress and preservation are not seen as complementary but have emerged as antagonists over the future of Galesburg.
>
> I am writing all this for two reasons. As an outsider, I need your advice on how to sensitize the people of Galesburg to their heritage, and second I wonder if you can write to the people of Galesburg through the *Register-Mail* or possibly revisit Galesburg, about the current trend of events. I will not see Galesburg this spring since my project will end by March 12th to go on to another town, but your story captured the essences of Galesburg, that I hope we are not too late from losing forever.

Finney replied on December 28, 1978, with his longest letter:

There has been a good deal of success here on the West Coast in only the last half dozen years or so in propagandizing the people of a town about the beauty and historical interest of some of their old buildings. And in San Francisco the preservation of its old structures is very much in, these days. Old so-called "Victorian" houses which would have been hard to give away fifteen years ago — and which were often torn down by the square block — are now very valuable, because people buy them and restore them. This has become so much the thing to do in S.F. that there is actually a new business firm, making a good profit, in making the old house ornamentation — the 'gingerbread' — that distinguishes these houses.

The town of Petaluma, not too far from here, has a lot of nice old buildings, many of them in the downtown area. A dozen years ago the store fronts of these were invariably modernized, and some were torn down. But now the town has been educated to think these things are beautiful, and part of their heritage, etc., and the thing to do now is paint and emphasize their 19th-century ornamentation.

I'm sure you know all these things as well as I do, but I mention them to make the point that I don't think it's too hard to make a town conscious of the value of its old buildings. I think all that has to be done is to find no more than a handful of informed, dedicated people willing to form a committee to preserve Galesburg's heritage, or something on that order. A series of articles in the *Register-Mail* done by someone who knows the town's history can — with photographs — make the people who have walked past the old buildings hardly aware of them, suddenly become aware. Most people — I among them — need someone else to point out to us what is beautiful. I see it in a painting when someone more discerning spells it out for me. I think that can happen with old buildings. People stop seeing them as old-fashioned, out-moded buildings that ought to be replaced; and now see them as attractive. And when they learn something of their histories, they walk past the familiar old places with new feelings about them.

I don't think it's hard to accomplish this with a town, or that it takes very long. Articles in the *R-M* ... nice plaques mounted on old buildings with some interesting historical facts about them ... old photos of those buildings enlarged and displayed in the windows ... etc.

And when the general population, rather than just a handful of preservationists, are swung around, banks hesitate about tearing down old buildings, and begin to see the wisdom of retaining them by adapting them to modern usage.

All this is obvious to you, I know. But I mention it because I think it has been effective out here.

There is one other thing: I read an article, which I think I can find if you want to pursue this, about a business firm which is making a very good profit by advising towns on how to effectively use fine old buildings. What happens is something like this. The town officials need, or think they need, more space, or different kind of space, than the old courthouse provides. They want to tear it down, and build a new building. But it costs money to tear down the old building, and more money to build a new one. They call in this firm which sends in a small team of experts, including structural engineers, architects, and whatever. They consult very closely with the town officials; learn what they think they need in working space, and why they think they need it. They then study the old structure, and — if it is practical — they then demonstrate to the town officials that by certain remodelings they can get the floor space they now need ... or that by certain remodelings they can augment the usefulness of the present space and did not really need the additional space they thought they did, etc. This is done with floor plans, specifications, models, etc., and their success has been in genuinely persuading the people involved that they are right.

Sometimes they report that they can't recommend restructuring the old building; it won't work. So that their reputation has to do with a kind of hard-headed practicality; they don't say it will work unless it really will. The result, when they have successfully demonstrated the value of saving and remodeling, is that everybody is happy; the preservationists have what they wanted, the bureaucrats have what they want, the taxpayers saved money, and the firm makes its fee.

They succeed because they provide a practical out for everybody. But we have preservationists here who don't seem to think. There is a fine old-fashioned, and very lovely old department store in San Francisco called The City of Paris. It went out of business because it couldn't compete; part of the loveliness everyone likes is pure empty space. From ground floor to ceiling is empty space, the floors above them being open to provide the space. So that it's lovely as you enter, you look up five stories past all the railing-protected floors to a wonderful stained-glass dome. And every Christmas they brought in an enormous Christmas tree that rose up to that dome five stories; it took a couple dozen men working all night to trim it, with special oversize ornaments. And everyone went to see it each year; it was a part of Christmas.

Merchandising changed, and the store couldn't compete because of all that empty space. They closed. The store stood empty; a closed-up blight on the downtown area. Neiman-Marcus bought the site; they wanted to tear down the old building, and put up a new one that conformed to modern merchandising ideas. They were and are willing to retain a kind of smaller rotunda, and even inset the old stained-glass dome. But the building would have no windows in order to provide more merchandise space.

No question but that the old building was far more attractive. So the preservationists here have gone to court and endlessly delayed Neiman-Marcus by simply, and I think stubbornly, insisting that Neiman-Marcus must use the old building as is. Neiman-Marcus won't do that, of course — that's the building the old store closed down. So Neiman-Marcus keeps submitting revised plans, which the preservationists reject.

The preservationists can never win this one; no one will reopen the old store; they are demanding the impossible. Eventually Neiman-Marcus will either win, or they will give up. They will sell the property, and open up in some other place. Who will then buy the old City of Paris, and open it up just as is, as though 1910 were back? No one will, of course. And meanwhile the store stands empty, a kind of blight in the area, which is dangerous because the San Francisco downtown area is in trouble like so many other downtowns.

The reason for this rambling is to make — again — an obvious point but I think a crucial one. I don't think it's enough to simply oppose tearing down a fine old building on nothing more than the ground that you prefer the old one. I think you must also demonstrate that keeping or remodeling the old structure makes sense for the owner, too. If there really is a way to preserve or partly preserve the old City of Paris, I think they ought to demonstrate this to Neiman-Marcus. But if there is not, no one can win. I like it better when everyone wins, because then the old structure really is saved. The stubborn alternative only delays the inevitable.

I've descended to preaching, I see; and of course you know all this long since, and a lot more. But it's the only reply I could think of to make. I do think that if the preservationists will be practical, they can often win. And if not entirely, at least partially. Etc. Etc. Etc.

I can't really offer to help you, even if it were in my power, which I doubt. I don't actually know very much about Galesburg's history, and what buildings ought to be saved, etc. It's a job for someone who lives there. I'm too far away, and do not expect ever again to even be in Galesburg. I hope very much that your efforts to help preserve the town will succeed; but I don't think I can really help.

As you see from the overlong nature of my reply, my sympathies are very much with you. Thanks for writing, and good luck.

Finney would exchange three more letters with the people at Knox College in the early 1980s. The first, dated August 25, 1982, appears to be in reply to a letter from Douglas L. Wilson, an English professor there. While the professor's letter is not in the Knox College collection, Finney's response is:

> Thank you very much for your nice note about my story, "I Love Galesburg," etc. It was written long ago, and it's very pleasant to know that someone has read it fairly recently. Not long ago I was in a discussion of sorts with friends, the subject of the moment being: What is your favorite city? And of course, Paris, Rome, Venice, etc., were prime candidates. I said Galesburg, however; my motive, of course, was simply to avoid the obvious answer, and to be mildly startling. But later I realized it had the merit of being true, besides. One of the shocks of my life was — some years ago now — to visit Galesburg and find the elms were gone, the streets naked between rows of giant stumps. Terrible. But my Galesburg was in the Twenties, visiting it every summer when I was a child, and it was a wonderful place. The elms shaded the streets, there were still horses and buggies, and medicine shows on Saturday night on the Square. And so on, and so on. I get out those memories every now and then, and run them through like old films.
>
> It would be nice to know that my "papers," such as they are, were in Seymour Library. (Seymour? Was it called that when I was in college in the Thirties? Are you sure you're not Director of Seymour *Hall*?) My papers don't amount to much, and I really cannot imagine anyone studying them. He wouldn't learn much. Nevertheless, it would be pleasant, I expect, to know that there they sat, waiting for posterity. The only reason I don't offer to send them on is that, like many another writer, I am hanging onto them until Congress gets around to restoring the tax break we used to get for donating such papers. I'm sure that's an old story to you, but maybe they'll recognize in time that a lot of writers are doing the same, and allow a tax deduction. If so, and if Knox wanted them, I'd be happy to send them on, along with my Boy Scout merit badges, some snapshots of my kids, and color slides of our last vacation.
>
> Meanwhile, your note was a pleasure, and I appreciate it. When you renovate the library, please restore it to precisely as it was in 1934, and the ghost in the corner will be me.

Finney must have kept up with the magazine for college alumni, because one of its articles seems to have led to his next letter, dated May 25, 1983, and addressed to E. Samuel Moon at Knox College:

> I enjoyed reading the interview with you and Robin Metz, published in a recent *Knox Alumnus*. And liked what you both said; I think Knox is lucky in having both your classes.

I'm writing because you said, "I believe (the Knox writing program) started with Proctor Sherwin...." I'm sure you're right, but I'd like to suggest that any history, however informal or brief, of writing classes at Knox should include Albert Britt. I'm sure you know he was president of the college in the Thirties; but he also taught at least one (was it two?) writing courses. And they, or it, were fine; he knew about writing and how to teach it. Knew a lot about a lot, in fact.

Britt continued to write when he was in his nineties. Published a couple of books in his nineties, and they are first rate. No concessions to age by the author; good tight stringent stuff; and no concessions required of the reader. He was something special, Albert Britt; I suspect the college may not fully appreciate him. A lot of college people, and some idiot townspeople, certainly didn't at the time. I hope you'll include him when you write the definitive history of writing as taught at Knox.

No reply needed, incidentally; just wanted to make sure Knox remembers A.B.

Knox did remember Albert Britt, as Sam Moon replied in his June 10, 1983 letter to Finney:

I enjoyed your letter about Albert Britt very much. We have not forgotten him, I assure you, and it is my impression too that he was "something special."

You are right; he taught The Short Story from 1926 until he left the college in 1936, Advanced Writing from 1927 to 1936, and a course called Voluntary Writing from 1929 to 1933.

I looked up your record and find that you took Advanced Writing as a junior and The Short Story as a senior. You also took a course called Narration, taught, I believe, by Mr. Beauchamp, in your senior year.

You might like to see the catalogue descriptions of Mr. Britt's courses:

The Short Story: A study of the short story with practice in the preparation of synopses and discussion of suggested story plots.

Advanced Writing: Practical work in different forms of professional writing; news stories, feature articles, editorials, reviews.

Voluntary Writing: The class meets on call to discuss whatever they may have written during the previous week. The instructor takes no responsibility other than that of leading the discussion.

This last course sounds like a marvelous experiment in freedom; it reminds me of a course I taught in the sixties, thinking it was quite new!

Thanks again, very much, for your letter. I'm turning it over to the Archives.

And with that, the collection of letters to and from Jack Finney held in the Knox College Archives comes to an end. What began in 1959 with a letter from Finney to the president of the college, asking for help verifying details of his story, "I Love Galesburg in the Springtime," developed over the course of almost twenty-four years into a more expansive discussion of writing, memory, and the way that the passage of time was affecting a small Midwestern town.

Internal evidence in the letters themselves suggests that Finney only visited Galesburg once, in early December 1959, and that that visit represented the one and only time he would return to his college town after having been graduated from Knox College in 1934.

Yet the town of Galesburg never seems to have lost its hold on the author. It pops up from time to time in his fiction, and the fact that he wrote the story "I Love Galesburg in the Springtime" and later titled his second collection of short stories after it suggests that the town was a strong influence on his thought and writing. In one of his last letters to the college, on August 25, 1982, he admits having come to the realization that Galesburg is his favorite city on Earth, and had been ever since he visited it regularly as a child.

All of the letters to Galesburg bear the same address for Jack Finney, in Mill Valley, California, and just before he died he told a reporter that he had lived in that house for about 40 years (Ickes 36). His readers grew familiar with the southern California setting of many of his tales, and the San Francisco area was one that he often explored in his fiction. But it was the small, college town of Galesburg, Illinois, that would remain closest to him, and it is likely that this town — which changed along with the rest of the small towns in America, so drastically — was one of the key influences on his body of work.

SEVENTEEN

Jack Finney on Stage

In his lifetime, Jack Finney wrote two plays. The first was a one-act play published in 1956 and entitled *Telephone Roulette*. According to *Play Index*, it was a romantic comedy in which a "telephone date with unknown young man is too much for Gloria but not for her roommate" (Fidell 103). The play featured roles for a man and two women and had one interior set. It ran only twenty-two pages. According to Gary K. Wolfe, it was an adaptation of a Finney story called "Take a Number," and the play was published by the Dramatic Publishing Company in Chicago (253). Research has revealed nothing further about this play or the short story upon which it was said to be based.

Finney may have chosen to forget about *Telephone Roulette* by 1966, when his second play, *This Winter's Hobby*, premiered, because he referred to the new play as his first (*Playbill* 34). An undated, unidentified newspaper clipping in the clippings file at the New York Public Library's Lincoln Center Library for the Performing Arts reports that Finney was to come east for rehearsals, which were scheduled to begin on February 15, 1966. A press release dated March 22, 1966, reports that the cast and crew of the play left New York that day for New Haven, Connecticut, where the play was to open ("'Hobby' Leaves for New Haven").

This Winter's Hobby opened in New Haven the next day, playing a Wednesday evening show at the famous Shubert Theater, where many plays had ironed out their problems before moving to Broadway. The play ran at the Shubert for four nights, from Wednesday, March 23, 1966, through Saturday, March 26, 1966, and there was also a Saturday matinee. Although the script has not been found, articles and reviews from 1966, along with a folder of dozens of black and white photographs of the play that are part of the Friedman-Abeles Collection at the Lincoln Center library and a copy of the *Playbill* from the brief run at Philadelphia's Walnut Street Theatre, allow for a reconstruction of the story.

This Winter's Hobby was a play in three acts, with two scenes each. The first scene takes place on a Friday evening in early September, as respectable businessman Charles Bishop, played by E. G. Marshall, misses the connecting train home and steps into a bar in White Plains, New York. He gets into a fight with a drunken bigot outside the bar and walks the four miles to his house in suburban Westchester County. His wife, Duffy, hears a report on the radio that the bigot is dead and that the police are seeking his unknown assailant. Instead of calling the police, the Bishops decide to follow through with their vacation, which had been set the start the following morning. They go off together, assuming all will be forgotten when they return.

Scene two of act one is set on a Saturday morning, five weeks later, putting it in early October, presumably after the Bishops have returned from vacation.

It seems that the "winter's hobby" of the title becomes clear in scene one of act two, which is set on a Friday in early January, late at night. Although Bishop thinks he has gotten off scot free, it turns out that there was a witness to his fight outside the bar, and that witness was a sadistic young man named Arnold, played by William Hickey. (Hickey would play a memorable role years later in the film *Prizzi's Honor*.) Arnold and his friend Tommy, played by Michael Beckett, are two young homosexuals who decide to blackmail the Bishops. Instead of demanding money, however, they insist that Bishop perform outrageous stunts. The stunts are rather mundane, such as answering the phone at two a.m. and wearing funny clothes downtown. The rest of the play apparently consists of scenes in which the two young men "torture, embarrass and menace the businessman" (Johnson, Florence). Act two, scene two is set "the following morning." Act three has two scenes, set "that evening" and "late that night." The play ends with the line, "we haven't got a chance."

Reviewers of the New Haven production were not kind to *This Winter's Hobby*. Don Rubin, writing in the *New Haven Register* on March 24, 1966, remarked that the "complications are stock" and that the play is "not that strong to sustain itself for three acts." He added that it had "the subtlety of a sledge hammer and ... the naiveté of a 10-year-old" and concluded his savage review by writing that it "never quite decides what it wants to be: a bitter-comic mystery, a suspenseful melodrama or simply a dramatic study."

The most positive review was written by Florence Johnson, who commented that the play started well but ended badly. Despite the poor reception, *This Winter's Hobby* moved on to the Walnut Street Theatre in Philadelphia, Pennsylvania, to continue its planned eleven-city tour (Little).

"A new playwright will be introduced here Monday evening ... he is Jack Finney, a San Franciscan by way of the Midwest," wrote Barbara Wilson in the *Philadelphia Inquirer* on March 27, 1966, the day before the play opened. She had interviewed the author by telephone the week before, while he was in New Haven. He began in his usual, self-deprecating way, by telling her "'I can't understand why any one would be interested in what I have to say.'" After telling the interviewer that his novels "have brought him monetary gains, primarily because of their screen sales," Finney added that

> "I think visually ... so when I write a book I really am thinking about a movie. With 'Good Neighbor Sam,' I had Jack Lemmon in mind from the very beginning.
>
> "I certainly have enjoyed the success, but I haven't liked the pictures they have made of my books. That's one thing that directed me toward the theater. At least it will be my fault if the play doesn't work. I had no control over the films and I always felt like hiding when a friend would mention one of them."

Finney then relates an incident in a San Francisco department store that gave him the idea for *This Winter's Hobby*:

> "A man, obviously a tourist ... stopped at a counter to admire the display of jade jewelry. He asked about it, not realizing how expensive it was, and he was one of those unfortunates who are unable to admit that they can't afford something. They are compelled to make excuses.

"The clerk was perfectly aware of this. I watched his face as he toyed with the man. He was enjoying it thoroughly. He had an absolutely malicious expression. He possessed the most chilling type of malice."

Finney then began plotting "his drama about a middle-aged realtor drawn into an accidental event in which a man dies." Finney then provided this bizarre summary of the next part of *This Winter's Hobby:* "'He becomes the victim of two blackmailers ... homosexuals of the most sadistic nature who require him to do humiliating stunts every week!'"

After shelving the play for a while, Finney came up with an ending and sent it to his agent, who found a producer in Hillard Elkins. Elkins and director Donald McWhinnie helped Finney overcome a "'terrible defect in the script'" and actors including E.G. Marshall, Nan Martin, and William Hickey were hired. The article ends with Finney describing a scene in the play that "'involves the blackmailers in a vegetable-throwing display of rage.'"

This Winter's Hobby opened at the Walnut Street Theater in Philadelphia on March 28, 1966, and ran for 16 performances.

Reviews of the Philadelphia production were not good. Most positive was a review signed by "Bone" in *Variety*'s March 30, 1966, issue. The reviewer wrote that the play had "an original theme" with "pungent dialog and good performances, a meritorious physical production and an at-times engrossing pace. However, the final punch that can make it a solid click is yet to come."

In the Philadelphia papers, two reviews appeared on March 30, 1966. Ernest Schier, writing in the *Philadelphia Bulletin,* called *This Winter's Hobby* "a mess" and "a hasty and confused piece of writing." He added that the play's final line ("we haven't got a chance") may be a prediction of the fate of the play as a whole.

Henry T. Murdock, writing in the *Philadelphia Inquirer,* called the play "one of the most inept melodramas in recent memory." *This Winter's Hobby* closed in Philadelphia on April 9, 1966, one day after an article by James Davis appeared in the *New York Daily News.* In this article, Davis reports that the play had been scheduled to move to Broadway in the fall of 1966 but that "author Finney will work on revisions at his California home in hopes of a new fall production." On that same day, Sam Zolotow wrote in the *New York Times* that the show's star, E. G. Marshall, had "signed a two-year contract to act in the suspense play" but that bookings through June 9, 1966, had now been canceled.

The play then appears to have disappeared, its planned move to Broadway never materializing. Two months later, in a June 30, 1966 article in the *New York Times*, Sam Zolotow reported that the producer, Hillard Elkins, had been accused of diverting money invested in a show entitled *Golden Boy* to help finance two plays, including *This Winter's Hobby*. Apparently, misappropriation of funds may have played a part in the failure of Finney's play.

Yet the details that survive suggest that the play was not one of the author's stronger works, and perhaps it is best left forgotten. Although Seymour Rudin wrote that the Studio Duplicating Service published it in 1966, research has revealed no copies of the play available today.

It was not until after his death that one of Jack Finney's works would finally make it to the New York stage, and even that came after years of revisions and delays. *Time and Again,* the novel that I have called Finney's masterpiece, has resisted all efforts to film it to date, but it has been adapted into a musical. According to a press release found in the *Time and Again* clippings file at the Lincoln Center Library for the Performing Arts, the musical *Time and Again* was first performed in summer 1993 at the Eugene O'Neill Theater Center in Waterford, Connecticut, as part of the National Music Theater Conference. This theater appears to be a workshop where shows are developed.

Time and Again had its world premiere at the Old Globe Theatre in San Diego, California, on May 4, 1996, and it officially opened on May 9, 1996. It ran there until June 9, 1996. The press release mentioned above lists the show's stars as Howard McGillin and Rebecca Luker. A May 10, 1996 review in the *San Diego Tribune* comments that "there's about half a good new American musical wound up inside *Time and Again*" (Phillips). Although the press release states that the show was to start performances on Broadway on September 24, 1996, and open officially on October 24, 1996, a July 11, 1996 article reports that the show received mixed reviews and was in "extensive rewrites." Another workshop was planned, as were more rehearsals, and the Broadway opening was postponed to spring or fall 1997 (Viagas).

It is not known what happened to *Time and Again* between 1996 and 1999, but the next record of the show is found in a program for "A Workshop of *Time and Again*," to be held at the Altman Building on Eighteenth Street in New York City on May 18, 20, 21, and 22, 1999. The cast was new and apparently so was much of the show, which had been reworked since its San Diego run. For these performances, Julia Murney played Kate, Si Morley's modern girlfriend, and Laura Benati played Julia, the object of Si's affections in the nineteenth century. Most of the other cast members were to change again before the show finally reached Off Broadway.

After at least eight years of rewrites, workshops, and rehearsals, *Time and Again* finally opened Off Broadway at the Manhattan Theatre Club on January 9, 2001. The book was by Jack Viertel and the music and lyrics were by Walter Edgar Kennon. Viertel was quoted in *Variety* as saying that enormous changes had been made to the show; he had tried to adapt the entire novel in earlier drafts but had later simplified the story and cut the production by 25 minutes. There was about 35 percent new music and the earlier production's 16 scenes had been cut to eight or nine (Hofler).

The Manhattan Theatre Club production ran from January 9, 2001, to February 18, 2001, and was directed by Susan Schulman. Lewis Cleale starred as Si Morley, and Julia Murney and Laura Benati returned as Kate and Julia. Television star David McCallum played scientist E.E. Danziger, among other roles. Near the end of the show's run, on February 16, 2001, the production was videotaped by The New York Public Library's Theatre on Film and Tape Archive.

On viewing the show today, it is a delight. With the help of the *Playbill*, the scenes and songs may be recreated. The show runs about two hours and five minutes, and is performed on a small stage in what appears to be a cozy theater setting, where the audience sits very close to the performers. The production opens with Si Morley standing alone on a dark stage, looking at paintings of a woman in eighteenth century attire. The lights come up to reveal that he is at a party in his apartment in New York City, and that the paintings are being used to advertise Nostalgia, which has recently become the best selling perfume in America.

Si painted the picture but seems uneasy about its success as part of an advertising campaign. His girlfriend Kate runs the ad agency and makes him a partner, yet he feels that he has betrayed the painting and the girl pictured in it. Si sings "Standing in the Middle of the Road," which explains some of his feelings: "I'm standing in the middle of the road, wondering which way to go." He tells the painting, "time and time again I thought I dreamed you" and "my mind and heart combined to make you art."

Si is joined by an older man named E.E. Danziger, who tells Si that he works for the federal government. He shows Si a framed picture from 1882 that bears an inscription from Simon Morley to Julia C., explains that he has been looking for Si for twenty years, and asks Si to give him twenty-eight days to try a time travel experiment. Danziger and Si sing "The Training" and the scientist explains that "then is just a different now." He wants to cut "the million tiny threads that bind you to today." He suggests using New York's Dakota Building as a portal to the past and wants to send Si back to January 20, 1882, to learn why he was there, why he painted Julia C., and how Danziger's grandmother came to have the picture. Kate fears that Si will go and not return. Danziger tells him that he must be a twig in the river of time, merely observing but not changing anything.

Si then goes to the Dakota and immerses himself in the details of 1882. Danziger visits him and explains that his grandmother was an actress living in a boarding house at 19 Gramercy Park in New York City; he sings ("At the Theater") of how his grandparents met on an opening night at the theater. His grandmother was the star of the show, and when she fainted she met Dr. Danziger, her future husband.

Si then travels back to 1882 and finds himself in a blizzard, which is recreated using lights on a darkened stage. Si sings "Who Would Have Thought It?" and revels in the new world he has found. He travels down Fifth Avenue on a trolley car and the singing conductor points out the sights. Arriving at the boarding house at 19 Gramercy Park, Si finds himself in the drawing room, where the various residents interact. A man named Felix composes a song at the piano for his new show, in which Emily (Danziger's grandmother) will star. She sings along as other residents come and go. Emily sings "The Marrying Kind," a catchy song that will recur throughout the show.

Si is stunned to see Julia, the woman in his painting and the landlady's niece. He sings of her beauty in "She Dies," and laments his realization that she will pass away before he is born. Julia speaks to Jake Pickering, another resident at the boarding house, telling him that she delivered a letter on his behalf to Edward Carmody, an important man. Jake wants to marry Julia but grows suddenly angry at her for delivering the letter by hand rather than by mail.

We learn that Julia works for the liberty campaign and is a suffragette. Si is captivated by her. Edward Carmody and his wife make speeches on behalf of the Statue of Liberty, which is arriving in pieces from France. Only the arm sits in New York City at this point, and a crowd protests the statute's impending arrival. Julia sings "The Lady in the Harbor" to try to turn the crowd in favor of the statute, and Si joins in to help her convince them. Soon, all join in the song, and Si makes various mistakes by referring to countries and things that do not yet exist. Si's sketch of the statue as it will one day appear helps convince the crowd that it will be beneficial.

The scene then shifts to Jake Pickering, who meets Carmody in a park. Jake sings "Carrara Marble," which explains that he plans to blackmail the wealthy man regarding a past embezzlement. Jake wants a million dollars in gold and the two plan to meet again on Monday at two a.m.

Back at the boarding house, all work on another song ("The Music of Love"), and Si is encouraged to sketch a portrait of Julia to give to her because it is her birthday. Past and present intertwine as Julia sings about her feelings for Si and Kate comes onstage as well, singing about Si's painting. She thinks that she inspired it, not realizing that she is seated next to the woman who was the picture's real source.

Jake comes home drunk and proposes to Julia, a proposition she accepts, much to Si's surprise. She sings to him and explains how love and marriage were different for women in 1882. Si decides to leave the past and takes the trolley back toward the Dakota, planning to return to 2001. The trolley man sings again ("For Those You Love"), and Si joins in, realizing that he loves Julia and must become more than a twig in the river of time in order to keep her from marrying Jake.

The first act of *Time and Again* ends with Si's decision to get involved in the events of 1882 and in Julia's life. This portion of the play lasts about 74 minutes and establishes all of the characters, although it cuts large amounts of exposition from the novel and combines all of the characters connected with The Project into the person of E.E. Danziger, who has very little time onstage. The strongest parts of the show thus far are the music, which is memorable, the singing, which is excellent, and the staging, which is evocative. The biggest problem with the show is that so many plot elements have been put in motion that the second act has trouble resolving them.

Act two opens on a high note as Emily, Dr. Danziger's grandmother, performs a very catchy song and dance number to "The Marrying Kind." This is revealed to be a preview of the new show that will open the next day; Felix, the pianist in the boarding house, has finally completed it and Emily is set to star. The audience knows that, at the show, Emily will faint and meet the man she is to marry, Dr. Danziger's grandfather. One interesting aspect of this production of *Time and Again* is that most of the actors play more than one role; for instance, David McCallum, who appears in the 2001 portion of the story as Dr. Danziger, also sings and dances in the 1882 story thread, playing the shotgun-toting father of the character who sings "The Marrying Kind." It appears from the *Playbill* that the only actors not to play multiple roles were those portraying Si and Julia.

The story resumes as Jake apologizes to Si for his brusque earlier behavior, and Si explains to Julia that he has discovered Jake's plot to blackmail Edward Carmody. Si fears for Julia's safety and cautions her against trusting Jake. The plot speeds up here, as Julia and Si go the *The World* building and barge in on the meeting between Jake and Carmody. Carmody lashes out at Jake with his cane, knocking over a lamp and starting a fire. "Carrara Marble" is reprised in this scene, and a song entitled "The Fire" is sung, but it is clear that the writer and director of the show had trouble fitting all of this in and staging it convincingly. The fire is conveyed with lights and shadows, and we soon learn from a newspaper report that Jake is dead. Si searches for the missing Julia, and they meet and hide in the torch held by the Statue of Liberty's arm, fearing that Carmody will blame them for the fire and have them hanged.

Julia finally asks Si where he comes from and he replies by singing the lovely "Time and Time Again." As a mob gathers outside, Si and Julia will themselves to New York in 2001, a bit of time travel that was handled with finesse in the novel but which makes little sense on stage.

We then see Julia in Si's apartment, watching television with fascination and enjoying the remote control. She sees a commercial for Nostalgia, the perfume that bears her likeness, and is surprised when Kate comes home. Kate quickly realizes who Julia is and where she comes from, and there are some funny lines as Kate tries to explain a thing or two about the modern world. Si arrives and he and Kate argue about Julia; Kate sings a song called "The Right Look," admitting that the look of love Si gives to Julia is quite different than the look he gives her. Julia Murney has a magnificent voice and her performance as Kate is one of the highlights of the show, even though she does not spend a great deal of time on stage.

Danziger arrives and provides some speedy exposition by telling Si and Julia that Edward Carmody shot himself in a fit of guilt a few days after the fire. The doctor plans to provide Julia with a valid 2001 identity and he is excited about the opportunity to reshape time using Si's ability to travel back and forth. He calls time travel "the ultimate weapon" and states that science cannot be stopped, no matter where it goes. Si agrees to bring Julia to The Project, but she disappears. He finds her at the site of the old boarding house, where all of the 1882 furniture is now covered with sheets. This scene is rather hard to believe, but it allows for a quick change in time. Julia and Si sing "I Know This House," and he professes his love for her. He then helps her return to 1882 using the boarding house as a portal, and the past returns as the furniture is uncovered and the residents drift onstage.

Si is left alone in the present and runs offstage. The show ends in 1882, as we see Emily performing "The Marrying Kind" again in her musical's opening night performance. After the show, she faints from excitement. Dr. Danziger arrives, but Si suddenly appears on the scene, masquerading as a doctor, and dismisses Danziger before he and Emily can have their fateful meeting. Si tells Felix, the piano player, to marry Emily instead, and all sing and waltz happily together as the lights fade.

Act two of *Time and Again* is shorter than act one, lasting about 54 minutes. The plot and its execution are a bit clumsy; the highlights are the songs. Overall, *Time and Again* is an enjoyable musical to watch, streamlining the novel's story in order to fit the format of musical theater. The production that was videotaped at the Manhattan Theatre Club is lovely but rather simple, with just two pianos accompanying the singers on a small stage. Most of the effects are done with lighting, since there is no large-scale scenery or scene changes. The singers in this production are very strong, and several of the songs — especially "The Marrying Kind" — are memorable.

Readers of *Time and Again* must have been surprised by the extensive changes that had been made in the story by the time it reached the New York stage. First and foremost is the elimination of the character of Ruben Prien, the former Army man and government employee whose devotion to The Project stems from a belief that time travel represents a valuable military option. Moving the story from 1970 to 2001 required a change in its politics, and the Vietnam-era questioning of authority that runs through the novel is absent onstage. Taking Prien out of the plot required the musical's writer, Jack Viertel, to make E.E. Danziger a composite character who loses the self-doubts found in the novel and replaces them with Prien's mania. The extensive training that Si Morley undergoes in the book is also gone, as is virtually all of his relationship with Danziger.

Another major plot point that is changed is the reason for Si's trip to the past. In the novel, he seeks clarification of the partially-burned letter that his girlfriend Kate inherited and its mysterious message involving "Destruction by Fire of the entire World." On stage, Danziger wants Si to find out why the picture of Julia was painted by someone named Si Morley in 1882.

Si's various trips back and forth between the past and the present that occur in the book become a single trip to 1882 and back in the musical, and the fire — which is a climactic point in the book — becomes a clumsy incident on stage. Finally, the twist in the book that has Jake Pickering survive to steal the identity of Edward (Andrew in the novel) Carmody is replaced by the much simpler explanation that Jake was killed in the fire and Carmody killed himself out of grief for causing the conflagration.

In short, the adaptation of *Time and Again* for the stage does not succeed in capturing the flavor of the novel, and the writing does not succeed in simplifying the book's complicated plot in a satisfactory way. It is in the staging and the music that the show succeeds most.

Time and Again did not receive good reviews in the press. The *New York Times* review asked, "how long can you listen to a music box, the sort that dribbles out a single tinkly melody, before you want to throw it out a window?" (Brantley). It seems that there had been major changes to the show in between its performances in San Diego and its arrival in New York, as Ken Mandelbaum pointed out in a review on *Theater.com*. "But for the most part," he noted, "the Old Globe version was faithful to the novel's action, and the result was, if not disastrous, plodding and overloaded with plot. The reason why the musical didn't vanish at that point was that, in addition to the appeal of its source, the show came to life on a number of occasions thanks to some ravishing songs...." After seeing the Manhattan Theatre Club's production of *Time and Again,* Mandelbaum complained that, "while the music has for the MTC version been attractively arranged for two pianos, it's a score that cries out for the full orchestration that would match the kind of operatic singing required of several of the principals."

Mandelbaum adds that the book underwent major changes from San Diego to New York, altering the plot and making Julia "more complex and assertive" than before. He suggests that James Hart, credited in the program with "additional story material," may have been the source of some of the changes. Still, he complains that the show "remains overplotted" and "can't compete with the Old Globe version, much less the novel..." and concludes that "perhaps Finney's novel should have been a movie."

Kenneth Jones, writing on *Playbill.com,* summed up the response to the show by noting that "the official opening Jan. 30 was followed by a flood of negative reviews in the New York dailies and magazines. Critics, in a collective sour mood, fell over themselves seeking adjectives to curse a show that many in the audience and industry regarded as having one of the craftier scores in recent seasons." He added that the show was still changing during the previews in January 2001, and that the song "The Primary Source" was replaced by "Standing in the Middle of the Road." Si's training was also cut back almost to nothing.

Perhaps the most positive review was written by an out of town critic — Clifford Ridley of the *Philadelphia Inquirer.* He called *Time and Again* an "irresistibly charming musical" and wrote that "it deserves a wide audience."

The show's New York run ended on February 18, 2001, and I have not been able to find evidence that it has been revived since that time. According to Kenneth Jones, "Thomas Viertel, one of the producers who first initiated the project, told the *New York Times* there are no longer hopes to take *Time and Again* to Broadway."

Jack Finney was a successful short story writer early in his career, and he became a successful novelist in the 1950s. Eventually, he gave up writing short stories and concentrated on novels until his death. His experiments in writing for the stage were few and they were not successful. After his death, his most admired novel, *Time and Again,* was adapted for the stage unsuccessfully. It seems that enjoyment of Jack Finney's work was found mostly on the printed page, for when his characters tried to come to life on stage they did not have the same appeal.

EIGHTEEN

Jack Finney on Television

Although Jack Finney never wrote directly for television, three of his short stories have been adapted for the small screen, one of them twice. "Such Interesting Neighbors" aired as "Time Is Just a Place" on the April 16, 1955 episode of *Science Fiction Theatre*. "All My Clients are Innocent" was adapted for *Alcoa Premiere* on April 17, 1962. "Such Interesting Neighbors" was adapted for a second time, under its original title, for *Amazing Stories* on March 20, 1987. Finally, "The Love Letter" aired as part of the *Hallmark Hall of Fame* series on February 1, 1998. None of Finney's novels has been adapted for television.

Science Fiction Theatre ran in syndication for two years, from April 1955 to April 1957. It was hosted by Truman Bradley and it stood out from most other television series of the time because it was filmed in color. It premiered on April 9, 1955, and its second episode was entitled "Time Is Just a Place" ("Science Fiction Theatre"). This was adapted from Jack Finney's story, "Such Interesting Neighbors," which had first appeared in the January 6, 1951 issue of *Collier's* magazine.

The show begins with an introduction by Truman Bradley, who remarks on how a plane can fly from New York to Chicago and land five minutes before it took off. He attributes this to the plane's ability to fly faster than the time difference between the two cities. He then introduces a robot, called "the man of tomorrow," that is able to do tasks that would be too dangerous for humans to attempt. He predicts

159

that, some day, we will all have automatic men around the house to do chores.

The story proper begins with a montage of modern scenes, including fast airplanes, a superhighway, and new homes. In one of these homes lives Al Brown, the protagonist of the story. He receives a telephone call from Colonel Peterson, who tells him that the test plane will not be ready until Monday. He thinks he has a free weekend to spend with his wife, Nell, until she tells him all of the chores he needs to do. Ironically, the chores involve repairing modern conveniences that have broken down, such as a garbage disposal and a clothes dryer.

Al then comments on how well the new neighbors have fixed up their house. The neighbor, Ted Heller, pulls his car into the driveway and gets out, looking around suspiciously before glancing up at the sky. Later, Al's attempt to watch television is thwarted by static interference. He goes outside to check the antenna and hears a strange whine from the Hellers' house. Looking through their window, he sees a small, round machine with a circular antenna. The machine is traveling across the floor. Heller emerges from his house and meets Al, explaining that the machine is a sonic broom that he has invented. It works by remote control and the "pressure of the noise under the hemisphere disintegrates the refuse." Al confides that he, too, is an inventor, and agrees not to tell anyone about Ted's new device.

Later that day, Al is in his workshop when he hears Ted having trouble starting his car. Al helps Ted get it started but notices that his new neighbor does not seem to know much about cars. Ted's wife, Ann, also seems strangely reticent and frightened when she brings her husband a flashlight without having been summoned. She warns him, "watch out, darling; be careful what you say" and runs back into her home.

Al and Nell discuss the neighbors' odd behavior just before their clothes dryer breaks again. Al goes downstairs to fix it and shines his flashlight at the fuse box, only to discover that the light acts as an x-ray machine. He realizes that he picked up Ted's flashlight by mistake and shows it to Nell, who is frightened. Before they can fully discuss their questions about who Ted is, where he comes from, and why he's there, the neighbor appears, angry at first. He takes back his flashlight and explains that he has not applied for a patent yet.

Al decides to show Ted what he is working on. Al is trying to find a metal that can withstand heat and pressure at supersonic speeds. He uses a model plane and a wind tunnel to demonstrate how the metal melts. Ted suggests he try a "corbelite." That evening, the Browns host the Hellers for cake and coffee. While Nell and Ann retire to the kitchen, Al bluntly asks Ted who he is and what "corbelite" is. Ted unconvincingly says that it is a new alloy that he read about in a science magazine.

Ted picks up a toy robot and Al remarks that he is a science fiction fan. The robot is a gag gift from Nell called the man of tomorrow (recalling the robot in the program's introduction). This leads Al to wonder what the world of tomorrow will be like. Ted tells him that it will not be much fun and surmises that, in 500 years, all of the fun and emotion will have gone out of living because civilization will have become so mechanized and scientific.

Ted remarks that he is toying with the idea of writing a science fiction story in which someone invents a time travel device. "Time is only a place," he tells Al. His story is interrupted by the beginning of a thunderstorm, which clearly frightens Ted. He asks Al if all of the transformers that supply power have ever failed at the same time, and Al assures him that it has only happened twice. Ted continues telling his story, adding that so many people begin to use time travel that they stop coming back. It seems that each person finds his "favorite place in time" and stays there. People spread out through time and know from history books how to adapt in order to fit in without being noticed.

Ted continues to say that the government eventually makes time travel illegal when it begins to affect the population. They send out investigators to track down those who have escaped back in time; each person may be traced by a distinct set of mental vibrations that are as individual as fingerprints, and the only way to avoid detection is to hide in an area filled with electronic circuits and magnetic force fields. Al remarks that the area where they both live would make a perfect hiding place. The electrical storm gets worse, and Ann returns from the kitchen, terrified. She and Ted go home.

Late that night, Al and Nell are talking as they lie in their twin beds. Al tells Nell that he thinks that Ted's science fiction story is true. A bolt of lightning strikes and the power fails. Ted and Nell hear a scream from next door. Ted gets up and looks out of his window, only to see a light rising by the Hellers' house, accompanied by a whine. The power comes back on and he and Nell go next door to investigate, only to find no trace of the Hellers, except for some clothes and debris on the floor. Ted ruminates and says that the neighbors will never be found because they were never really there.

"Time Is Just a Place" was directed by Jack Arnold from a script by Lee Berg ("Science Fiction Theatre — Time Is Just a Place"). It stars Don DeFore as Al Brown and Marie Windsor as Nell Brown. DeFore was a familiar face in early television, appearing in a recurring role as a neighbor on *The Adventures of Ozzie and Harriet* from 1956 to 1960 and in a starring role on *Hazel* from 1961 to 1965 ("Don DeFore's Television Credits"). Windsor is familiar from numerous television roles, but is best remembered for parts in such films noir as *The Killing* (1956). She is an odd choice for Nell Brown, too voluptuous for the role of Don DeFore's homemaking wife ("Marie Windsor"). Ted Heller is played by Warren Stevens, who brings a nervous intensity and intelligence to the role of the visitor from the future. Stevens appeared in numerous television shows from the late 1940s on, and is familiar from guest starring roles on such well-remembered series as *Alfred Hitchcock Presents* and *The Twilight Zone* ("Warren Stevens").

"Time Is Just a Place" is filmed on a very small set, which gives it a claustrophobic feeling. The characters spend the entire story either in the Browns' house or in the driveway between the two houses. The story is also changed from its source in some significant ways. The most notable change comes at the end, when the Hellers presumably are caught and killed by an investigator from the future. While this makes for a more exciting conclusion to the television show, it begs the question of why the government of the future would bother to track down escapees through time only to kill them, if its goal was to keep the population at an acceptable level.

Also awkward are the attempts to fit hard science into the somewhat whimsical tale. The introductory comments by Truman Bradley seem to have little to do with the story that follows, and the nonsense about electrical fields and test planes seems out of place. The scene in which Al shows Ted a model of a plane and demonstrates how it burns up at high speeds does little to move the story along.

The next story by Jack Finney to be adapted for television was "All My Clients Are Innocent," which was published in the July 1959 issue of *Cosmopolitan*. The story was broadcast as the April 17, 1962 episode of the prestigious drama series *Alcoa Premiere*, which aired every Tuesday night on the ABC television network ("Television"). Adapted by Jameson Brewer ("Alcoa Premiere — All My Clients Are Innocent"), the program starred Barry Morse as attorney Max McIntyre and Richard Davalos as his junior partner, Alan Michaels. The brief note in that day's *New York Times* television listings summarizes the plot: "a criminal lawyer tries to prevent his junior partner's marriage." This appears to follow the plot of the short story.

"All My Clients Are Innocent" also features Vic Morrow as the accused criminal, Carl Balderson ("Guest Appearances for 'Alcoa Premiere'"). The series, *Alcoa Premiere,* ran on ABC for two seasons, from 1961 to 1963, and was later syndicated as *Fred Astaire's Premiere Theatre.* The programs do not appear to have been broadcast in many years, and the only print of this episode available for viewing is a non-circulating research copy on 16 mm film at the UCLA Library's Film and Television Archive in Los Angeles, California ("Alcoa Premiere. All my clients are innocent").

Jack Finney's stories were absent from television from 1962 until March 20, 1987, when "Such Interesting Neighbors" aired as an episode of the series, *Amazing Stories.* This series ran for two years on the NBC network and this episode appeared near the end of the show's run ("Amazing Stories Episode Guide"). This time, the story is set in a new housing development in the Arizona desert. Al Lewis, a buffoon-like husband and father of a precocious boy, comes home from work, followed by his very-pregnant wife, Nell. They have recently moved into a new house and are surprised by things like the dead rattlesnake son Randy brings in from the back yard. Nell asks, "what else have we got to look forward to?"

They soon find out, as they see that the unfinished house across the street has suddenly become occupied. Al sneaks across the street, baseball bat in hand, to investigate, but retreats when he sees a man inside the house destroying a futuristic machine. The next day, the Lewises pay a visit to their new neighbors, the Hellenbecks, who sit strangely in dining room chairs around a pot of water in an unfinished section of the house. Their clothes and manners are strange, and Ted Hellenbeck tells Al that he "vivisects information" on "sociological substructures" and that his wife Ann is a "cataloguer" who is "working on atomic deformities in the rare earths." While the adults chat, Randy steals the pieces of the futuristic machine from the Hellenbecks' garbage.

Randy goes home and rebuilds the gizmo, which proceeds to cause heat-seeking spheres to appear all over the house and burn through anything warm. This leads to some excitement as the Lewises try to avoid the spheres by directing them into the toaster, the oven, and so on, until Ted Hellenbeck rushes over to provide an explanation. He tells the startled Lewises that he and his family are visitors from 400 years in the future, and that they fled after having their son naturally. It seems that, in their time, babies are made scientifically, and their decision to have one the old-fashioned way made them criminals.

A futuristic robot appears at the door, looking like a person wrapped in tinfoil with a cooking pot on his head. Al and Ted are able to subdue and destroy the machine, and the Hellenbecks say goodbye and disappear. Al remarks that they "sure were interesting neighbors."

Unlike the 1955 adaptation of Finney's short story, this version of "Such Interesting Neighbors" is hard to watch. The acting is uniformly awful, the special effects are an embarrassment, and the changes to the storyline make little sense. The wry humor that made the original story so effective has been replaced with forced humor wrung from poorly developed characters. In the short story, the Hellenbecks simply move away, leaving the narrator to wonder just who they were. In the 1955 teleplay, this was apparently too dull an ending, and the neighbors presumably are killed by police from the future. In the 1987 teleplay, the Hellenbecks simply disappear, and it is not clear where they go or why. The entire episode leaves a bad taste in the viewer's mouth and makes one glad that this series did not adapt any other stories by Jack Finney.

The last television adaptation of a Jack Finney story was broadcast on February 1, 1998, when "The Love Letter" premiered on the CBS network as part of the *Hallmark Hall of Fame* series. The Hallmark greeting card company began sponsoring television programs in 1951, and "The Love Letter" was the 317th broadcast of the sporadic series that had been running for 37 years ("Hallmark Hall of Fame — Episode List"). To expand a several-page story to fill a two-hour time slot required considerable fleshing out, and the screenplay, by James Henerson and Pamela Gray, expands the original tale in a manner consistent with Jack Finney's vision.

The program begins in present-day Boston, Massachusetts, where Scott Corrigan and his fiancée, Debra Zabriskie, buy a nineteenth-century desk in an antique shop. Scott is a Civil War buff who discovers a hidden compartment in the desk after he has brought it home and cleaned it. In the compartment is a letter by Elizabeth Whitcomb, dated April 16, 1863. She is a 29-year-old woman who wrote this letter to an imaginary lover and hid it in her desk. Scott does not take the letter seriously at first, writing a reply on his modern word processor and signing it, "Rhett Butler."

At work the next day, Scott thinks about the desk, the letter, and its writer. He telephones the antique dealer from whom he bought it and learns that the dealer had purchased the desk in a town called Willoughby, near the town of Salem.

The writers of "The Love Letter" appear to have known Jack Finney's work well, because this important addition to the original story is also a reference to an episode of the television series, *The Twilight Zone,* which Stephen King has suggested was influenced by Finney's time travel stories of the 1950s. In "A Stop at Willoughby," written by Rod Serling, a weary businessman escapes from his unhappy modern life by getting off of a commuter train in the town of Willoughby, which exists perpetually in about the year 1900. The town is idyllic and represents all that the man wishes existed in his own life.

Viewers of "The Love Letter" who are familiar with the work of both Finney and Serling will appreciate this choice of name for a town where the Civil War sweetheart of Scott Corrigan's imagination used to live. Scott drives to Willoughby and visits the house from whence the desk had come; it is located at 3 Mill Plain Road, perhaps another reference to Finney, who lived for much of his career in Mill Valley, California. Scott is prevented from entering, though, by an old black woman who guards the elderly resident of the home from her relatives, who want to put her in a nursing home. In essence, Scott is not serious enough about Whitcomb's letter yet, so he is not allowed to enter the past in any way.

Scott's interest in the letter is encouraged by his eccentric mother, who speaks to him about time travel. His fiancée Deb, on the other hand, reads the letter but shows no interest nor support. Scott's mother's encouragement continues as she gives him a one cent stamp from 1863 and a vintage bottle of ink. She tells him, "it's got to be perfect or we don't have a prayer of erasing the barrier." This remark, and the actions that follow, suggest that the authors of the screenplay were familiar with Finney's time travel work, especially "Second Chance," where an antique car is able to take its driver back in time when the conditions are right, and, most of all, *Time and Again*, where the method of time travel is based on the creation of accurate conditions.

Scott's mother locates a post office that was built in 1857. She says that it is the only pre–Civil War post office in existence and prods her son to go there to mail his letter to Elizabeth Whitcomb. After some restless attempts at sleep, Scott writes a letter to Elizabeth using the old pen and ink. No longer sarcastic, he signs it, "A friend," and mails it at night at the old post office.

The scene then switches to 1863, as we meet Elizabeth Whitcomb, a pretty young woman who is more interested in composing a poem in her garden than she is in responding to the advances of a dull suitor. Her father is pressuring her to marry but she is stunned when she receives and reads Scott's letter. She looks in the secret compartment of her desk and confirms that her own letter is gone. Elizabeth and Scott then begin an exchange of letters; she leaves hers in the desk's secret compartment and they disappear; he mails his at the old post office. He writes that "the connection between us is so strong that we're able to talk to each other across the chasm of time."

We learn that Elizabeth is a poet who has sent her verses to Ralph Waldo Emerson and others in an attempt to get them published. Her relationship with Scott deepens with each letter. However, his relationship with Debra, his fiancée in the present, begins to suffer as his mind and heart are drawn toward the past. This leads Scott to stop writing to Elizabeth and to take another trip to the house in Willoughby. This time, having demonstrated his resolve and having established a relationship with Elizabeth, he is allowed to enter and explore the house, where he meets Clarice, an elderly woman. She is the niece of Elizabeth Whitcomb, but she does not answer Scott when he asks if her aunt ever married. While in the house, Scott feels a connection with Lizzie, one that she also appears to feel in 1863. His visit to Willoughby leads him to resume his correspondence, and he promises not to be silent again. Elizabeth sends Scott a photograph of herself, as well as her final poem — criticism from her suitor has led her to give up poetry writing.

Scott sends Elizabeth a photo of himself and encourages her to keep writing poetry. His encouragement does not extend to his present fiancée, however, and their relationship grows increasingly strained.

The plot takes a surprising twist at this point, wholly invented for the television adaptation. Scott is injured in a bicycle race and lies comatose for a long period. In 1863, Lizzie meets Colonel Caleb Denby, who looks exactly like Scott, and they fall in love. Their romance is interrupted by Denby's need to return to the battlefield, and we learn that he is heading for Gettysburg. In the meantime, Scott awakens from his coma and reads Elizabeth's letters about Denby. Research reveals that Denby died at Gettysburg, and Scott rushes a letter to Elizabeth to try to save her lover. He is able to mail the letter at the old post office, which is burning down in a fire as he does so. This scene is reminiscent of the fire at *The World* building in Finney's novel, *Time and Again*.

The letter reaches Elizabeth, who races to Gettysburg, only to find Denby on his deathbed. In a touching scene, she recites her poem to him as he dies. Back in the present, Scott finally shows Debra the letters from Elizabeth, and he confesses his love for the dead woman. They break off the engagement, and Scott visits the old Whitcomb house in Willoughby one last time. Clarice has died, leaving the house to her caretaker. Scott again has the sensation that Lizzie is in the room with him, and Lizzie feels the same thing in her era. The old caretaker gives Scott a box of Elizabeth Whitcomb's letters, poems, and journals, and in it he finds the photograph of himself that he had sent to her.

The teleplay ends as Scott visits an old churchyard and finds Elizabeth's grave. On her headstone is carved the phrase, "I never forgot." The story has one more twist, however, as Scott meets a woman who is Elizabeth's double and they go off together to have coffee. She tells him that her name is Beth. As the credits roll, the camera focuses in on a bookstore window, where the newly published volume of Elizabeth Whitcomb's poetry — edited by Scott — is displayed.

"The Love Letter" is a wonderful adaptation of Jack Finney's short story. The acting is outstanding, especially by Campbell Scott and Jennifer Jason Leigh in the two lead roles. The writers have done an excellent job of expanding the short story to fill a two-hour time slot, using plot devices and ideas that are in keeping with Jack Finney's other time travel tales. No other television programs based on Finney's work have appeared since 1998, but "The Love Letter" stands as a fine example of what can be done with this source material and a creative approach.

NINETEEN

Jack Finney on Film

In May 1955, the first film to be adapted from a Jack Finney novel was released: *5 Against the House* was a Columbia Pictures production, directed by Phil Karlson and adapted by Stirling Silliphant, William Bowers, and John Barnwell. The credits state that it was based on the *Good Housekeeping* story by Jack Finney. This may be because the story was sold to the studio before the novel was written or published, or it may be that the producers thought that the name of the popular magazine might carry some weight with the public.

The film stars Guy Madison as Al Mercer and Kim Novak as Kay Greyleg (Tina in the book). Brick is played by Brian Keith. Jerry Weiner and Guy Cruikshank in the book become Ronnie and Roy, played by Kerwin Mathews and Alvy Moore, respectively. The only other character worth noting is Eric Berg, the man who pushes the money cart at Harold's Club and who is held up by Brick and his friends. Berg is played in the film by William Conrad, whose career spanned many years in radio and television.

The film version of *5 Against the House* is in black and white, and it is very different from the novel. The story and characters are established in the film's first section, which takes place in Reno, Nevada. Al and his three friends drive to the gambling mecca from their Midwestern university to visit Harold's Club, have fun, and gamble. Each of the four young men is introduced in scenes that provide quick snapshots of their characters. Al Mercer is serious, carefully watching the time as they spend their planned hour in the casino. Ronnie is from a wealthy family and wears an ascot around his neck; he has a system that does not seem to result in much winning. Roy is the comedian of the group, and Brick is the somewhat more mature ladies' man. The unusual casino parking lot is shown, where cars are lifted to upper levels by means of a mechanical lift. We also see an attempted robbery in the casino, as well as the heavy security there that prevents it from succeeding. A policeman who almost arrests two of the foursome tells them that it's "easier to knock off Fort Knox."

On the drive back to Midwestern University, Al begins to consider the challenge of robbing Harold's Club. Back at college, hijinks abound and we learn that Al and Brick served in Korea together. Brick saved Al's life, and Al feels a bond to the obviously shell-shocked veteran. Al's girlfriend Kay is introduced as a former department store worker who has metamorphosed over the summer into a sultry nightclub chanteuse. In between comedy relief involving college boys, scenes depicting the trouble that Al and Kay are having over the decision to get married, and Brick's hair-trigger state of mental health, Ronny works out a plan to rob Harold's Club. To him, it is an intellectual puzzle, since he clearly does not need the money. To Brick, however, it represents the promise of financial freedom and escape from the tensions of school and career preparation that threaten to push him over the edge of sanity.

Ronny, Brick, and Roy prepare for the heist and bring Al in at the last minute, tricking him into joining them on a trip to Reno but not telling him their plan. Kay decides to accompany them in order to take advantage of the laws in Nevada that allow for quick marriage.

Near the end of the long drive to Reno, Al learns of the plan to rob the casino and does not want to be involved. Brick threatens him with a gun and forces Al to drive the rest of the way at gunpoint.

Arriving in Reno, the four young men enter the club and carry out their plan. Things go awry and Brick runs off with the stolen money, hiding in the upper level of the Harold's Club parking deck that had been shown early in the movie. Al finds Brick and talks him into giving up; as the film ends, Brick is taken away by the police as Al and Kay are driven off in another police car. It is a curiously calm and happy ending, where Al and Kay are relieved by the knowledge that Brick will finally be treated for his mental problems that stem from his war experience.

5 *Against the House* is a minor film that takes a very different approach from the novel that was its source. First of all, the male members of the film's cast are much too old to be playing college boys. While Al Mercer is nineteen years old in the novel, actor Guy Madison was in his early thirties when the film was made. Brian Keith and Alvy Moore were each a year older than Madison. Kerwin Mathews was a "boyish" 29. Only Kim Novak, at 22, was about the right age for her part, carrying on the Hollywood tradition of pairing older men with younger women.

The novel's focus is on the caper itself and on Al's attempt to justify robbery as a moral choice. The film puts the caper aspects of the story on the back burner and concentrates on two major plot threads: the relationship between Al and Kay, and the relationship between Al and Brick. Al and Kay's relationship is superficial in the film, and the waitress of the novel has become a glamorous lounge singer in order to give Kim Novak a chance to sing and look seductive. One sequence in particular, where Novak sings to Madison as he drives to Reno, is quite awkward.

The other relationship, between Al and Brick, is the central issue in the film and one that was absent from the book, at least in the way the film portrays it. The film's creators decided to make Al and Brick veterans of the Korean War, and Brick's experience left him shellshocked. This is used to explain all of Brick's unorthodox behavior, and the crazed look in actor Brian Keith's eyes when he starts to be "possessed" by the memory of Korea borders on the humorous.

5 *Against the House* is a mediocre and forgotten novel today; the film has also been justly forgotten.

The second film to be adapted from Jack Finney's work was *Invasion of the Body Snatchers,* a film that has been far from forgotten. Released in 1956 by Allied Artists, the film sticks closely to its source and is considered a classic. It begins with the well-known framing sequence, which was added at the studio's insistence to tone down the film's level of terror. Kevin McCarthy plays Miles Bennell, a small town doctor, who is brought by police to see a psychiatrist at a hospital. He insists he is not insane, and tells the story of the film in flashback —

"it started last Thursday," he remarks, adding that "something evil had taken possession of the town."

As the tale begins, we see Dr. Bennell return by train from a conference that has kept him away from the small California town of Santa Mira for two weeks. Patients were lining up to see him while he was gone, refusing to see anyone else. As Miles drives back to his office, he sees Jimmy Grimaldi, a small boy he knows, run into the street in terror, and he notices that the Grimaldi family's formerly prosperous vegetable stand has fallen into disrepair.

Back at his office, Miles is greeted by the lovely Becky Driscoll, who is back in town after a five-year absence. She and Miles had been sweethearts before they had each married other people; both are now divorced, and it takes little time for the romance to begin again. Like author Jack Finney and his first wife, Miles and Becky have both recently been divorced in Reno, Nevada.

A sense of uneasiness begins to set in as Miles meets patients who insist that their family members are not who they seem. Jimmy Grimaldi, the boy who had run down the street in terror, claims his mother is not his mother. Becky's cousin Wilma insists that her Uncle Ira is not her Uncle Ira. Throughout the first part of *Invasion of the Body Snatchers,* the sense of dread and unease grows slowly. The film has been hailed as a classic of science fiction cinema, but its success lies more in its film noir qualities. Miles's voiceover narration recalls similar narration by Humphrey Bogart in *The Big Sleep* and other classic private eye films; the movie is shot in black and white and shadows are used to suggest horrors not yet revealed.

Miles's friend, psychiatrist Danny Kaufman, provides the voice of cold reason in the film, explaining that Santa Mira's citizens are exhibiting signs of mass hysteria, probably caused by worry about what's going on in the world. Later events are foreshadowed as Miles tells Becky, "I'd hate to wake up some morning and find out you weren't you." The relief provided by Dr. Kaufman's rational explanation doesn't last long, however, as Miles and Becky are called to the home of Jack and Theodora Belicec. Jack is a writer (like author Jack Finney, whose given name he shares), and he shows Miles a body on his basement pool table. The body is strangely unformed but resembles Jack. At this point, the eerie feeling that has dominated the film so far is replaced by something tangible. Becky Driscoll and the viewers are shocked by the sudden alarm of a cuckoo clock in the Belicecs' basement; this subtly suggests that everything in the film has suddenly turned "cuckoo"— or crazy.

Miles begins to suspect a connection between the alleged mass hysteria in Santa Mira and the body double. There is another brief respite from the suspense as Miles takes Becky home and she refuses to let him stay the night. "That way lies madness!" she quips, to which he replies, "What's wrong with madness?" Her answer, "Madness!" implies that madness itself is something to be avoided and feared. The scene then shifts back to the Belicecs' house, where the couple have dozed off, only to be awakened by the cuckoo clock, signaling more of the sort of madness that Becky wants to avoid. The body on the pool table opens its eyes, and we see that it has now become more clearly a replica of Jack.

Jack and Theodora rush to Miles's house. Miles calls Dr. Kaufman and asks him to come over, then rushes to Becky's house, fearing for her safety. He breaks in through a basement window, opens a storage bin, and sees a partially formed replica of Becky. More than ever in the film, Miles is the detective in a film noir world at this point — his voiceover narration explains his descent into a world gone mad. He finds Becky in bed and carries her off in his arms when he is unable to awaken her. Doing so saves her life for a time, though we don't realize it until later in the film.

Back at Miles's house, Dr. Kaufman has arrived and once more the voice of reason attempts to take over and calm the growing sense of chaos and madness. Kaufman, Miles, and Jack return to Jack's house, where they find that the body has disappeared. They then go to Becky's house, where there is also no body. Explanations by Dr. Kaufman and a policeman make sense to the characters in the film but not to the viewers, who have seen more than any of the characters and know that something is wrong.

The next day, Friday — hard to believe that all of this has happened in one day!—finds things strangely calm in Santa Mira. Miles's patients line up to tell him that they are fine and claim that their worries were groundless. But Miles is not convinced, and his voiceover narration reveals his concern about the sudden turn of events. The horror of the situation soon explodes as Miles discovers large seed pods in his greenhouse; they are photographed at an odd angle and begin to open, revealing replacement bodies for Miles, Becky, Jack, and Theodora. Miles quickly deduces that the pod-bodies replace the originals and that the change occurs when one falls asleep. Suddenly, all of the eerie feelings and frightening suggestions in the film are revealed to be real. Miles's attempt to call the FBI fails, and he destroys his own replacement pod but cannot bring himself to destroy Becky's. Just as he had saved her by waking her up the night before, this act of weakness seals her doom.

Miles and Becky flee. The "pods," as they have been known since the film premiered in 1956, realize that the couple pose a threat and begin to search for them, sealing off the town's borders. Miles and Becky take refuge in his office, taking pills to keep themselves awake all night. Miles remarks that, in his practice, he has seen people allow their humanity to drain away, but it usually happens slowly — not all at once.

Saturday morning begins, with the fugitive couple still locked in the medical office. Outside, they observe replacements preparing seed pods to be taken to nearby towns, like "a malignant disease spreading through the whole country." Their safety ends when a changed Jack Belicec leads the pods to the office. This represents one of the biggest changes from the source, for in the serial and novel upon which the film was based the Belicecs survive, along with Miles and Becky.

Dr. Kaufman, who has taken on the role of the scientist in the film, explains that the pods are seeds that drifted through space for years before taking root in a farmer's field. Miles resists the change, noting that the new bodies "have no feelings, only the instinct to survive." Miles and Becky escape their captors by injecting them with sedatives, and they race into the hills at the edge of town, pursued by the townspeople.

Miles and Becky take refuge in a cave-like tunnel, hiding in an abandoned mine shaft as the crowd searches for them. Becky falls asleep and changes into a replacement, marking the second major change from the source material. This changeover has puzzled filmgoers for almost fifty years, since up to that point the replacement bodies have had to be different than the original humans. However, the filmmakers seem to have decided that logic was not necessary when reaching for a suspenseful effect, and Becky's awakening as a pod-person is one of the classic scary moments in 1950s cinema.

Miles, now alone, reaches the highway, and runs wildly among the cars and trucks, trying in vain to warn everyone that the pods are coming and will replace them. He yells into the camera, "They're here already — you're next!" This was the film's original ending, but the release print adds the conclusion of the framing story with which the film had opened. Miles, still in the hospital, finishes telling his story to the skeptical doctors. Their skepticism changes to fear when they learn that a truck filled with giant seed pods has overturned on the road from Santa Mira. The film ends as the authorities are summoned, presumably to defeat the aliens once and for all.

Invasion of the Body Snatchers is a wonderful film, which uses film noir techniques to tell a story that is part science fiction, part horror, and part detective story. Jack Finney was said to have thought it "marvelous," and it is recognized as a landmark film of the 1950s.

The third film to be adapted from a Jack Finney novel is not as well known, but is quite well made. "The House of Numbers" first appeared as a novelette in the July 1956 issue of *Cosmopolitan*. It was then expanded to novel form and published as a paperback original by Dell in 1957. That same year, it was released as an M-G-M motion picture, and the credits state that it is "based on the Cosmopolitan magazine novel by Jack Finney." Thus, like the filmed versions of "5 Against the House" and "The Body Snatchers," this third film to be made from Jack Finney's work seems to have been based on the original, shorter version rather than the longer book version that followed. It is quite possible that the stories were sold to Hollywood studios and that these movie deals led to book deals for the author.

House of Numbers is filmed in gritty black and white, like the two movies that precede it, and is a fine example of the suspenseful crime films that were made by studios in the 1950s. It features a short sequence before the opening titles, in which a montage of prison scenes concludes as an inmate attacks a guard by grabbing his ankles and throwing him over a railing to the floor far below. The titles then appear, stamped on the screen by a hand holding a rubber stamp and superimposed over a shot of the prison exterior. Thanks are given to warden Harley O. Teets and others, as well as to real San Quentin officers and inmates who appear in the film. Jack Finney had also thanked Warden Teets for his help in researching the novel. After a voiceover tells viewers how hard it is to escape from the prison, the story begins as we meet

Bill and Ruth Judlow, who have four days to help Bill's brother Arnie escape from prison. Ruth is Arnie's wife and he is serving a life sentence. Much as the five college friends do in *5 Against the House,* Bill and Ruth shop for various items to use in the planned escape. Arnie has given them a list and presumably a plan; the details of the plan unfold as the film unwinds.

Ruth knew Arnie for only twelve days before they wed, and Arnie killed a man who Ruth had dated when he thought that the man was paying too much attention to her. Arnie was jealous and controlling, and Ruth clearly fears him and is anxious about being reunited. Still, both she and Bill believe that they owe it to Arnie to help him escape, and they rent a house near the prison in order to carry out the plan.

They hear a radio report that states that the guard who was attacked at the beginning of the film is recovering and will likely name his attacker when he awakes. Bill explains that Arnie would be put to death under California law for assaulting the guard, even though the guard did not die. A problem develops when they meet their new neighbor, Henry Nova, who is a guard at the prison. He recognizes Ruth from her visits to the jail and promises to keep an eye on Arnie, much to their chagrin.

That night, Ruth drives Bill to the prison and he climbs the wall in the remote industrial area, where he hides among a stack of crates. He switches places with his brother the next day and takes his place among the prison inmates. Jack Palance plays both Bill and Arnie Judlow, and the difference between the two characters is apparent. As played by Palance, Bill is quieter than Arnie, with a look of fear in his eyes but a moral center. Arnie, on the other hand, is wild-eyed and nervous. Bill's time as a prisoner does not go smoothly, as he lights up a cigarette in the mess hall and is reported for the infraction. This attracts Nova's attention and, while the guard does not realize that he is speaking to Bill and not Arnie, the attention is unwanted, as is Nova's unsavory attraction to Ruth.

That night, under cover of darkness, Arnie comes out of hiding from among the crates and digs a grave-sized hole in the industrial area yard. He then covers the hole with plywood and camouflages it before returning to his hiding place. The next day, Arnie and Bill switch places again. That night, Bill escapes over the wall and Ruth picks him up and brings him home. At this point, it is unclear what is going on, other than the fact that Arnie has managed to dig a hole in the yard and hide it from view.

The next morning, as Bill carves a realistic-looking gun from a block of wood, we learn that Arnie has been squandering opportunities at Bill's expense for many years. Arnie went to college, so Bill could not afford to go, yet Arnie dropped out and became a boxer. He later killed a man with his hands and was convicted of assault with a deadly weapon. Both Bill and Ruth feel guilty about Arnie's fate, even though he has clearly taken advantage of them. This guilt provides the rationale for their helping him to escape.

Back at the prison, Arnie takes advantage of a momentary distraction to hide in the hole he had prepared. A subsequent count of inmates comes up short and the alarm is sounded. Guards search the prison as Arnie remains hidden underground.

On the outside, Bill hijacks a car and plants evidence to make it appear that Arnie was the culprit. Police investigate and confirm that Arnie has escaped from prison. This leads the warden to turn off the alarm, which means that the search of the prison area comes to an end and the wall in the industrial area is again unguarded.

Bill and Ruth return home to find Henry Nova waiting for them in their living room. He tries to blackmail them, having guessed the truth, and Bill goes to the prison to help Arnie escape as Nova supposedly awaits his return. Bill climbs the wall back into the prison and a suspenseful scene ensues as Arnie and Bill hide in the hole while a guard walks by, inspecting the area. The problem with this scene is that the area is dirt, yet the guard's footsteps echo loudly as if he were walking on a platform. While this allows Arnie and Bill to listen to him as he passes, and also allows for maximum suspense in the film, it is utterly implausible that footsteps would make this sound on dirt.

Arnie and Bill avoid the guard and climb the wall, only to find Nova waiting for them on the other side. Yet Nova does not realize that there are two of them, and he is tackled from above. Arnie nearly kills Nova and Bill has to intervene; he sees first hand how dangerous and unstable Arnie is. Bill then takes Arnie home to Ruth, who resists his affection. Ruth chooses to stay with Bill and Arnie leaves, swearing never to go back to jail.

Later, Bill and Ruth are summoned to the prison by the warden, who received a tip from an anonymous caller. The warden has also guessed what happened, but his concern is with getting Arnie back safely, and he convinces them to reveal his hiding place. Bill tells Ruth that Arnie was the one who called the warden anonymously and turned them in, and the film ends as Bill's anguished face shows the dismay that his brother has caused.

House of Numbers is a gripping suspense film, with an outstanding performance by Jack Palance as the Judlow brothers and good supporting work by Barbara Lang as Ruth and Harold J. Stone as Nova. Edward Platt, who would later gain fame as the Chief on the television series, *Get Smart,* is convincing as the warden. *House of Numbers* is effective film noir, making good use of shadows, night scenes, close quarters (characters are often seen in cars), and suspenseful music. Like other classics of the genre, it features tough characters caught in a web from which they seem unable to escape.

After having his first three novels made into movies that were released three years in a row, Jack Finney would have to wait another seven years before another film of his work was released. This time, it would be in color, a comedy very different in tone from the three movies that preceded it.

Good Neighbor Sam was released by Columbia Pictures in 1964. Finney was quoted in a 1966 interview as saying that he wrote the book with actor Jack Lemmon in mind (Wilson), and Lemmon starred in the adaptation of the 1963 novel. This film marked a big departure from the three films that had preceded it. It was in color, it had a big budget, and it was a comedy. Set in and around San Francisco, *Good Neighbor Sam* is a film that still holds up forty years later as great entertainment.

Sam Bissell is a likeable young man raising a family in the suburbs and commuting to work each day at the office of Burke and Hare, an advertising agency where the executives are successful but less than ethical. Early in the film, Sam laments his boring nine-to-five life, foreshadowing similar complaints that would be raised in Finney's 1977 novel, *The Night People.* Sam's wife is the lovely, blonde Minerva, whom he calls Min.

The film's plot follows two main threads. One concerns an ad campaign for Nurdlinger Eggs. Mr. Nurdlinger is played by Edward G. Robinson, who enjoys the role of the puritanical dairy man who threatens to fire the Burke and Hare agency because all of their executives are libertines. This leads Sam's boss to promote him from the art department to account executive in charge of the Nurdlinger egg campaign — Sam is the only man in the company who appears to live a clean, family-oriented life. Sam's intention to "strip away the sham and pretension" from advertising is bound to fail.

The second thread concerns Min's old school friend, Janet Lagerlof, who moves in next door to the Bissells after returning from Europe. While Janet in the novel was simply an attractive next-door neighbor, in the film she is a rather exotic woman with a foreign accent and a devil-may-care attitude, played by Austrian actress Romy Schneider. Sam must pose as her husband in order for her to inherit fifteen million dollars from her late grandfather, who left a will insisting that her marriage be sound for the inheritance to be paid.

The theme of the film is simple: the older generation, represented by Mr. Nurdlinger and Janet's dead grandfather, do not approve of the loose morals of the younger generation, and they use their wealth to try to force younger men and women to behave in ways they believe are appropriate. Nurdlinger wants a clean ad campaign, and Sam tries to give it to him. Janet's grandfather wanted a happily married granddaughter, and Sam also attempts to provide this. The irony of both situations is that they can only come true through falsehoods, with Sam — truly a good neighbor to all — the hapless participant in both shams.

Of course, neither lie is easily maintained, and the film finds its humor in Sam's attempts to keep up a good front as his life grows ever more complicated. Sam's interior monologue from the novel is gone, as is much of the novel's racy content — Sam is barely tempted by Janet's charms in the film, except for one scene where he imagines the result of an attempt at seduction. In the end, all is well, as Sam returns to his life with Min and Janet presumably inherits fifteen million dollars — a million of which she promised to give to the Bissells. The novel's final twist is missing; in the book, a second will is discovered that deprives Janet of her inheritance. In the film, the money is forgotten in the end as everyone lives happily ever after in a suburban world of artifice maintained by a series of deceptions.

Two years after *Good Neighbor Sam* was released, another big-budget color adaptation of a Jack Finney novel hit the movie screens. This time, it was *Assault on a Queen*, adapted from Finney's 1959 novel of the same name, which had been written and published four years before the novel that served as a basis for *Good Neighbor Sam*. The film version of *Assault on a Queen* was written by Rod Serling, whose television series, *The Twilight Zone*, is said to have owed a debt to Finney's time travel stories of the 1950s. This film had its premiere the same spring that Finney's play, *This Winter's Hobby,* ran briefly in Connecticut and Philadelphia before closing.

Assault on a Queen stars Frank Sinatra as Mark Brittain, a sailor who is down on his luck. He is recruited by Vic Rossiter and Eric Lauffnauer, who are relying on money supplied by Rosa Lucchesi to dive for sunken treasure. Set to a jazzy score, the film is a star turn for Sinatra who, at age 51, romances the lovely 29-year-old Italian actress, Virna Lisi. Unlike the novel, where Lauffnauer plans to raise the submarine from the start and rob the *Queen Mary,* everything in the film happens by coincidence. Mark discovers the sunken U-boat while diving for sunken treasure; Lauffnauer happens to have been a U-boat commander and suggests "why not play pirates?"

Rosa finances the operation for no particular reason, and Mark raises the sunken sub so quickly and easily that it is not a very impressive accomplishment. The sub is towed to dry-dock and repaired; an expert mechanic named Tony Moreno is brought in to get it shipshape. There are some awkward moments with Mark's friend Linc, a black man with an English accent who comes across as little more than a token attempt to appear relevant in the era of civil rights demonstrations. Rossiter sneers and calls him a "freedom rider" at one point; Linc later replies, sarcastically, that Rossiter should bring him a "nice, shiny watermelon."

The robbery is planned with little suspense. The only tension in the film comes from the relationships between the members of the gang who plan to rob the ship. There is a love triangle between Mark, Vic, and Rosa, but she obviously prefers Frank Sinatra to Tony Franciosa (though Franciosa is much closer to her age, at 37) and the expected confrontation over the beautiful Italian woman never materializes.

The robbery of the *Queen Mary* is also rather different on film than in the novel. On film, Mark, Vic, and Eric board the luxury liner and rob the bank and the bullion room. Mark and Eric escape by boat after Vic is distracted by a large diamond ring on a female passenger's hand. He tries to pull it off of her finger and is shot by a chivalrous sailor.

Gone is the plan to rob the passengers one by one; gone, too, is the Nazi subplot of the magazine serial.

Mark and Eric make it back to the sub but leave the money in the boat in their haste to escape a U.S. Coast Guard destroyer that has spotted them. There is an effective sequence where the sub hides underneath the *Queen Mary*, but the film ends with a cliché as Eric wants to torpedo the Coast Guard cutter and Mark tries to stop him. Eric pulls a gun, Rosa deflects his arm, and Tony Moreno is shot in the back. Mark, Linc, and Rosa escape by diving off of the sub's deck into the ocean, leaving Eric to be killed as the Coast Guard cutter rams the sub full steam ahead.

Assault on a Queen ends with a sequence where the three survivors climb aboard a raft and start paddling for South America, happy to have escaped with their lives.

Assault on a Queen was a novel with problems, and it was made into a movie that wasted the talents of writer Rod Serling and a number of good actors. Jack Finney's works would not be filmed again for twelve years, until a remake of *Invasion of the Body Snatchers* appeared in 1978. The world of 1978, as depicted in Philip Kaufman's reworking of Don Siegel's original film, is much different than the world of 1956. Viewers of the new film were expected to have some familiarity with the story already, and the mystery of whether the main characters were sane or insane is not a part of the new film.

Instead, it opens with a scene where the space spores drift away from their own planet and across outer space, landing on Earth and sticking to plants in San Francisco. The entire film has a strange, disoriented feeling right from the start, courtesy of director Kaufman's penchant for using odd camera angles and spooky music. Instead of a small-town doctor, Matthew (not Miles) Bennell is now a big-city health inspector, and Elizabeth Driscoll (no longer Becky) also works for the city. Matthew's job is to look below the surface of things to find the disease and decay that lie beneath — as is shown when he finds a "rat turd" in the kitchen of a fancy restaurant.

From the start of the film, nothing in San Francisco seems right, but no one notices. People run through the streets in fear and there is a general sense of paranoia and unease. Soon enough, characters begin to suspect that loved ones are not themselves. One of the many updates to the 1970s is the suspicion — voiced by various characters — that a conspiracy is afoot, much like the government conspiracies that were widely believed to exist at the time. Symbolism is plentiful in the film, including Matthew's cracked windshield through which he sees the world. Yet the jaded health inspector is so used to things being broken that he doesn't notice anymore.

Director Kaufman pays homage to the 1956 film twice: with actor Kevin McCarthy, who runs in front of Matthew's car, still warning drivers that "you're next!" as if he has been doing it since the prior film ended; and with director Don Siegel, who plays a sinister taxi driver who tries to turn Matthew and Elizabeth over to the pod people.

The basic plot remains the same, as Matthew and Elizabeth are slowly drawn into the horror of realization that people are being replaced by emotionless pods. This time, Jack and Nancy (not Theodora) Belicec run "The Belicec Mud Baths" and psychiatrist Mannie Kaufman is now best-selling pop psychiatrist David Kibner, played by *Star Trek*'s Leonard Nimoy. Kibner tries to rationalize his friends' concerns with 1970s psychobabble; Nancy's biggest concern upon discovering the replacement pod for her husband is that it is infected with some sort of disease.

The film as a whole is disquieting, featuring color, shock, and gore, where the original succeeded through subtlety and suspense. About two-thirds of the way through, it becomes an elongated chase, losing any mood and thoughtfulness that it had built up in exchange for an attempt at excitement. The mood of the era surfaces again when Kibner and Jack Belicec trap Matthew and Elizabeth in Matthew's office; Kibner tells Matthew, "you'll be born again into an untroubled world," and suddenly the pods seem like members of a religious cult.

Near the end, Matthew destroys a large greenhouse full of pods in a series of explosions and fires. While this scene somewhat recalls the conclusion of the novel, where Miles sets fire to a field full of pods, the visuals and the sound are so shrill that the effect is lost. True to form for a 1970s film, the 1978 version of *Invasion of the Body Snatchers* ends on a downbeat note — Nancy Belicec meets Matthew on a San Francisco street, only to learn that he has been replaced by a pod. His scream that reveals her as human fades in to the closing credits.

Invasion of the Body Snatchers would be remade a second time in 1993, but first one of Jack Finney's latter novels, *Marion's Wall*, would be adapted as *Maxie* and released in 1985. *Maxie* is as bright and cheerful as *Invasion of the Body Snatchers,* released only seven years before, was dark and gloomy. It stars Glenn Close as Jan Cheney, who is possessed by the spirit of deceased silent movie actress Maxie Malone (Marion Marsh in the novel). The story has been changed considerably in the transition to film. Jan is now an efficient secretary to a bishop, and Nick is a librarian pursued by an amorous female boss.

The character of Nick's father, who provides the link to Marion/Maxie in the novel, is replaced by that of Mrs. Lavin, played by Ruth Gordon. She is the Cheneys' eccentric landlady, and six decades before she was Maxie's dancing partner. The film's plot generally parallels that of the novel, with one important alteration in tone. Where Marion Marsh was saddened and eventually disgusted by what she saw of the modern world, Maxie Malone is delighted and finally vindicated by her experiences. Glenn Close switches back and forth from Jan to Maxie effortlessly, changing her accent and her behavior to suit each character.

The film's point, which is rather different than that of the novel, is that Jan needs to wake up and start enjoying life. This is expressed humorously by her boss, the bishop, when she tells him of her actions upon first being possessed. He tells her in reply: "that's not known as possession, that's known as living." The characters of Hugo Dahl, the former prop boy, and Ted Bollinghurst, the aged film collector, have been eliminated and, while Maxie does succeed in getting a part in a movie (this time, as the star of a remake of *Cleopatra*), she is entranced by the filmmaking experience. This is quite a contrast to the scene in the novel, where Marion performs nude in a movie and is disgusted by modern film.

The conflagration that ends the novel is also absent; in the film, Maxie voluntarily fades off into the spirit world, leaving Nick and Jan to drive off happily into the California sun. *Maxie* is an entertaining, funny film, but it has little in common with the novel *Marion's Wall* beyond the general premise and the skeleton of the plot. Still, it would have been a much better farewell on film to Jack Finney's works than the abominable *Body Snatchers.* Released in 1993, the third and final adaptation of Finney's novel, *The Body Snatchers,* is the last film adapted from his works to date.

The story is nearly unrecognizable, and it must have been puzzling for those viewers unlucky enough to see this film without knowing the premise in advance. This time, the story has been updated to

1993, and takes place almost entirely at a military base somewhere in the U.S.A. Instead of Dr. Miles Bennell or Matthew Bennell, the main character is teenaged Marti Malone, whose voiceover narration is heard briefly at the beginning and end of the film.

Marti moves to a military base with her family and problems begin right away. Her father is a rather weak man who is there to test chemical waste for the Environmental Protection Agency. Her stepmother is a poorly-drawn character, played by Meg Tilly, who demonstrates some of the film's worst acting when she tells Marti about halfway through that there is nowhere to run or to hide. There is also a little brother, Andy, who is in preschool. The child actor playing Andy is unappealing, and the viewer is not moved when his replacement is thrown from a moving helicopter near the end of the film.

Many words could be wasted explaining what is wrong with this film, which features considerable nudity, four-letter words, and graphic violence, but which is devoid of a single likeable character. Suffice it to say that the screenwriters and director appear to have watched Philip Kaufman's 1978 version of *Invasion of the Body Snatchers* and tried to spice it up. Forrest Whitaker plays Dr. Collins, overacting wildly in his few scenes, and when he shoots himself in the head (filmed in loving detail and living color), the viewer wishes he could share the doctor's fate rather than watch another minute of this miserable film.

Fortunately, *Body Snatchers* was not the end for admirers of Jack Finney's work. The television adaptation of "The Love Letter" aired in 1998, and the musical version of *Time and Again* finally made it to the New York stage in 2001. As of this writing, in 2006, no more of Finney's works have appeared on screen or stage, but his many short stories and novels remain a rich source of material that may be mined again in the future, hopefully to good result.

Appendix I.
Writings by Jack Finney

NOVELS

1954   *5 Against the House*
1955   *The Body Snatchers*
1957   *The House of Numbers*
1959   *Assault on a Queen*
1963   *Good Neighbor Sam*
1968   *The Woodrow Wilson Dime*
1970   *Time and Again*
1973   *Marion's Wall*
1977   *The Night People*
1995   *From Time to Time*

SHORT STORIES AND SERIALS

1947

Manhattan Idyl. *Collier's.* April 5, 1947.
The Widow's Walk. *Ellery Queen's Mystery Magazine.* July 1947.
I'm Mad at You. *Collier's.* December 6, 1947.

1948

Cousin Len's Wonderful Adjective Cellar. *Ladies' Home Journal*. April
   1948.
Breakfast in Bed. *Collier's*. May 15, 1948.
It Wouldn't Be Fair. *Collier's*. August 28, 1948.
Long-Distance Call. *Collier's*. November 6, 1948.

1949

Something in a Cloud. *Good Housekeeping*. March 1949.
You Haven't Changed a Bit. *Collier's*. April 16, 1949.
The Little Courtesies. *Collier's*. June 25, 1949.

1950

Sneak Preview. *Collier's*. April 29, 1950.
Week-end Genius. *Collier's*. May 20, 1950.
I Like It This Way. *Collier's*. June 24, 1950.
My Cigarette Loves Your Cigarette. *Collier's*. September 30, 1950.
The Third Level. *Collier's*. October 7, 1950.

1951

Such Interesting Neighbors. *Collier's*. January 6, 1951.
Husband at Home. *Ladies' Home Journal*. April 1951.
One-Man Show. *Collier's*. June 30, 1951.
Swelled Head. *Collier's*. July 14, 1951.
Quit Zoomin' Those Hands Through the Air. *Collier's*. August 4,
   1951.
I'm Scared. *Collier's*. September 15, 1951.
Sounds in the Night. *Collier's*. November 24, 1951.

1952

Stopover at Reno. *Collier's*. January 5, 1952.
Obituary. *Collier's*. February 2, 1952 (with C.J. Durban).
Tiger Tamer. *Collier's*. May 31, 1952.
There Is a Tide. *Collier's*. August 2, 1952.
Man of the Cocktail Hour. *Collier's*. September 20, 1952.
Diagnosis Completed. *Collier's*. October 18, 1952 (with F.M. Barratt).
Behind the News. *Good Housekeeping*. November 1952.

1953

5 Against the House (part one). *Good Housekeeping.* July 1953.
5 Against the House (part two). *Good Housekeeping.* August 1953.
5 Against the House (part three). *Good Housekeeping.* September 1953.

1954

The Body Snatchers (part one). *Collier's.* November 26, 1954.
The Body Snatchers (part two). *Collier's.* December 10, 1954.
The Body Snatchers (part three). *Collier's.* December 24, 1954.

1955

Legal and Tender. *Good Housekeeping.* February 1955.
Of Missing Persons. *Good Housekeeping.* March 1955.
Tattletale Tape. *Collier's.* March 4, 1955.
A Man of Confidence. *Good Housekeeping.* August 1955.

1956

Second Chance. *Good Housekeeping.* April 1956.
The House of Numbers. *Cosmopolitan.* July 1956.
Contents of the Dead Man's Pocket. *Collier's.* October 26, 1956.

1957

Rainy Sunday. *Good Housekeeping.* April 1957.
Expression of Love. *Good Housekeeping.* June 1957.
Fast Buck. *Good Housekeeping.* September 1957.
A Dash of Spring. *The Third Level.* 1957.

1958

Vive La Différence! *Good Housekeeping.* June 1958.

1959

Seven Days to Live. *Saturday Evening Post.* January 10, 1959.
Bedtime Story. *Good Housekeeping.* May 1959.
All My Clients Are Innocent. *Cosmopolitan.* July 1959.
The Love Letter. *Saturday Evening Post.* August 1, 1959.
The U-19's Last Kill (part one). *Saturday Evening Post.* August 22, 1959.
The U-19's Last Kill (part two). *Saturday Evening Post.* August 29, 1959.

The U-19's Last Kill (part three). *Saturday Evening Post*. September 5, 1959.

The U-19's Last Kill (part four). *Saturday Evening Post*. September 12, 1959.

The U-19's Last Kill (part five). *Saturday Evening Post*. September 19, 1959.

The U-19's Last Kill (part six). *Saturday Evening Post*. September 26, 1959.

Take One Rainy Night ... *McCall's*. October 1959.

1960

The Other Wife. *Saturday Evening Post*. January 30, 1960.

Crazy Sunday. *McCall's*. February 1960.

I Love Galesburg in the Springtime. *McCall's*. April 1960.

1961

An Old Tune. *McCall's*. October 1961.

1962

Where the Cluetts Are. *McCall's*. January 1962.

The Man with the Magic Glasses. *McCall's*. March 1962.

Old Enough for Love. *McCall's*. May 1962.

Hey, Look at Me! *Playboy*. September 1962.

The Sunny Side of the Street. *McCall's*. October 1962.

Time Has No Boundaries. *Saturday Evening Post*. October 13, 1962.

1965

Double Take. *Playboy*. April 1965.

NONFICTION

Where Has Old-Fashioned Fun Gone? *New York Times*. Sept. 24, 1970: 47.

Off to the Golden West. *New York Times*. Oct. 29, 1970: 43.

St. Nicholas Monthly's Xmas List. *New York Times*. December 18, 1970: 39.

When Felony Had Style. *New York Times*. February 5, 1971: 31.

Getting It Right This Time. *New York Times.* June 11, 1973: 35.

Man's First Flight: Over Manhattan, 1876. *New York Times.* Aug. 1, 1973: 39.

Esprit de Postal Corp. *New York Times.* Dec. 21, 1973: 35.

Forgotten News: The Crime of the Century and Other Lost Stories. 1983.

SHORT STORY AND NOVEL COLLECTIONS

The Third Level. 1957.

Contents: The Third Level. Such Interesting Neighbors. I'm Scared. Cousin Len's Wonderful Adjective Cellar. Of Missing Persons. Something in a Cloud. There Is a Tide ... Behind the News. Quit Zoomin' Those Hands Through the Air. A Dash of Spring. Second Chance. Contents of the Dead Man's Pockets.

I Love Galesburg in the Springtime. 1962.

Contents: I Love Galesburg in the Springtime. Love, Your Magic Spell Is Everywhere. Where the Cluetts Are. Hey, Look at Me! A Possible Candidate for the Presidency. Prison Legend. Time Has No Boundaries. The Intrepid Aeronaut. The Coin Collector. The Love Letter.

About Time: Twelve Stories. 1986.

Contents: The Third Level. I Love Galesburg in the Springtime. Such Interesting Neighbors. The Coin Collector. Of Missing Persons. Lunch-Hour Magic. Where the Cluetts Are. The Face in the Photo. I'm Scared. Home Alone. Second Chance. Hey, Look at Me!

Three by Finney. 1987.

Contents: *The Woodrow Wilson Dime. Marion's Wall. The Night People.*

PLAYS

Telephone Roulette. Dramatic Publishing. 1956.

This Winter's Hobby. 1966.

FILM ADAPTATIONS

Five Against the House. 1955.
Invasion of the Body Snatchers. 1956.
House of Numbers. 1957.
Good Neighbor Sam. 1964.
Assault on a Queen. 1966.
Invasion of the Body Snatchers. 1978.
Maxie. 1985.
Body Snatchers. 1993.

TELEVISION ADAPTATIONS

"Time Is Just a Place." (Adaptation of "Such Interesting Neighbors.")
    Science Fiction Theatre. First broadcast on April 16, 1955.
"All My Clients Are Innocent." *Alcoa Premiere.* First broadcast on
    April 17, 1962.
"Such Interesting Neighbors." *Amazing Stories.* First broadcast on
    March 20, 1987.
"The Love Letter." *Hallmark Hall of Fame.* First broadcast on Febru-
    ary 1, 1998.

Appendix II.
Credits for Adaptations
of Jack Finney's Work

FILM

5 Against the House
Released in 1955 by Columbia Pictures
Screenplay by Stirling Silliphant, William Bowers, John Barnwell
Based upon the *Good Housekeeping* Magazine story by Jack Finney
Produced by Stirling Silliphant, John Barnwell
Directed by Phil Karlson
  • Cast •
Al Mercer — Guy Madison
Kay Greyleg — Kim Novak
Brick — Brian Keith
Roy — Alvy Moore
Ronnie — Kerwin Mathews
Eric Berg — William Conrad
Francis Spieglebauer — Jack Diamond
Virginia — Jean Willes

Robert Fenton — John Zaremba
Jack Roper- George Brand
Brad Lacey — Mark Hanna
Mrs. Valent — Carroll McComas
Pat Winters — Hugh Sanders
    (Additional cast information from "5 Against the House (1955)."
3 Sept. 2003 <http://movies.go.com/filmography/Credits?movie_id=
31756>.)

Invasion of the Body Snatchers

Released in 1956 by Allied Artists Pictures Corporation
Screenplay by Daniel Mainwaring
Based on the *Collier's* Magazine serial by Jack Finney
Produced by Walter Wanger Pictures, Inc.
Directed by Don Siegel
   • Cast •
Dr. Miles Bennell — Kevin McCarthy
Becky Driscoll — Dana Wynter
Dr. Dan Kauffman — Larry Gates
Jack Belicec — King Donovan
Theodora Belicec — Carolyn Jones
Nurse Sally Withers — Jean Willes
Police Chief Nick Grivett — Ralph Dumke
Wilma Lentz — Virginia Christie
Uncle Ira Lentz — Tom Fadden
Stanley Driscoll — Kenneth Patterson
Officer Sam Janzek — Guy Way
Anne Grimaldi — Eileen Stevens
Grandma Driscoll — Beatrice Maude
Eleda Lentz — Jean Andren
Jimmy Grimaldi — Bobby Clark
Dr. Ed Pursey — Everett Glass
Mac Lomax — Dabbs Greer
Baggage man — Pat O'Malley
Restaurant owner — Guy Rennie
Martha Lomax — Marie Selland
Charlie, the meter reader — Sam Peckinpah
Pod carrier in Miles's office — Harry J. Vejar

Dr. Harvey Bassett — Richard Deacon
Dr. Hill — Whit Bissell
Ambulance driver — Robert Osterloh
with Frank Hagney
        (Additional cast information from "Invasion of the Body Snatch-
ers (1956)." *Amazon.com.* 11 Sept. 2003 <http://www.amazon.com/
exec/obidos/tg/detail/-/0782009980/002-0306956-8512019?vi=con
tents>.)

House of Numbers

Released in 1957 by Metro-Goldwyn-Mayer
Screenplay by Russell Rouse and Don M. Mankiewicz
Based on the *Cosmopolitan* magazine novel by Jack Finney
Produced by Charles Schnee
Directed by Russell Rouse
    • Cast •
Bill Judlow/Arnie Judlow — Jack Palance
Henry Nova — Harold J. Stone
Warden — Edward Platt
Ruth Judlow — Barbara Lang
        (Additional cast information from "House of Numbers (1957)."
29 Sept. 2003 <http://movies.go.com/filmography/credits?movie_id=
882>.)

Good Neighbor Sam

Released in 1964 by Columbia
Screenplay by James Fritzell, Everett Greenbaum, and David Swift
From the novel by Jack Finney
Produced and directed by David Swift
    • Cast •
Sam Bissel — Jack Lemmon
Janet Lagerlof — Romy Schneider
Minerva Bissel — Dorothy Provine
Howard Ebbets — Michael Connors
Mr. Burke — Edward Andrews
Reinhold Shiffner — Louis Nye
Earl — Robert Q. Lewis
Girl — Joyce Jameson

Irene — Anne Seymour
Jack Bailey — Charles Lane
Edna — Linda Watkins
Phil Reisner — Peter Hobbs
Sonny Blatchford — Tris Coffin
Larry Boling — Neil Hamilton
Miss Halverson — Rizza Royce
Millard Mellner — William Forrest
The Hi-Los — The Hi-Los
Simon Nurdlinger — Edward G. Robinson
Taragon — Bernie Kopell
Wyeth — Patrick Waltz
Hausner — William Bryant
Jenna — Vickie Cos
Ardis — Kym Karath
Marsha — Quinn O'Hara
McVale — Hal Taggart
Gloria — Jan Brooks
French waiter — Peter Camlin
Assistant director — Tom Anthony
Mrs. Burke — Bess Flowers
Hertz commercial man — Dave Ketchum
Drunk — Gil Lamb
Milkman — Harry Ray
Postman — Joe Palma
TV director — David Swift
Belly dancer — Zanouba
Receptionist — Barbara Bouchet
    (Additional cast information from "Good Neighbor Sam (1964)."
5 Nov. 2003 <http://movies.go.com/filmography/Credits?movie_id=
28893>.)

Assault on a Queen

Released in 1966 by Paramount
Screenplay by Rod Serling
From the novel by Jack Finney
Produced by William Goetz
Directed by Jack Donohue

• **Cast** •

Mark — Frank Sinatra
Rosa — Virna Lisi
Rossiter — Tony Franciosa
Moreno — Richard Conte
Lauffnauer — Alf Kjellin
Linc — Errol John
Captain — Murray Matheson
Master-at-arms — Reginald Denny
Bank manager — John Warburton
Doctor — Lester Matthews
Trench — Val Avery
1st officer — Gilchrist Stuart
2d officer — Ronald Long
3d officer — Leslie Bradley
4th officer — Arthur E. Gould-Porter
Junior officer — Laurence Conroy

Invasion of the Body Snatchers

Released in 1978 by United Artists
Screenplay by W.D. Richter
Based on the novel *The Body Snatchers* by Jack Finney
Produced by Robert H. Solo
Directed by Philip Kaufman

• **Cast** •

Matthew Bennell — Donald Sutherland
Elizabeth Driscoll — Brooke Adams
Jack Bellicec — Jeff Goldblum
Nancy Bellicec — Veronica Cartwright
Geoffrey — Art Hindle
Katherine — Lelia Goldoni
Dr. David Kibner — Leonard Nimoy
Running man — Kevin McCarthy
Taxi driver — Don Siegel
Ted Hendley — Tom Luddy
Stan — Stan Ritchie
Mr. Gianni — David Fisher
Detective — Tom Dahlgren

Boccardo — Gary Goodrow
Restaurant owner — Jerry Walter
Chef — Maurice Argent
Street barker — Sam Conti
Mr. Tong — Wood Moy
Mrs. Tong — R. Wong
Outraged woman — Rose Kaufman
Beggar — Joe Bellan
Policeman #1 — Sam Hiona
Policeman #2 — Lee McVeigh
Rodent man — Albert Nalbandian
School teacher — Lee Mines

Maxie

Released in 1985 by Orion Pictures
Screenplay by Patricia Resnick
Based upon *Marion's Wall* by Jack Finney
Produced by Carter De Haven
Directed by Paul Aaron
  • Cast •
Jan/Maxie — Glenn Close
Nick — Mandy Patinkin
Mrs. Lavin — Ruth Gordon
Bishop Campbell — Barnard Hughes
Miss Sheffer — Valerie Curtin
Father Jerome — Googy Gress
Cleopatra Director — Michael Ensign
Commercial Director — Michael Laskin
Art Isenberg — Lou Cutell
Bartender — Nelson Welch
E.T. Reporter — Leeza Gibbons
Channel 4 Announcer — Evan White
Mr. Chu — Harry Wong
Policeman — Charles Douglas Laird
Assistant Director — David Sosna
Charity Patron — Hugo Stanger
Trainer — John O'Neill
Usher — Eddie Wong

Exercise Class Ladies —
  Pauline Bluestone
  Rebecca Greenfield
  Jinaki
  Jobyna Phillips
  Gayle Vance
Chinese Movie Patrons —
  Glen Chin
  Nancie Kawata
  Conan Lee
Mr. San Francisco — Cyril Magnin
Reporter — Michael Jordan
Magazine Attendant — Alan Gin
Street Bum — Tony Amendola
Al the Dog — Nelson

Body Snatchers

Released in 1993 by Warner Brothers
Screenplay by Stuart Gordon, Dennis Paoli, and Nicholas St. John
Screen story by Raymond Cistheri and Larry Cohen
Based on the novel *The Body Snatchers* by Jack Finney
Produced by Robert H. Solo
Directed by Abel Ferrara
  • Cast •
Marti Malone — Gabrielle Anwar
Steve Malone — Terry Kinney
Tim Young — Billy Wirth
Jenn Platt — Christine Elise
Gen. Platt — R. Lee Ermey
Pete — G. Elvis Phillips
Andy Malone — Reilly Murphy
Mrs. Platt — Kathleen Doyle
Dr. Collins — Forest Whitaker
Carol Malone — Meg Tilly
Platt's aide — Stanley Small
Teacher — Tonea Stewart
Soldier at gas station — Keith Smith
Gas attendant — Winston E. Grant

MP gate captain — Phil Neilson
MP #1— Timothy P. Brown
MP #2 — Thurman L. Combs
Soldier #1— Sylvia Small
Red — Adrian Unveragh
Neighbor — Johnny L. Smith
MP #3 — Allen Perada
Medic — Candy Orsini
Man in infirmary — Marty Lyons
MP #4 — Rick Kangrga
MP #5 — Michael Cohen
Pod soldier — Kimberly L. Cole
G.I. #1— James P. Monoghan
G.I. #2 — Craig Lockhart
Alien woman — Darian Taylor
Body double Meg — Jennifer

TELEVISION

"Time Is Just a Place"

Broadcast on April 16, 1955, in syndication as part of the series, *Science Fiction Theatre*
Screenplay by Lee Berg
From a short story by Jack Finney
Directed by Jack Arnold
   • Cast •
Al Brown — Don DeFore
Nell Brown — Marie Windsor
Ted Heller — Warren Stevens
Ann Heller — Peggy O'Connor

"All My Clients Are Innocent"

Broadcast on April 17, 1962, on the ABC television network as part of the series, *Alcoa Premiere*
Teleplay by Jameson Brewer
Story by Jack Finney

• Cast •

Max McIntyre — Barry Morse
Alan Michaels — Richard Davalos
Carl Balderson — Vic Morrow
Cora Pierson — Joan Staley
Martha — Mari Aldon
Nurse — Lillian Bronson
    (Credits and cast from "Guest Appearances for 'Alcoa Premiere.'"
15 Mar 2005 <http://www.imdb.com/title/tt0054513/guests> and
"Alcoa Premiere — All My Clients Are Innocent." *TV Tome.* 17 Dec.
2044 <http://www.tvtome.com/tvtome/servlet/GuidePageServlet/
showid-4345/epid-187926>.)

"Such Interesting Neighbors"

Broadcast on March 20, 1987, on the NBC television network as part
    of the series, *Amazing Stories*
Teleplay by Mick Garris and Tom McLoughlin
Based upon the story by Jack Finney
Directed by Graham Baker

• Cast •

Al Lewis — Frederick Coffin
Nel Lewis — Marcia Strassman
Randy Lewis — Ian Fried
Ann Hellenbeck — Victoria Caitlin
Ted Hellenbeck — Adam Ant
Brad Hellenbeck — Ryan McWhorter
    (Credits and cast from Brown, Michael L., and Loren Heisey.
"Amazing Stories." 12 May 2004 <http://www.innermind.com/my
guides/guides/am_story.htm>.)

"The Love Letter"

Broadcast on February 1, 1998, on the CBS television network as part
    of the *Hallmark Hall of Fame* series
Screenplay by James Henerson and Pamela Gray
Based on a story by Jack Finney
Produced by Dan Curtis and Lynn Raynor
Directed by Dan Curtis

• **Cast** •
Scotty Corrigan — Campbell Scott
Elizabeth Whitcomb — Jennifer Jason Leigh
Everett Reagle — David Dukes
Beatrice Corrigan — Estelle Parsons
Debra Zabriskie — Daphne Ashbrook
Clarice Whitcomb — Myra Carter
Warren Whitcomb — Gerrit Graham
Mae Mullen — Irma P. Hall
Jacob Campbell — Richard Woods
    (Credits from Joyner, Will. "Television Review; A May-December, of Sorts." *New York Times* 31 January 1998: B13.)

STAGE

This Winter's Hobby
Performed in New Haven, Connecticut, from March 23, 1966, to
    March 26, 1966, at the Shubert Theater
Performed in Philadelphia from March 28, 1966, to April 9, 1966, at
    the Walnut Street Theater
Written by Jack Finney
Directed by Donald McWhinnie
  • **Cast** •
Charles Bishop — E.G. Marshall
Duffy Bishop — Nan Martin
Arnold — William Hickey
Tommy — Michael Beckett
Laura Amling — Martha Bundy
Sheriff McCarthy — Norman Bly

Time and Again
Performed in Waterford, Connecticut, in summer 1993 at the Eugene
    O'Neill Theater Center
Performed in San Diego from May 4, 1996, to June 9, 1996, at the Old
    Globe Theater
Performed in New York from May 18, 1999, to May 22, 1999, at The
    Altman Building, and from January 9, 2001, to February 18, 2001,
    at the City Center Stage II

Book by Jack Viertel
Music and lyrics by Walter Edgar Kennon
Based on the novel by Jack Finney
Directed by Susan H. Schulman
• **Cast (2001)** •
Si — Lewis Cleale
Kate — Julia Murney
Julia — Laura Benanti
Danziger — David McCallum
with Melissa Rain Anderson, Ann Arvia, Jeff Edgerton, Eric Michael
Gillett, Gregg Goodbrod, Christopher Innvar, Patricia Kilgarriff, Joseph
Kolinski, George Masswohl, Amy Walsh, and Lauren Ward.

   (Credits from "MTC 2000–2001 Season." 23 Oct. 2001 <http://
www.mtc-nyc.org/season/time_and_again.htm>; <http://stag ing.the
atre.com/www_mtc-nyc_org/season/time_and_again_photos. htm>;
<http://staging.theatre.com/www_mtc-nyc_org/season/time_and_
again_press.htm>.)

Works Cited

Quotations in the text from works by Jack Finney are from first editions or first magazine publications, except where noted below.

5 Against the House. Dir. Phil Karlson. Columbia, 1955.
"5 Against the House (1955)." 3 September 2003. http://movies.go.com/filmog raphy/Credits?movie_id=31756.
Adams, Phoebe-Lou. Rev. of *Forgotten News: The Crime of the Century and Other Lost Stories. The Atlantic Monthly.* May 1983: 104–05.
Advertisement for *The Woodrow Wilson Dime. Alibris.* 11 November 2003. http:// www.alibris.com/search/detail.cfm?chunk=25&mtype=&qwork=7281917&5=R &bid=8124641747&pqtynew=08page=1&matches=16&qsort=r.
Advertisement for *Time and Again* Walking Tour of Manhattan. *New York Times.* 3 August 2001: E35.
"Alcoa Premiere — All My Clients Are Innocent." *TV Tome.* 17 December 2004. http://www.tvtome.com/tvtome/servlet/GuidePageServlet/showid-4345/epid-187926.
"Alcoa premiere. All my clients are innocent." UCLA Library Catalog, Film and Television Archive. 21 February 2005. http://cinema.library.ucla.edu.
"Amazing Stories Episode Guide." 21 February 2005. http://www.geocities.com/ TelevisionCity/studio/8849/amazimag/episodes/SUCHIN.HTM.
Assault on a Queen. Dir. Jack Donohue. Paramount, 1966.
Bannon, Barbara A. Rev. of *Forgotten News: The Crime of the Century and Other Lost Stories. Publisher's Weekly.* 4 February 1983: 356.
_____. Rev. of *Marion's Wall. Publisher's Weekly.* 19 February 1973: 70.
_____. Rev. of *The Night People. Publisher's Weekly.* 12 September 1977: 120.

_____. Rev. of *The Woodrow Wilson Dime. Publisher's Weekly.* 5 February 1968: 64.

_____. Rev. of *Time and Again. Publisher's Weekly.* 9 March 1970: 81.

Beard, Michael. "Jack Finney." *Twentieth-Century American Science-Fiction Writers. Part 1: A-L.* Detroit: Gale, 1981. 182–85.

Beatty, Jerome Jr. [Editorial.] *Collier's.* 24 December 1954: 18.

Beres, Cynthia Breslin. "Time and Again/From Time to Time." 2003. *MagillOn-Literature.* 4 March 2003. http://web15.epnet.com/delivery.asp?tb=1& ug=dbs+ 0+1n+en-us+sid+43EACF6F-C3BF-4....

Bettack, Francis T. Letter. *Collier's.* 5 January 1952: 4.

Blackburn, Sara. Rev. of *Time and Again. The Washington Post.* 28 June 1970: 6.

Blosser, Fred. "Of Time and Pods: The Fantastic World of Jack Finney." In McCarthy and Gorman. 49–56.

Body Snatchers. Dir. Abel Ferrara. Warner Bros., 1993.

"*Body Snatchers* Author Dies at 84." *Dayton Daily News.* 17 November 1995: 6B.

Bone. "Show Out of Town." *Variety.* 30 March 1966: n. pag.

Bosky, Bernadette Lynn. "Finney, Walter Braden ("Jack")." *The Scribner Encyclopedia of American Lives.* Vol. 4: 1994–1996. New York: Charles Scribner's Sons, 2001. 172–73.

Boucher, Anthony. "Criminals at Large." *New York Times.* 7 March 1954: 7.27.

Brantley, Ben. " A Flight of Fancy to 1882 to Channel a Quirky Past." *New York Times.* 31 January 2001: E5.

Breen, Jon L. "The Fiction of Jack Finney." In McCarthy and Gorman. 23–36.

Brown, Michael L. and Loren Heisey. "Amazing Stories." 12 May 2004. http:// www.innermind.com/myguides/guides/am_story.htm.

Clute, John. "Finney, Jack." *The Encyclopedia of Fantasy.* New York: St. Martin's Press, 1997.

"Collier's Weekly." 16 December 2001. Spartacus Educational. 30 May 2002. http://www.spartacus.schoolnet.co.uk/USAcolliers.htm.

Crane, Ruth. Letter. *Collier's.* 5 January 1952: 4.

"Crowell-Collier Publishing Company (Collier's Weekly Magazine Publisher)." *Scripophily.com.* 10 September 2003. http://www.scripophily.net/crowcolpubco. html.

Cuff, Sergeant. "The Criminal Record." *Saturday Review.* 3 April 1954: 60.

_____. "Criminal Record." *Saturday Review.* 21 May 1960: 37.

"Current Magazine Story Features Galesburg." *Register-Mail* (Galesburg, IL). 21 March 1960: n. pag.

Dannay, Frederic. Introduction. "The Widow's Walk." By Jack Finney. *Ellery Queen's Mystery Magazine.* July 1947. Qtd. in Breen 24–25.

Davis, James. "New Play Withdrawn; Run of 'Circle' Extended." *New York Daily News.* 8 April 1966: 40.

De Haven, Tom. "Life in the Past Lane." *Entertainment Weekly.* 24 February 1995: 108–09.

Dirda, Michael. "Tinkering With the Past." *Washington Post Book World.* 12 February 1995: 6–7.

"Don DeFore's Television Credits." 5 January 2005. http://www.defore.net/tv credits.html.

Dove, Bryan. Letter. *The Saturday Evening Post.* 31 October 1959: 6.

Elliott, Gwendolyn W. Rev. of *Forgotten News: The Crime of the Century and Other Lost Stories. Library Journal.* 1 April 1983: 740.

Epstein, Bennett. "Six People and their Fantastic Plot." *New York Herald Tribune Book Review.* 13 September 1959: 5.

Ermelino, Louisa. Rev. of *From Time to Time. People.* 10 April 1995: 29, 32.

Fidell, Estelle A., and Dorothy Margaret Peake. *Play Index, 1953–1960.* New York: H.W. Wilson, 1963.

Finney, Jack. *5 Against the House.* 1954. New York: Pocket Books, 1955.

_____. *The Body Snatchers.* 1955. New York: Dell, 1967.

_____. "Crazy Sunday." *Love and Marriage: 22 Stories.* Ed. Margaret Cousins. Garden City, NY: Doubleday, 1961. 233–47.

_____. "Double Take." *The Playboy Book of Science Fiction and Fantasy.* 1966. Chicago: Playboy, 1968. 293–313.

_____. "Hey, Look at Me!" *About Time.* 203–19.

_____. *I Love Galesburg in the Springtime.* 1962. London: Pan, 1968.

_____. *Invasion of the Body Snatchers.* 1978. New York: Dell, 1979.

_____. Letter to Douglas L. Wilson. 25 August 1982. Special Collections and Archives, Knox College Library, Galesburg, IL.

_____. Letter to E. Samuel Moon. 25 May 1983. Special Collections and Archives, Knox College Library, Galesburg, IL.

_____. Letter to M.M. Goodsill. 14 December 1959. Special Collections and Archives, Knox College Library, Galesburg, IL.

_____. Letter to M.M. Goodsill. 27 April 1960. Special Collections and Archives, Knox College Library, Galesburg, IL.

_____. Letter to M.M. Goodsill. 8 September 1966. Special Collections and Archives, Knox College Library, Galesburg, IL.

_____. Letter to Mr. Kilkenny. 7 November 1966. Special Collections and Archives, Knox College Library, Galesburg, IL.

_____. Letter to Mr. Kosin. 28 December 1978. Special Collections and Archives, Knox College Library, Galesburg, IL.

_____. Letter to The President, Knox College. 14 November 1959. Special Collections and Archive, Knox College Library, Galesburg, IL.

_____. *Marion's Wall.* 1973. *Three By Finney.* 117–246.

_____. *The Night People.* 1977. *Three By Finney.* 247–416.

_____. *The Third Level.* 1957. New York: Dell, 1959.

_____. *Time and Again.* 1970. New York: Simon and Schuster-Fireside, [1978].

_____. *The Woodrow Wilson Dime.* 1968. *Three By Finney.* 1–115.

"Finney, Jack." *The Author's and Writer's Who's Who,* 4th ed. London: Burke's Peerage, 1960.

"Finney, Walter Braden." *Contemporary Authors,* Vol. 110. Detroit: Gale, 1984.

"Finney, Walter Braden." *Contemporary Authors,* Vol. 150. Detroit: Gale, 1996.

Fleming, Thomas. "Inventing Our Probable Past." *New York Times.* 6 July 1986: 7.1, 7.20.

Gehle, Quentin. "Time and Again." *Survey of Contemporary Literature.* Englewood Cliffs, NJ: Salem, 1977. 7644–46.

"George H. Fitch Papers." 3 March 2005. http://catalog.knox.edu/archives/manu scripts/fitch_george_h.htm.

Good Neighbor Sam. Dir. David Swift. Columbia, 1964.

"Good Neighbor Sam (1964)." 5 November 2003. http://movies.go.com/filmog raphy/Credits?movie_id=28893.

Goodsill, Max. Letter to Jack Finney. 26 March 1960. Special Collections and Archives, Knox College Library, Galesburg, IL.

Goodsill, M.M. Letter to Jack Finney. 16 November 1959. Special Collections and Archives, Knox College Library, Galesburg, IL.

_____. Letter to Jack Finney. 18 December 1959. Special Collections and Archives, Knox College Library, Galesburg, IL.

_____. Letter to Jack Finney. 22 March 1960. Special Collections and Archives, Knox College Library, Galesburg, IL.

_____. Letter to Jack Finney. 22 April 1960. Special Collections and Archives, Knox College Library, Galesburg, IL.

_____. Letter to Walter B. Finney. 1 September 1966. Special Collections and Archives, Knox College Library, Galesburg, IL.

Greenbaum, Everett. Letter. *New York Times.* 9 April 1995: 6.18.

"Guest Appearances for 'Alcoa Premiere.'" 15 March 2005. http://www.imdb.com/ title/tt0054513/guests.

Haagen, Lucy. "Time and Again." *English Journal.* February 1979: 45–46.

"Hallmark Hall of Fame — Episode List." *TV Tome.* 17 January 2005. http://www. tvtome.com/tvtome/servlet/EpisodeGuideServlet/showid-4152/Hallmark_Hall_ of_Fame.

Hirschfeld, Neal. "Is the Time Finally Ripe for 'Time and Again'?" *New York Times.* 20 March 1994: 13, 20.

"History of the World Fantasy Conventions." *World Fantasy Convention.* 22 March 2004. http://www.worldfantasy.org/retro.html.

Holfer, Robert. "Second Chances." *Variety.* 29 January 2001: 61.

House of Numbers. Dir. Russell Rouse. Metro-Goldwyn-Mayer, 1957.

"House of Numbers (1957)." 29 September 2003. http://movies.go.com/filmog raphy/credits?movie_id=882.

Ickes, Bob. "As Time Goes By; Jack Finney." *New York Times Magazine.* 19 March 1995, 34–37.

Invasion of the Body Snatchers. Dir. Don Siegel. Allied Artists, 1955.

Invasion of the Body Snatchers. Dir. Philip Kaufman. United Artists, 1978.

"Invasion of the Body Snatchers (1956)." *Amazon.com.* 11 September 2003. http:// www.amazon.com/exec/obidos/tg/detail/-/0782009980/002-0306956-8512019 ?vi=contents.

"Jack Finney — Bibliography Summary." 20 December 2000. http://www.sfsite. com/isfdb-bin/exact_author.cgi?Jack_Finney.

Johnson, Florence. "Shubert Play Promises to Rise Above Flaws." Unidentified newspaper, New Haven, CT, c. 24 March 1966: n. pag.

Johnson, Glen M. "'We'd Fight.... We Had To.' *The Body Snatchers* as Novel and Film." *Journal of Popular Culture.* 13.1 (1979): 5–14.

Jones, J. Sydney. "Finney, Jack." *Something About the Author.* Vol. 109. Detroit: Gale, 2000.

Jones, Kenneth. "Time and Again's Time Has Come—and Gone." 11 February 2005. http://www.davidmccallumfansonline.com/Time%20and%20Again. htm.

Kilkenny, William J. Letter to Jack Finney. 3 November 1966. Special Collections and Archives, Knox College Library, Galesburg, IL.

Killheffer, Robert K.J. "Books." *The Magazine of Fantasy and Science Fiction.* September 1995: 19–27.

King, Stephen. *Danse Macabre.* New York: Everest House, 1981.

Kobel, Peter. "Hollywood's Honeymoon With Time." *New York Times.* 20 January 2002: 11, 26.

Kosin, Robert. Letter to Jack Finney. 13 December 1978. Special Collections and Archives, Knox College Library, Galesburg, IL.

Landon, Brooks. "Time and Again." *Survey of Modern Fantasy Literature.* Englewood Cliffs, NJ: Salem, 1983. 1938–42.

Lask, Thomas. "Of Time and the River." *New York Times.* 25 July 1970: 24.

Levin, Martin. "Reader's Report." *New York Times.* 14 April 1968: 7.31.

Little, Stuart W. "'The Defender' on ..." New York *Herald Tribune.* 3 March 1966: n. pag.

"The Locus Index to SF Awards." 22 March 2004. http://www.locusmag.com/ SFAwards/Db/Imaginaire.html.

The Love Letter. Dir. Dan Curtis. CBS. 1 February 1998.

MacLachlan, Suzanne. "A Sidetracked Mission in Time-Travel Sequel." *Christian Science Monitor.* 28 February 1995: 14.

Mandelbaum, Ken. Rev. of *Time and Again.* 11 February 2005. http://www.david mccallumfansonline.com/Time%20and%20Again.htm.

"Marie Windsor." 5 January 2005. http://us.imdb.com/name/nm0934798.

Maxie. Dir. Paul Aaron. Orion, 1985.

McCarthy, Kevin, and Ed Gorman, eds. *"They're Here...": Invasion of the Body Snatchers; A Tribute.* New York: Berkley Boulevard, 1999.

McCarty, John. "An Interview with Kevin McCarthy." In McCarthy and Gorman. 187–273.

McCormick, Donald. Rev. of *Marion's Wall. Library Journal.* 15 February 1973: 563.

Mendelssohn, John Ned. Rev. of *Forgotten News: The Crime of the Century and Other Lost Stories. Los Angeles Times Book Review.* 29 May 1983: 8.

Moon, Sam. Letter to Mr. Finney. 10 June 1983. Special Collections and Archives, Knox College Library, Galesburg, IL.

Moran, John F. Rev. of *The Third Level. Library Journal.* July 1957: 1777.

Mott, Schuyler L. Rev. of *The Woodrow Wilson Dime. Library Journal.* 1 April 1968: 1500.

"MTC 2000–2001 Season." 23 October 2001. http://staging.theatre.com/www_ mtc-nyc_org/season/time_and_again_photos.htm.

"MTC 2000–2001 Season." 23 October 2001. http://staging.theatre.com/www_ mtc-nyc_org/season/time_and_again_press.htm.

"MTC 2000–2001 Season." 23 October 2001. http://www.mtc-nyc.org/season/time_and_again.htm.

Murdock, Henry T. "E.G. Marshall Heads Cast of Thriller." *Philadelphia Inquirer.* 30 March 1966: n. pag.

Newman, Kim. "Finney, Jack." *St. James Guide to Fantasy Writers.* New York: St. James, 1996.

Oliver, Myrna. "Jack Finney; Wrote 'The Body Snatchers.'" *Los Angeles Times.* 17 November 1995: A32.

Otten, Robert M. "Jack Finney." *Beacham's Popular Fiction in America.* Vol. 2. Washington, DC: Beacham, 1986.

Palmer, Jean. Rev. of *Time and Again* and *From Time to Time* audio books. *Kliatt.* May 1995: 52.

Phillips, Michael. Rev. of *Time and Again.* Qtd. in Haun, Harry, and Robert Viagas. "*Time and Again* Opens in San Diego 10-May-96." 10 May 1996. http://wheat.symgroup.com/cgi-bin/plb_newfe_show?show+news+1498.

Photographs. *This Winter's Hobby.* Friedman-Abeles Collection. New York Public Library, Lincoln Center Library for the Performing Arts. (1966.)

Playbill. This Winter's Hobby. Walnut Street Theatre. Philadelphia, PA. (March 1966.)

Playbill. Time and Again. Manhattan Theatre Club. New York, NY. (January 2001.)

Powers, Richard Gid. Introduction. *The Body Snatchers.* 1955. Boston: Gregg, 1976. v–xi.

Press release. "'Hobby' Leaves for New Haven." 22 March 1966.

Press release. "Time and Again." New York Public Library, Lincoln Center Library for the Performing Arts Clippings File. 1 May 1996.

Pringle, David. *Modern Fantasy: The Hundred Best Novels.* New York: Peter Bedrick Books, 1989. 136–38.

Program. A Workshop of Time and Again at The Altman Building, 135 W. 18th St., New York. 18 May 1999.

Pronzini, Bill, and Marcia Muller. *1001 Midnights: The Aficionado's Guide to Mystery and Detective Fiction.* New York: Arbor House, 1986.

"Proviso East High School." 5 June 2003. http://www.proviso.k12.il.us/EastNew/penew.htm.

Raymer, Anne Carolyn. "Time and Again." *Survey of Science Fiction Literature.* Vol. 5. Englewood Cliffs, NJ: Salem, 1979. 2283–86.

Relling, William Jr. "A Nice Place to Visit, But..." In McCarthy and Gorman. 63–68.

Resnick, Mike. "Forgotten Treasures." *Magazine of Fantasy and Science Fiction.* October/November 1997: 84+.

Rev. of *About Time. Washington Post Book World.* 31 August 1986: 12.

Rev. of *Assault on a Queen. Bulletin from Virginia Kirkus' Service.* 15 July 1959: 506.

Rev. of *Assault on a Queen. The New Yorker.* 26 September 1959: 192–93.

Rev. of *Forgotten News: The Crime of the Century and Other Lost Stories. Kirkus Reviews.* 15 January 1983: 97.

Rev. of *From Time to Time*. *Kirkus Reviews*. 1 December 1994: 1559–60.

Rev. of *I Love Galesburg in the Springtime*. *Times Literary Supplement*. 10 June 1965: 469.

Rev. of *Marion's Wall*. *Kirkus Reviews*. 1 February 1973: 137.

Rev. of *Marion's Wall*. *The Booklist*. 15 October 1973: 221.

Rev. of *The Night People*. *Booklist*. 1 December 1977: 600.

Rev. of *The Night People*. *Kirkus Reviews*. 15 August 1977: 867.

Rev. of *The Third Level*. *Bulletin from Virginia Kirkus' Service*. 15 June 1957: 426.

Rev. of *The Woodrow Wilson Dime*. *The Kirkus Service*. 1 February 1968: 135.

Rev. of *Three By Finney*. *Washington Post Book World*. 23 August 1987: 12.

Rev. of *Time and Again*. *Kirkus Reviews*. 1 March 1970: 272.

Rich, Frank. "'The 20th Century Should Have Been the Best.'" *New York Times*. 19 February 1995: 7.10.

Ridley, Clifford A. "Laura Benati: Remember That Name." *Philadelphia Inquirer*. N.d. 11 February 2005. http://www.davidmccallumfansonline.com/Time%20 and%2020Again.htm.

Roberts, Sam. "The Ten Best Books About New York." *New York Times*. 5 February 1995: 13.1, 14–15.

Rogers, W.G. Rev. of *Time and Again*. *New York Times*. 2 August 1970: 7.24.

Rothenberg, Kelly. "Jack Finney: It's About Time." November 1996. 19 December 2000. http://members.aol.com/Lemarchand/articles/finney.html.

Rubin, Don. "A Try-Out for E.G. Marshall." *New Haven Register*. 24 Mar 1966: 27.

Rudin, Seymour. "Finney, Jack." *St. James Guide to Crime and Mystery Writers*, 4th ed. Detroit: St. James, 1996.

Sandoe, James. "Mystery and Suspense." *New York Herald Tribune Book Review*. 28 February 1954: 14.

Schier, Ernest. "The Final Line May Bespeak Fate of Implausible 'This Winter's Hobby.'" *Philadelphia Bulletin*. 30 March 1966: n. pag.

Schuldt, Steven W. "Message of Love." j-j-l.com. 13 December 2000. http://www. j-j-l.com/reviews/ReviewLoveLetter.html.

"Science Fiction Theatre." *TV Tome*. 3 January 2005. http://www.tvtome.com/tv tome/servlet/ShowMainServlet/showed-6057.

"Science Fiction Theatre — Time is Just a Place." *TV Tome*. 17 December 2004. http://www.tvtome.com/tvtome/servlet/GuidePageServlet/showid-6057/epid-126764.

Seeley, George R. Letter. *Saturday Evening Post*. 31 October 1959: 6.

Shakespeare, William. *Julius Caesar*. 1599. *The Riverside Shakespeare*. Ed. G. Blakemore Evans. Boston: Houghton Mifflin, 1974. 1100–34.

Shane, Ted. "The Week's Work." *Collier's*. 5 April 1947: 8.

_____. "The Week's Work." *Collier's*. 15 May 1948: 10.

_____. "The Week's Work." *Collier's*. 28 August 1948: 8.

_____. "The Week's Work." *Collier's*. 6 November 1948: 10.

Sheff-Cahan, Vickie. "Talking With ... Jack Finney." *People*. 10 April 1995: 32–33.

Singer, Barry. "'Youngsters' Reach Broadway Bearing Gifts: Musical Scores." *New York Times*. 27 August 2000: 5.

"Siwash." *Merriam-Webster Online Dictionary.* 3 March 2005. http://www.m-w.com/cgi-bin/dictionary?book=Dictionary&va=Siwash.

Sloan, DeVillo. "The Self and Self-less in Campbell's *Who Goes There?* and Finney's *Invasion of the Body Snatchers.*" *Extrapolation* 29.2 (1988): 179–88.

Sparks, Leah. "Jack Finney." 15 December 2001. 25 October 2002. http://members.aol.com/leahj/finney.htm.

Steinberg, Sybil S. Rev. of *From Time to Time. Publisher's Weekly.* 28 November 1994: 42.

"Such Interesting Neighbors." Writ. Mick Garris and Tom McLoughlin. *Amazing Stories.* Dir. Graham Baker. 20 March 1987.

"Television." *New York Times.* 17 April 1962: 54.

The 1935 Gale. Galesburg, IL: Knox College, 1935.

"They Broke the Prairie." *University of Illinois Press.* 7 January 2005. http://www.press.uillinois.edu/preqs/0-252-06094-6.html.

Time and Again. Videotape. Dir. Susan H. Schulman. Rec. 16 February 2001. New York Public Library Theatre on Film and Tape Archive. NCOV 2493. 125 min.

"Time Is Just a Place." Writ. Lee Berg. *Science Fiction Theatre.* Dir. Jack Arnold. Introd. Truman Bradley. 16 April 1955.

Timpone, Anthony. "Robert H. Solo, Pod Producer." In McCarthy and Gorman. 125–47.

Van Gelder, Lawrence. "At the Movies." *New York Times.* 25 May 1990: C8.

———. "Some Time Later, a Sequel to 'Time and Again.'" *New York Times.* 13 December 1994: C.22.

Viagas, Robert. "*Time and Again* in 'Extensive Rewrites.'" 11 July 1996. http://piano.syngrp.com/cgi-bin/plb_newfe_show?show+news+1498.

"Walter B. Finney, '34." *The Knox Alumnus* winter 1960: 22.

"Warren Stevens." 5 January 2005. http://www.tvtome.com/tvtome/servlet/PersonDetail/personid-9674.

Weinraub, Bernard. "Shhh. There's a New Musical. It's Hush-Hush." *New York Times.* 11 June 2000: 4, 29.

"What's in this Issue." *Good Housekeeping.* March 1955: 2.

Wilson, Barbara L. "The Theme Is 'Malice.'" *Philadelphia Inquirer.* 27 March 1966: 5.1.

Wolfe, Gary K. "Finney, Jack." *Twentieth-Century Science-Fiction Writers,* 2d ed. Chicago: St. James, 1986.

Young, B.A. Rev. of *I Love Galesburg in the Springtime. Punch.* 7 April 1965: 525.

Zolotow, Sam. "Producer Barred from Fund Pleas." *New York Times.* 30 June 1966: 28.

———. "'Winter's Hobby' Closing on Road." *New York Times.* 8 April 1966: n. pag.

Index